Knossos and the Near East

A contextual approach to imports and imitations in Early Iron Age tombs

Vyron Antoniadis

ARCHAEOPRESS PUBLISHING LTD
Gordon House
276 Banbury Road
Oxford OX2 7ED

www.archaeopress.com

ISBN 978 1 78491 640 4
ISBN 978 1 78491 641 1 (e-Pdf)

© Archaeopress and V Antoniadis 2017

Cover: A view of Knossos Valley from the east slopes of the Acropolis Hill (Image by the author).
A Steatite Scarab from Khaniale Teke Tholos tomb (Hutchinson and Boardman 1954).

All rights reserved. No part of this book may be reproduced, or transmitted, in any form or by any means, electronic, mechanical, photocopying or otherwise, without the prior written permission of the copyright owners.

Printed in England by Oxuniprint, Oxford

This book is available direct from Archaeopress or from our website www.archaeopress.com

'We necropolitans know more of the ways of the living than the inhabitants of their cities do'.

-Neil Gaiman, *The Sandman.*

Contents

Preface and Acknowledgements ix
Abbreviations xi
Introduction 1
    i. Contextual Analyses vs. Empirical Accounts 1
    ii. Aim and Method 3
    iii. General Remarks on Knossos 5

Chapter 1: Death and her Objects: Theoretical Approaches 9
    i. Interpreting the Mortuary Evidence 9
    ii. Funeral Rites: Cremation or Inhumation? 14
    iii. Imports, Imitations and Numbers 16
    iv. The Problem of Names: Implications on Chronology and Terminology 21

Chapter 2: Would you like your tomb with or without dromos? Tombs and Society in EIA Knossos 27
    i. Tomb Typology 27
    ii. History of Discoveries and Spatial Distribution of Tombs and Cemeteries .. 29
    iii. Funerary Rites and Rituals in Knossian Context 41
    iv. Who Used the Cemeteries? 44
    v. EIA Cemeteries and BA Tradition 53
    vi. Additional Archaeological Evidence 58
        a. From the BA palace to the EIA settlement 58
        b. Cult activity 64
    vii. Conclusion 67

Chapter 3: The Near Eastern Connection: The Finds and their Contexts ... 69
    i. Revisiting the Evidence: 69
    ii. The Catalogue 71

Chapter 4: Who gets the Imports and who the Imitations? 91
    i. First-level Analysis: The Finds 91
        a. Provenance of the objects catalogued as imports................................... 91
        b. Provenance of the objects catalogued as imports or local imitations 99
        c. The significance of the imitations in relation to their prototypes: the pottery factor.. 103
    ii. Second-Level Analysis: Imports, Imitations and Society......................... 115
    iii. Cluster Analysis... 131
    iv. Conclusion.. 134

Conclusion: An Overview of the Knossian Early Iron Age Society 136

Appendix I: The Tombs and the Burials 141

Appendix II: Imports and Imitations 148

Bibliography 154

List of Figures

Figure 1: Map 1: Knossos and the Eastern Mediterranean. 6
Figure 2: Map 2: The area of Knossos, the BA Palace and Modern Heraklion. 8
Figure 3: Terminology of the chamber tomb. 27
Figure 4: A shaft grave and a pit-cave grave. 28
Figure 5: Map 3: The location of EIA tombs. 30
Figure 6: Map 4: The burial sites within KNC 33
Figure 7 Map 5: Fortetsa SE Tombs. 36
Figure 8: Kouskouras beneath Heraklion Hospital 51
Figure 9: Map 6: The settlement of Knossos. 63
Figure 10: Scarab from Tomb II, Khaniale Teke 98
Figure 11: Scarab from Al-Bass, Tyre 98
Figure 12: Pots from a modern workshop at Knossos and at Rethymnon 114
Figure 13: Distribution of Imports at KMF 122
Figure 14: Distribution of Imports at Teke 125
Figure 15: Distribution of imports at Fortetsa NE 125
Figure 16: Distribution of imports at Khaniale Teke 126
Figure 17: Distribution of imports at Fortetsa SE 128
Figure 18: Distribution of imports at Ayios Ioannis 129

List of Tables

Table 1: A basic chronological sequence of Knossos 25
Table 2: Graph 1: Numbers of tombs per type. 41
Table 3: Graph 2: Maximum and minimum of cremation urns... 52
Table 4: Graph 3: Cremations per year... 52
Table 5: Graph 4: Construction of new Tombs per period. 52
Table 6: Graph 5: Construction of new Tombs during the PG period. 53
Table 7: Graph 6: Construction of new Tombs during the G period... 53
Table 8: Graph 7: Provenance of imports.. 92
Table 9: Graph 8: Pottery style in relation to the quantities found at the Knossian Cemeteries.. 95
Table 10: Graph 9: Near Eastern objects and pots per period. 96
Table 11: Graph 10: Material of imports. 97
Table 12: Graph 11: Numbers of imports or local imitations. 100
Table 13: Chart 1: imported and locally made pottery. 104
Table 14: Chart 2: Evolution of local shapes deriving from Near Eastern pots. (1) 108
Table 14: Chart 2: Evolution of local shapes deriving from Near Eastern pots. (2) 109
Table 14: Chart 2: Evolution of local shapes deriving from Near Eastern pots. (3) 110
Table 15: Graph 12: Shapes and quantities of Near Eastern Pottery found at Knossos Cemeteries... 111
Table 16: Graph 13: Shapes of Local Imitations of Near Eastern Pottery and quantities Found at Knossos Cemeteries.. 111
Table 17: Graph 14: Chronological sequence and quantity of imported pots and of their imitations. 112
Table 18: Classification of tombs according to imports. 117
Table 19: Graph 15: The ten richest tombs across all cemeteries... 119
Table 20: Graph 16: Dendrogram of tomb clusters... 133

Preface and Acknowledgements

Knossos was one of the most important settlements of the EIA Aegean. Elite groups manifested their social position and ideology by burying their dead in different clusters of tombs and cemeteries around Knossos. This book is a contextual study of the Near Eastern imports which reached Crete during the EIA and perhaps slightly earlier and that were deposited in the Knossian tombs. Cyprus, Phoenicia, North Syria and Egypt are the places of origin of imports used as burial offerings in Knossian cemeteries of the various elite groups. The present study reveals the ways in which imported commodities were used to create or enhance social identity. It is interesting to explore the reasons that made Knossians deposit imported objects in their graves as well as investigate whether specific groups could control not only the access to these objects but also the production of their imitations.

The locally produced imitations of Near Eastern objects, pots in their vast majority, are discussed since they offer a glimpse on the political, economical and also aesthetic preferences of the society. The extensive use of locally produced imitations in burial rituals along with their association with their imported prototypes found inside the same tombs signifies their importance. After more than a hundred years of excavations in the area, one revolution, two World Wars and intensive building activity, there have been many challenges in the preservation of the archaeological record. Therefore this study uses the evidence coming from 166 known and previously published Knossian tombs. Investigation includes descriptive analysis, statistics, quantification of pots and other objects and ethnographic examples, to further understanding of burial customs and material culture of these tombs.

I am grateful to my former PhD supervisor, Professor Maria Eugenia Aubet, Pompeu Fabra University, who suggested an investigation of the Knossian cemeteries from the perspective of the Near Eastern imports. Hence, I proceeded to a contextual study liberated from the traditional questions of migration, invasion and cultural dominance. She also kindly permitted me to reproduce photos from the excavations at Tyre, Al-Bass Cemetery. I am indebted to Dr Antonios Kotsonas, Assistant Professor at the University of Cincinnati, for engaging discussions on the subject and to share with me some of his unpublished articles, which were invaluable for the development of this study. Dr Konstantinos Kalogeropoulos, Academy of Athens and Dr Ourania

Vizyinou, Archaeological Society at Athens, made very useful suggestions on cult activity and burial rites; I truly thank them. I would also like to thank the British School at Athens for kindly permitting me to use photos and plans from the *Annuals* and the *Knossos North Cemetery* and *Fortetsa* publications. Friends and colleagues, my family and my girlfriend constantly supported me throughout this investigation. This book is dedicated to them.

Abbreviations

Bich.	Bichrome	M	Minoan
BoR	Black on Red	LM	Late Minoan
CG	Cypro-Geometric	SM	Sub-Minoan
CA	Cypro-Archaic	PG	Proto-Geometric
DA	Dark Age	EPG	Early Proto-Geometric
EIA	Early Iron Age	MPG	Middle Proto-Geometric
H.	Height	LPG	Late Proto-Geometric
KMF	Knossos Medical Faculty	PGB	Proto-Geometric B
KNC	Knossos North Cemetery	EG	Early Geometric
BA	Bronze Age	MG	Middle Geometric
LBA	Late Bronze Age	LG	Late Geometric
RS	Red Slip	EO	Early Orientalizing
WP	White Painted	MO	Middle Orientalizing
WoB	White on Black	LO	Late Orientalizing

Introduction

i. Contextual Analyses vs. Empirical Accounts

The present book derives from my PhD thesis.[1] However, the need for a contextual analysis of EIA Near Eastern imports discovered at Knossos resulted from an attempt, prior to the PhD research. Initially, I wanted to study and understand the distribution primarily of Phoenician and secondly Cypriot imports in Greece for a period which is still called by some scholars as 'the Greek Dark Age'.[2] They use this term mainly because of the supposed isolation of the post-BA Aegean from the world outside.[3] In this first attempt, the major problem I faced was that the evidence for such a study came from very old archaeological investigations[4] or unpublished rescue excavations. There were also irrelevant book-catalogues of museum collections with unprovenanced finds. Most of these collections were very interesting for the art market but of limited use for modern archaeology.

The second issue I noted during this first approach was that many relevant books and articles were concerned with the traditional issue of the early presence of Phoenicians in Greece.[5] There were also archaeologists that proposed the opposite view and argued for an early Greek presence in the Near East since the Mycenaean Period.[6] Long before the theories on the Afro-Asiatic roots of Ancient Greece,[7] debates concerning ethnicity and issues of 'cultural transmission' were very heated not only among historians but also among archaeologists.[8] Reading the articles of the archaeologists for the importance of the presence of the Phoenicians and other Near Eastern people in Greece[9] and vice versa,[10] one could claim that they seem to be defending an important cause, which, however, lacks any real social context. For many authors, the question of who transported those imports to Greece holds more importance than the imports' function within the local Aegean communities. A typical example of this approach, concerning not Greece itself but the Near East, is the site of Al Mina and the debate on whether it

---

[1] Antoniadis 2012.
[2] Dickinson 2006, 6.
[3] For the debate and definition of the Dark Age see Kotsonas 2016a, Papadopoulos 1994, 438; Dickinson 2006, 6. For earlier approaches see Desborough 1972 and Snodgrass 1987; 2000 xxiv.
[4] See Clara Rhodos (Jacobi 1938).
[5] Negbi 1992, 39-40.
[6] Boardman 1980, 75; Popham 1994, 11-34.
[7] Bernal 1988; 1991; 2001.
[8] Kossinna 1911; Childe 1929.
[9] Negbi 1992, 39-40.
[10] Sherratt and Sherratt 1993; Popham 1994, 11-34.

was an Early Greek emporium or not.[11] The importance and function of this port from the point of view of the local kingdoms is still largely ignored.

At the same time, there are other questions which are not related to traditional and historical debates. For example, why local people adopt, use and copy foreign objects and incorporate them into their society. The mechanisms of commercial activities and how an import travels to its destination are certainly important issues but the function of this import in the 'foreign' land and the way that local societies perceive it, deserves also attention. A good example of a region with an ample amount of well-published evidence is Knossos. I decided to study an EIA society where Near Eastern imports have been found and registered properly in numerous excavations at different periods over the last 117 years. Additionally, local imitations of Near Eastern imports were also discovered there. I believe that this is the best way to understand the function of Near Eastern imports and, above all, why and how Knossians used them.

I, therefore, propose a contextual analysis of Near Eastern imports and of their imitations discovered in the Knossian tombs. A decisive step to proceed to the imports' analysis is the detailed study of the EIA cemeteries at Knossos. This synthesis is needed because, after more than a century of excavations, revolutions, a disastrous Second World War and intensive building activity, many notes, small finds and even the location of some tombs have been lost. In fact, I consider that the study of the tombs and their spatial distribution must be of equal importance to the study of the imports. Attention is also given to the BA past of the area: there are Minoan characteristics, which might have been passed on to the EIA Knossian society.

The present study is not the first contextual analysis of archaeological evidence from Knossian tombs. There are books and articles written on the imports of EIA Crete[12] in general and of Knossos in particular. The first two books[13] were very detailed, up-to-date catalogues of imports discovered in all kinds of contexts in EIA Crete. Hoffman's book focused not only on Near Eastern imports but also on the possible presence of Near Eastern people in Crete. Jones, on the other hand, studied all EIA imports discovered in Crete regardless of their provenance. These two books were published after the KNC[14] publication. They did not, however, include the entire amount of information from this essential publication but they made use of preliminary reports written by the same authors.

---

[11] Wooley, 1948; 1953; Boardman 1980; Coldstream 1982; Waldbaum 1997; Kearsley 1999; Luke 2003; Lehman 2005, 61-92.
[12] Hoffman 1997; Jones 2000; Kotsonas 2006.
[13] Hoffman 1997; Jones 2000.
[14] Coldstream and Catling, 1996.

Kotsonas' article[15] focused mostly on contextual analysis and a specific archaeological argument of Boardman[16] about the ethnicity of the deceased of Teke Tholos Tomb. It also contained a catalogue of luxury imports. In another article,[17] he used a quantitative approach for the cinerary urns found at Knossos. This approach will have an important value also in the present book. It must be noted that in the books by Jones and Hoffman artefacts were classified first by type and then by context.[18] They were analysed more as valuable objects and not as part of a burial context, even if the context of the tombs was mentioned. I give priority to context. Archaeologists have pointed out the need for such an analysis as well as the possible difficulties: the tombs contained burials which in many cases were disturbed by other burials or plundering.[19] Since the scope of this book focuses on one main objective (i.e. highlighting the relationship between Near Eastern imports and burial groups), I believe that the nature of the tombs is not an obstacle.

ii. Aim and Method

The present book investigates the social structure and behaviour of the EIA Knossian society based on the mortuary evidence. The main tool employed in this study is a contextual analysis of the Near Eastern imports and their imitations discovered in the various burial sites. This is a contextual small- and large-scale comparison between the tombs, their locations and the quantities of Near Eastern imports and their imitations found in each context. This is an appropriate method for understanding the social relationships within the same community.[20] Special attention is given to the relation between the various elite groups as suggested by the mortuary evidence.

By using the term 'context' I refer to the tombs containing archaeological material dated to the EIA. The groups of tombs and the location of the various cemeteries of the area constitute part of a wider context, which is also of interest for this project. The impact of Near Eastern imports to the Knossian community will also be thoroughly studied in relation to their local copies. Context is one of the most important parameters of this study. It is the *"contextual approach that places social and archaeological context in the forefront of any analysis"*.[21]

Quantification is another important parameter. Descriptive statistics, measurements of distances between tombs and cemeteries will also be

---

[15] Kotsonas 2006.
[16] Boardman 1967, 57-75.
[17] Kotsonas 2011b.
[18] Hoffman 1997, 23.
[19] Whitley 1986; 1994; 1998, 613; Kotsonas 2006, 150.
[20] For the complex relationship between society and burial activity see Chapter 2.
[21] Whitley 1994, 52; Hodder 1991.

very important instruments for this study. Cluster analysis is crucial for understanding a variety of evidence. Ethnography is also important regarding theoretical issues. The cemeteries at Knossos are a special case: most of the chamber tombs were used for more than two generations and in some cases more than 40 inurned burials can be found in a chaotic state inside the same tomb. This puts in question whether the contextual approach can be the sole theoretical agenda of this book. I feel that one should not follow only one approach in order to understand the social relationships between the various groups that form a society.

For this reason, understanding the burial practices and social structure should involve archaeological evidence provided from other contexts as well. This is namely the evidence regarding the settlement and the cult activity at Knossos. This integrated approach follows a theoretical[22] agenda which proposes an interpretive rapprochement for combining and balancing multiple lines of evidence.[23] The only differentiation from this approach is that in Knossos mortuary evidence is much more excessive in comparison to all the other kinds of evidence.

The present book is divided into four chapters and two distinct parts. In Chapter 1, I discuss theoretical issues of contextual archaeology and the use of mortuary evidence for a better understanding of the nature and function of a society. The concept of imports and imitations is also assessed. Certain issues of terminology and chronology of the EIA in Crete are also discussed. The archaeological theory, however, is a very complex matter and cannot be restrained to a single chapter as a section separated from the rest of the book. There are issues concerning society, rites, rituals, grave goods and other objects found in the tombs that need to be discussed and in some cases tested against specific archaeological evidence. Therefore, further theoretical considerations are used throughout the book.

Chapter 2 is concerned with the nature of archaeological evidence and the distribution of tombs and cemeteries. It offers a history of the excavations of the EIA tombs and cemeteries at Knossos and their relation to the settlement. Apart from the two main publications written about the cemeteries,[24] in this investigation are included all the other final publications of tombs discovered in the region. All tombs will be grouped according to their location and type. The second chapter also presents evidence from the Knossos area regarding the society besides the mortuary evidence. An important part of this discussion regards the debates concerning the nature of the EIA settlement. Finally,

---
[22] Keswani 2004, 6-21.
[23] Ibid., 31-4.
[24] Brock 1957; Coldstream and Catling 1996.

another very significant issue is the cult activity in the EIA Knossos and its possible connection to the Minoan past.

Chapters 3 and 4 which constitute the second part of the book concern the appreciation of the Near Eastern imports and their imitations by Knossian society. In Chapter 3, I present and analyse all the Near Eastern imports in relation to their context, which is the tombs. Other categories to be presented are the objects of uncertain provenance (which are either Near Eastern or local imitations) and finally, the imitations of Near Eastern finds, the prototypes of which have also been found in Knossos. The presentation of the above categories is made in a detailed catalogue. This enables the detection of possible patterns in their location. Imports are not always found in fully published tombs, but in some cases, they originate from unpublished ones. Unfortunately, archaeologists occasionally publish the most spectacular find from a tomb and not the complete assemblage of the context. Regardless of how brilliant or important a find is, if it published isolated from the rest of the objects that belong to the same assemblage, it distorts any study regarding this context. Since this study takes into serious consideration the entire context of the tomb, imports from not fully published tombs will not be included. In Chapter 4, I attempt to make the analysis and at the end a synthesis of all the different evidence and categories presented in Chapter 3. There is a series of questions, concerning the evidence, which I will attempt to answer.

In the Conclusion, there is a summary of the evidence. This is an attempt to describe the EIA from the point of view of the mortuary evidence, in relation to the Near Eastern imports and their imitations. Appendices are placed at the end of the book. Maps, plans and graphs deemed crucial for the development of the analysis will be placed within the body of the text.

iii. General Remarks on Knossos

The name Ko-no-so was recorded in the Linear B clay tablets. The region of Knossos, with its most prominent archaeological feature, the heavily reconstructed Palace of Minos, is located in the north-central part of Crete, about 5km from the north coast, near the modern capital of Heraklion. Knossos is a lowland area with small river valleys. The most prominent river is Kairatos, which runs just to the east of Minoan Palace.[25] The natural borders of the area are low hills in the south and even lower in the north, while various streams run in the eastern and western borders of the lowland. Due to the presence of the rivers and of various springs and despite the non-alluvial conditions, Knossos is a well-watered area.

---

[25] Hood and Smyth 1981, 1.

FIGURE 1: MAP 1: KNOSSOS AND THE EASTERN MEDITERRANEAN.

The first archaeological investigation at this site was made in 1878, when local antiquarian Minos Kalokairinos identified, after a series of soundings, the BA Palace of Knossos in 1878-79.[26] Crete was then under the Ottoman rule and Cretans feared that, if Kalokairinos had conducted more excavations, the archaeological finds would be transferred by the Turks to the Imperial Museum of Istanbul.[27] This was exactly the case of the famous marble sarcophagus depicting Alexander the Great discovered in Sidon in 1887. For this reason, in 1879, Kalokarinos was asked by the Cretans to stop his investigations.[28] An autonomic Cretan state, under the sovereignty of the Sultan, was established in 1896. Four years later, Arthur Evans and the director of the British School at Athens, David George Hogarth, began a series of excavations and surveys in the area, a part of which had already been bought by Evans.[29] After a series of restorations, initially for protecting the freshly excavated ruins, Evans created the Palace of Minos, a structure that would be called later as *"the most eccentric archaeological reconstruction ever to achieve scholarly acceptance"*.[30]

Crete was united with the Hellenic State in 1913. Eleven years after in 1924, Arthur Evans handed over his Knossos state to the British School at Athens. By

---

[26] Kotsonas 2016b, 299; Kopaka 1995.
[27] Castleden 1990, 22.
[28] Ibid.
[29] Panagiotaki 2004; Coldstream and Catling 1996, 1; Evans 1921, v.
[30] Gere 2009, 5.

the end of the World War II, the BSA faced great economic difficulties. For this reason, all the properties of the School in Knossos (apart from the Stratigraphic Museum) were donated to the Hellenic State.[31] At the same time, an agreement was made between the British School and Greek authorities that the School should always be able to conduct excavations and make publications of the archaeological area of Knossos, subject to prior authorisation by the Greek antiquities service (*Ephoria*).[32]

There is a particular problem concerning excavations and primary archaeological reports written before the World War II. Following the battle of Crete in 1941, the island was occupied by the Germans for four years. From the onset of the war, there was a huge effort by the local archaeological service to safeguard and conceal from the foreign army the most important archaeological objects in sealed vaults. However, in many occasions during the occupation, the German authorities transferred the archaeological material that had remained outside the vaults from one gallery to another.[33] At the same time, most of the British archaeologists had to leave the island, while others like John Pendlebury stayed and fought.[34] Many of their archaeological notes were lost. After the end of the war, most of the archaeological material was found and rescued. However, it was occasionally difficult to rematch the objects and the pieces with the inventory catalogues or to sort out pottery without the archaeologists' preliminary notes. This was also the case with small finds. Additionally, a further difficulty in understanding the archaeological evidence is that archaeologists Humfry Payne and Alan Blakeway who had excavated many EIA tombs died in 1936 before the final publication of the finds.

After World War II, Greek authorities established two archaeological zones in Knossos. The main archaeological area was around the Palace (Archaeological zone A) and it was protected by modern constructions. In the second much more extended area (Archaeological zone B), building activity was permitted to a certain degree, but only after a thorough archaeological investigation. However, the borders of the two zones were not precisely defined and did not remain stable. For this reason, the most important benefit from the initial agreement between Greek authorities and the British School was that the Archaeological Zone A remained relatively intact. This permitted to archaeologists to conduct investigations without the pressure of the constructors. Unfortunately, after 1950 the situation changed and the constructions of the Venizeleion Hospital

---

[31] Coldstream and Catling 1996, 1.
[32] Ibid.
[33] Brock 1957, xii.
[34] Pendlebury joined the British army and became liaison officer between British troops and Cretan military. He was executed by the Germans in 1941 (Fermor 2003).

(Sanatorium) and later of the University Medical Faculty have resulted in the shrinking of the archaeological zones, not to mention the constant pressure by the locals for extension of the urban zone into the protected areas. In 2010 the Hellenic Ministry of Culture excluded 3000 m² of land from archaeological zone A (near Fortetsa) in order to allow urban development in it.[35] This building activity will result in a further environmental degradation and change of the landscape which constitutes part of the archaeological monuments of the area.[36]

FIGURE 2: MAP 2: THE AREA OF KNOSSOS, THE BA PALACE AND MODERN HERAKLION.

---

[35] Kontrarou-Rassia 2010.
[36] Ibid.

Chapter 1: Death and her Objects: Theoretical Approaches

i. Interpreting the Mortuary Evidence

Fundamental to this book is the belief that the analysis and interpretation of mortuary evidence (either human remains or grave goods and other objects along with tomb structure and architecture) may offer to archaeologists some explanation about the structure and behaviour of a given society. In other words, the way that the world of the dead is structured can provide some evidence for the world of the living. Although this statement seems straightforward, it requires an explanation from the point of view of archaeological theory, as this has been developed at least since the 'New Archaeology' at the 1960s. This analysis will demonstrate that there is differentiation in the way archaeologists interpret the relationship between death and society.

The subject of death and society was not first approached by the archaeological theory. As a social phenomenon, is related more to the work of social anthropologists.[37] According to the functional approach, after the death of an individual, society is disturbed by the shock and must gradually regain its balance through a series of ceremonies during the period of mourning.[38] In other words, there is always a need for equilibrium after such a devastating event. For functionalists, religion plays a great role during the funeral since: *"...it counteracts the centrifugal forces of fear, dismay, demoralisation, and provides the most powerful means of reintegration of the group's shaken solidarity and of the re-establishment of its morale."*.[39]

Gennep and Hertz provided archaeologists with an analysis of the concept of the three-stage ritual. The three stages are the rite of separation, the rite transition (rite de marge) and finally the rite of aggregation or reincorporation. These rites have become known as the 'rite of passage', i.e. the funeral.[40] Functionalism, however, was criticised for its preference to religion as a system that cannot practically explain the social and cultural change, especially on the basis of

---

[37] The differentiation between archaeology and social anthropology in the USA is not as sharp as in Europe.
[38] Danforth 1982, 26; Hertz 1960, 82 and 86.
[39] Malinowski 1954, 35; Danforth 1982, 26.
[40] Hertz 1960; Van Gennep 1960, 164-165; Morris 1987, 31.

an analysis of the death rituals.[41] Functionalism cannot provide explanations related to real archaeological evidence, since *"archaeologists excavate burials and not funerals"*.[42] In this respect, the four rules of cult behaviour are very crucial:[43]

1. Verbal testimony
2. Direct Observation of funerary practices
3. Study of non-verbal records
4. Study of the material remains of the funerary activities themselves

The fourth rule is the most important regarding the burial evidence from EIA Knossos because there are only archaeological finds from the era and naturally no verbal testimonies nor direct observation of funerary practices. The third rule could be useful only if one considers that the Homeric epics can be used in this investigation. Homer cannot be entirely overruled since modern concepts such us 'objects' biography' can be found in his verses.[44] There is no doubt that the most important part of the fourth rule is related to the direct interpretation approach in archaeology. The social status and the mortuary treatment have been linked with the aid of direct interpretation and ethnography[45].

This link between social status and mortuary treatment is very important: *"the overall complexity or variability of the mortuary ritual within a given society would be a direct reflection of social complexity in terms of both vertical or hierarchical and horizontal or non-hierarchical groupings"*.[46] The essential need to study a past society not with the aim of making it part of a historical explanation but for trying to understand it, is one of the major contributions of processual archaeology and one of the pillars of this book. Another key factor introduced with New Archaeology is the use of a broad range of statistical techniques. For example, cluster analysis and models, which in many cases put some order in the chaos of pottery evidence and styles. They are also useful for analysing various types of artefacts and materials and propose different answers.

However, for other archaeologists, the way that direct interpretation links the worlds of the dead and the living is not very satisfactory. Some have stressed the fact that there are high-status burials with no visible remains.[47] Others claim that post-depositional processes can change the context of the archaeological record.[48]

---

[41] Danforth 1982, 26; Geertz 1973, 142-143.
[42] Morris 1987, 36.
[43] Renfrew 1985, 12.
[44] Such as the story of Achilles'crater (*Iliad* 23.740-45).
[45] Keswani 2004, 7; Saxe 1971; 1970; Binford 1972.
[46] Keswani 2004, 7; Binford 1972, 232-5.
[47] Braun 1981; Brown 1981.
[48] Keswani 2004, 7; O'Shea 1984.

One of the most astonishing examples of a rich burial which cannot be traced archaeologically (especially from the point of view of the ritual) is the Viking burial of a chieftain on the banks of Volga, as described by Ahman Ibn Fadlan.[49] Another example of an 'invisible' ritual and performance can be by Achilles' preparation of Patroclus' funeral: gathering of graves goods, the sacrifice of Trojan captives and various animals, post-burial games etc. It is not certain that Achilles role was institutional in the organisation of the funeral and all his acts and tasks are, archaeologically speaking, untraceable, excluding perhaps the dead Trojans.

Post-processualism argued against the processual approach to the direct interpretation. For most of the post-processualists, the mortuary variation is not an exact representation of social roles and social hierarchy within the living society.[50] Post-processualists believe that the aspect of symbolism as manifested through the various visible and invisible rites and rituals is far more important than direct interpretation. Other archaeologists claim that mortuary rituals are a ritualised expression of social structure in which empirical relationships can be denied, reflected or exaggerated.[51]

One might add that even processes of burial practice that are easier for archaeologists to trace, such as the gradual shift from inhumation to cremation after the end of the BA in the Aegean societies, are only partly reflected in visible material remains. Again, the ritual or symbolic part of the activity, which is the funeral, is ignored.[52] In fact, many archaeologists still use the direct interpretation in order to understand a context.[53] An example of direct interpretation is that of the LBA tombs, where a lot of weapons has been found. These tombs have been interpreted as the resting plays of warriors. It is not always certain whether the dead was a male, a child or an adult.[54] In the same line of thought, others have interpreted theses graves as a practice that is related to the warlike Mycenaean ideology.[55] In his investigation on the differences between BA and EIA 'warrior' burials, Whitley puts great emphasis on the subject of identity, ideological claims and the symbolic aspects of a 'warrior burial' which involve status, hierarchy and gender.[56]

---

[49] Parker Pearson 1999, 1-3.
[50] Keswani 2004, 8; Pader 1982; Parker Pearson 1982; 1984; 1993; Shanks and Tilley 1982.
[51] Morris 1987, 39.
[52] Morris 1992, 13-14.
[53] Ibid., 24-26; Hodder 1982, 141-146.
[54] Whitley 2001, 169.
[55] Morgan 2009; Davies and Bennet 1999.
[56] Whitley 2002, 227.

Two ethnographic examples from contemporary Greece suggest the relativity of direct interpretation: when an unmarried girl dies, her funerary clothes are a wedding dress. The same applies to young boys, who are buried dressed in wedding attire.[57] A few decades ago, in rural areas of Greece, most of the unmarried persons (regardless of their age) were buried dressed as if they were to get married. On the contrary, when a young married woman or man died, relatives did not dress them as bride or groom. In this example, there is a very strong symbolism with death functioning as a metaphor of marriage.[58] This symbolism occurs during a funeral which is held by a priest but, has nothing to do with the Christian religion.[59]

The second example is related to grave goods. In Greek orthodox religion, grave goods are not officially accepted, yet Greeks sometimes place inside the coffin objects of minor value for the afterlife. The strange thing is that these objects are not always offered to the person who is inside the coffin. A few years ago, I was present at a funeral in the town of Marathon in Attica. In this funeral, the cousin of the deceased placed inside the coffin a packet of cigarettes that the deceased would give to the long-gone father of the cousin. This act has a very strong symbolism: a son that still remembers his dead father and his everyday habits. The symbolism becomes even stronger when it takes place in front of relatives during the funeral of another person of the same family. In both ethnographic examples, the direct interpretation would not help an archaeologist to understand the symbolic and social implication of an old lady in a coffin dressed as a bride, or a packet of cigarettes inside a coffin of a man. Additionally, it would be meaningless to assume any social difference between rich and poor dead people in these rituals.

Regarding grave goods, some archaeologists approach them as a manifestation of the attitude of the living rather than as a characterisation of the dead.[60] At the same time, though, they admit that grave goods cannot simply be expressions of the status of the burying group.[61] For example, in a typical marble sarcophagus in 5th Century BC Athens it is not unusual to find a stleggis (body scraper) as a grave good next to a male skeleton. That does not necessarily mean that this person was an athlete but at the same time leaves this possibility wide open. For this reason, one must stress the importance of quantification and measurements. If for example, all male skeletons were accompanied by the same grave good that might be more likely to be a symbolic act.

---

[57] Danforth 1982, 80.
[58] Ibid., 81.
[59] Alexiou 1974, 24-35.
[60] Dickinson 2006, 177-178.
[61] Ibid., 178.

These examples have shown that the direct interpretation of funerary evidence in the way it was used in the past (and still used) has serious weaknesses. However, it cannot be entirely disregarded as a method. There is always a possibility that a Mycenaean shaft grave with a male skeleton accompanied by a sword and a dagger is the tomb of a warrior. Direct interpretation remains a valuable tool but at the same time, one should be conscious of the importance of unofficial rituals which lay outside the typical religious ceremonies and could have been powerful and unrelated to the social status of the deceased. To study the EIA Knossians, I take for granted that society exists and past societies have also existed. At the same time, I am conscious of the post-processual critique that processual archaeologists should not take the concept of society so seriously as to exclude the individual from their study.[62] The critique of post-processualism and subsequently post-modernism is very important in order to approach the concept of a society without heavily relying on functionalism. Individuals are very important and their agency must be studied wherever it is detectable in the archaeological record.

In the present book, I have consciously avoided making broad use of the term 'grave goods', since, in the quantitative approach I use, all the objects found in each tomb are placed in a single category of objects. For this reason, a distinction between grave goods and other objects would have been pointless. It is also true that what does not seem to be considered as grave good is the pottery since its function is more related to funeral ceremonies. Therefore, I make a distinction between pots and other objects. One must not disregard the role of pots found in a grave. In the case of Knossos cemeteries, most of the Near Eastern imports are ceramic vases and almost all of them were found inside extremely rich chamber tombs. The role of these imports will be thoroughly analysed in Chapters 3 and 4.

Another theoretical approach, which is based more on post-processualism, pays attention not only to archaeological evidence but also to the subjective agent of the archaeological investigation, namely the archaeologist. An archaeologist will never be free from his or her prejudices and this can sometimes influence possible interpretations, a fact that has happened more than once in the past.[63] The idea that each scholar interprets the evidence according to his or her understanding and views constitutes a factor that makes the post-processual approach valuable. For example, all archaeologists seem to agree on what a grave is, or that a dromos (entrance passage) is part of chamber tomb. The

---

[62] Shanks and Tilley 1987, 29-57.
[63] See for example the influence of Modernism on Evans (Gere 2009).

analysis, however, of a dromos as an architectural/structural or symbolic feature depends on the archaeologist conducting the investigation.

Tombs contain individuals but in the case of EIA Knossos, each tomb usually contains more than one individual. In this wider group of individuals, archaeologists may trace and assign common artefacts and behaviours (or patterns) to the same or distinctive groups of people and might make common observations and probably interpretations. In other words, the process of understanding a group through observation does not always have to be related to the historical context.[64] Concluding this section, I argue that a contextual approach can be a very useful guide for understanding many aspects of the past.

ii. Funeral Rites: Cremation or Inhumation?

One of the most notable changes regarding mortuary evidence and funeral rites between the BA and the EIA is the shift from inhumation to cremation. Cremations outnumber inhumations after the beginning of the EIA. This shift does not mean that cremation previously was an unknown practice. It became, however, the dominant rite in some regions, especially from the 10th century onwards.[65] This change was not sudden neither occurred everywhere at the same time. In fact, in some regions cremation never became the dominant rite. In Corinth, for example, it was a very rare phenomenon.[66]

Cremation did not appear for the first time in the EIA. It probably first occurred in the Greek peninsula as early as the Early Neolithic Period (about 5500 BC). This is demonstrated by the burned human remains from the settlement of Souphli Magoula in Thessaly.[67] Cremations from all phases of the Neolithic Period were discovered in a cave at Lavrion, Attica.[68] There are few examples of cremation from the MBA, one on the island of Leukas and another in MH III Argos.[69] It is also attested in LBA Greece and Crete, but mostly as an isolated rite.[70] There are older theories connecting this rite with the invasion of Dorians from the North and the Homeric heroes.[71] Such theories though cannot be supported archaeologically and Mylonas rejected them almost 70 years ago.[72]

---

[64] Shanks and Tilley 1987, 59.
[65] Snodgrass 2000, 164-170; Coldstream 1977, 48; Cavangh 1996, 652; Dickinson 2006, 185-189.
[66] Blegen *et al* 1964.
[67] Gallis 1982, 32 and 48.
[68] Melas 1984, 25; Vavritsas 1968, 235-6.
[69] Melas 1984, 25; Dörpfeld 1927, 210-237; Benton 1931-32; 229-30.
[70] Snodgrass 2000, 165; Cavanagh 1996, 675.
[71] Ridgeway 1901, 506-7.
[72] Mylonas 1948, 79.

Others suggest that there was a continuity of the cremation rite from the Neolithic down to the EIA.[73] Melas does not share this view.[74] He maintains that despite the few examples of cremation in Greece, this burial custom was introduced from Anatolia in the mid-14th century BC. There were cultural and commercial relations of the Mycenaean sites of the Eastern Aegean and southwestern Anatolia with the Hittites and the Trojans.[75] The popularity of cremation in Anatolia must not be omitted.[76] Cremation emerges as a dominant rite in Greek sites with overseas connections the same period that became popular in the Levantine coast.[77] Other archaeologists stress the associations between LBA burials in Peloponnese and Crete with Italian imports.[78] After 1100 BC, in many cemeteries, cremation coexisted with inhumation and it seems that the adoption of this rite does not necessarily mean a shift in the wider context of burial rituals and beliefs.[79] Inhumation, on the other hand, did not really disappear from the archaeological record and in the case of Knossos there are few inhumations dated at the end of the EIA.

The reasons for the rise of cremation in EIA, especially after the PG period, are not clear. The most probable cause though is that cremation became associated with the luxurious funeral ritual display, since the consumption of wood involves a great use of energy and manpower and it is considered a very expensive operation.[80] Tarlas[81] reflects on several reasons which made the Athenian elite of the EIA to adopt cremation as the main funeral rite. He sees a series of different socio-economic reasons such as the superior productive capacity of the elite which eventually led to an unequal society.[82] In order to increase this inequality, the elite manipulated and elaborated ideological means such as selective formal burial and eventually cremation. He also maintains that selective formal burial and cremation are symbolically linked.[83]

There are more complicated issues concerning cremation and its impact on the society that practises it. Mylonas[84] claims that cremation can simply be the

---

[73] Galis 1982, 32, 48.
[74] Melas 1984, 26-33.
[75] Mylonas 1948, 80; Lorimer 1950, 107; McFadden 1954, 134; Iakovidis 1969-1970, n. 53; Snodgrass 2000, 157-8.
[76] Dickinson 2006, 188-189.
[77] Ibid.; Aubet 2001, 65.
[78] Ruppenstein 2013,188.
[79] Melas 1984, 33; Dickinson 2006, 180.
[80] Dickinson 2006, 189.
[81] Tarlas 1994.
[82] Ibid., 327.
[83] Ibid.
[84] Mylonas 1948, 80.

quickest way for the separation of the body from the soul. It is perhaps for this reason that it was first adopted for warriors who died overseas. For the scholar, this need could have been created during the Trojan War. Again, Anatolia is the region for where cremation rite originated. He claims that the change of the rite does not bring any change to the rest of the rituals and the grave goods.[85] This can be a further proof that cremation does not have to be related to a change in the religious beliefs of the society which adopts it.

Cavanagh[86] investigated the rite of cremation from the point of view of religion and superstition.[87] He claimed that "*the graves at Dypilon (Kerameikos, Athens) suggested a belief in wilful and demanding spirits surviving death and cremation*".[88] Gallis[89] argues that the mortuary evidence from Neolithic, Bronze and Iron Age Greece concerning cremation are related to the belief of the ancient Greeks that the soul survives death. He paid particularly to the grave goods prepared especially for the dead[90] .One must not forget Elpenor's ghost begging Odysseus for a proper burial.[91] According to Melas, there are some universal feelings, such as fear, insecurity, love etc.[92] In this way, cremation can be interpreted as a manifestation of an ancient fear towards the return of the dead person. Fire, apart from purifying the dead, also ensures the dead will not return.[93] What, however, is not well explained by Melas is why there is the coexistence of funeral rites (cremation and inhumation) or shifts from the one to the other practice.

iii. Imports, Imitations and Numbers

Imports and imitations are concepts and certainly objects which have concerned archaeologists since almost the beginning of the discipline.[94] German archaeologists studied the impact of Roman imports in the Northern Germanic regions. Additionally, imports and imitations found in Neolithic Germany were used for cross-dating and for the discovery of new 'cultures'.[95] However, in this book imports and imitations are studied primarily as objects and not as concepts or techniques. Therefore, the theoretical framework adopted

---

[85] Ibid.
[86] Cavanagh 1977
[87] Ibid., 20; Helbig 1900; Poulsen 1905.
[88] Cavanagh 1977, 20.
[89] Gallis 1982, 178.
[90] Ibid.
[91] *Odyssey* XI.1-332.
[92] Melas 1984, 28.
[93] Ibid., 23.
[94] Hansen 2008, 1.
[95] Ibid.

is related to the studies of the 'anthropology of things' and its implication for economy, politics and display. Undoubtedly, one of the most important contributions in this field is a collection of essays edited by Appadurai,[96] where concepts such as the cultural biography of objects[97] and the commodity and value in ranked societies[98] were thoroughly discussed. In an intriguing article, Koppytoff[99] parallels commodity to slavery, in order to argue that objects also have biographies (cultural, though) and that the status or cultural context of commodities can be modified during their 'lifetime'. Of course, the commodity is related to exchange and in this respect, an import is the best example of a product with an extensive and extremely rich biography.

One of the best examples of such an object is a Phoenician silver crater, which was used as a price by Achilles in the games that followed the burial of Patroclus.[100] In the Iliad, one reads that this crater was made in Sidon and was offered by Phoenician merchants to the King of Lemnos. After a series of exchanges at the highest levels of the Aegean elites, it ended up as a ransom gift to Achilles. Such a 'cultural biography' cannot be detected by the archaeologist who discovers similar artefacts in excavations.[101] The text of the Iliad is an indication that prestigious objects such as silver plates, bronze tripods etc might have longer lives than other objects such as ceramic vessels. Especially, in the case of the EIA Knossian cemeteries, there were imports from the Near East, mostly bronze objects, of a much older date than the rest of the context of the tomb.[102]

The Greek word *keimelia* (in singular *keimelion*) describes all these objects.[103] This word can be translated as heirloom. However, in English language an heirloom is an object that, apart from being old and valuable, is also related to the same family for at least more than one generation. As Whitley[104] points out not all keimelia are heirlooms. He claims that an antique object which is not an heirloom can also be very important because of its deeply entangled biography.[105] Gift-exchange, however, between Greek and in many cases Phoenician elite members[106] during the LBA and EIA is only one of the options for the circulations of objects. Craftsmen and trading networks actively

---
[96] Appadurai 1986.
[97] Kopytoff 1986, 64-91.
[98] Renfrew 1986, 141-168.
[99] Ibid., 65.
[100] Aubet 2001, 130-1; *Iliad* 23.740-45
[101] Aubet 2001, 130-1.
[102] See Catalogue at Chapter 3.
[103] Aubet 2001, 130-1.
[104] Whitley 2013, 402.
[105] Ibid.
[106] Aubet 2001, 107.

participated in the distribution of goods in the Ancient Mediterranean. These activities echo in Herodotus[107] when he describes how Phoenicians abducted women from Argos after they had first sold most of their commodities. Soon after, Cretans landed at Tyre and kidnapped princess Europa.

These cases suggest the need for contextual studies in archaeology, where the differences between objects found in the same context can be better appreciated. Over the last years, there have been studies concerning the theoretical issues of imports and imitations.[108] Wijngaarden[109] explores the concept of authenticity concerning Mycenaean imports and their imitations in LBA Cyprus, Levant and Italy. The author is concerned with how the origin of Mycenaean vessels were used and appreciated in Antiquity.[110] In the case of Levant and in urban and mortuary sites such as Vile Basse at Ugarit, Ashdod, Tell Abu Hawan, Tell Dan, Sarepta, Tell Nami and Beth Shean in Megiddo, archaeologists found LH IIIA and LH IIIB Mycenaean pots alongside Cypriot imitations thereof.[111] Wijngaarden[112] believes that in LBA Levant Mycenaean pots and their imitations were regarded as international goods but not as prestige items because in the Levantine cities they were related to all the aspects of life. He even suggests that they were suitable for the material expression of the urban middle classes.[113]

In Cyprus, the author argues that Mycenaean pots were incorporated into the local culture to such an extent that it did not matter whether they were local or not, while in Italy the same pots were more important for their function than their provenance.[114] The method used by Wijngaarden to establish his association is undoubtedly the context, the spatial distribution and the function of the pot. The quantity of the pots in the context is also important. The aforementioned analysis is important to the present book since it reveals the active role of the recipient and it can be compared to the case study of the Near Eastern pottery and their appreciation by the Knossians.

The value of quantified studies in these case studies must be highlighted: the importance of the quantification of ceramic finds in the EIA Cretan tombs has recently been stressed by Kotsonas.[115] In his theoretical analysis, he argues for

---

[107] Herodotus 1.1-2.
[108] Biehl and Rassamakin 2008, 1.
[109] Wijngaarden 2008, 126-145; 2002.
[110] Ibid., 129.
[111] Ibid., 13; Leonard *et al* 1993; Killebrew 1998; Khalifeh 1988; Balensi 1980.
[112] Wijngaarden 2008, 132.
[113] Ibid.
[114] Ibid., 135.
[115] Kotsonas 2011a, 129; 2008.

three types of inferences from pots of any assemblage, including burials as they were defined by Orton.[116]

a) Inferences on the number or amount of vessels in an assemblage, either as a total or by type.
b) Inferences on the composition of different assemblages and the proportions of different types.
c) Comparisons over the composition of different assemblages.

Kotsonas argues that mainly type b and at lesser degree type c can be used in the burials. From the three proposed references, only the second and the third are used by Kotsonas in his case study on the collective tombs at Knossos and Eleutherna and he considers that Cretan urns are a set that favours quantification. Although Kotsonas uses quantification in order to explain a different archaeological question, it is interesting to see in the present book how these inferences can be applied to the imports and imitations discovered in EIA Knossian tombs. As one may see in the section in the section of the catalogue in Chapter 3, there are assemblages of import and imitations of these imports discovered in the same tombs.

At the same time, there are other tombs that have only imports or only imitations. Type b fits better to the analysis of the imports. The function of the imported pots (unguent vessels in their vast majority) suggest that they were probably used only once in the mortuary context. Certainly, pots have the advantage of quantity in the archaeological record, but not all the finds share the luck of the ceramics. For various reasons, such as the cost of production, the exclusiveness of use etc., objects like for example bronze rod tripods appear in rare cases in the mortuary record of Knossos. In this case, apart from the quantified approach, there are other methods which should be used for analysing this material. Such a method can be the combination of different evidence from the same context, for example, a descriptive analysis between tombs containing metal objects and tombs which do not contain such objects. Snodgrass[117] has done such a study at Knossos but only for the site of KNC publication, in an attempt to compare it with the cemetery of Fortetsa.[118] Other ways can be a cluster analysis combining more than one variable to distinct groups.

Apart from the theoretical issues about import and imitation in general, there other matters concerning imports and imitations at Knossos itself in relation to Knossian society. First, it cannot be argued that all the imports that reached

---
[116] Ibid., 130; Orton 1993, 178-180; Orton *et al* 1993, 166-167, Orton and Tyers 1990, 88.
[117] Snodgrass 1996.
[118] Brock 1957.

Knossos during the EIA were end-products nor were all of them imitated by the locals. At the same time, not all the imports ended up in cemeteries and not all the imports were indeed imports. There is a variety of products very different from one another. There is also a range of other products for which archaeologists cannot decide whether they were imports or a result of advanced local production (i.e. exact copies). Certainly, different questions arise concerning the manufacture and use of these products. The most relevant questions conserving the use of imports and imitations are:

- Did Knossians know that the Near Eastern imports were indeed imports and not imitations? And if yes did they care?
- As an extension to the previous question: Did an exact local copy of an import have the same function as the imported object? Was it considered of the same social value and status?
- Was there any restriction to the access to those of imports and their imitations?

Al these different questions are closely related to the main purpose of the book, which is an effort to understand the EIA Knossian society through the study of cemeteries and of Near Eastern imports discovered in them. An answer to the first question must again be quantity. Additionally, in the case objects produced outside the community but used (or consumed) by community members, the importance of quantity is even greater. For this reason, the relation between the amount of the local grave goods and Near Eastern imports and imitations is thoroughly studied below.

In the next two questions, apart from quantity, equally important is the context of the imports in relation to local objects and imitations. First, it must be made clear that as import I mean only end-products and not raw materials, such as metal commodities or ivory.[119] Another important matter is the distinction between imports and exact local copies. There is a series of metal objects such as bronze rod tripods, bowls and stands on which there is a still a debate on their provenance. There are scholars who support that these objects are reaching Crete from Cyprus.[120] Others claim that they were locally produced by Cretans[121] or foreign craftsmen in Crete.[122] This occurs because this category of objects has hitherto been seen by most of the scholars as prestige or high-status goods.

---

[119] See also Hoffmann 1997, 19.
[120] Catling 1996c, 647.
[121] Hoffman 1997, 191-234.
[122] Boardman 1967, 56-57.

The main purpose of this book is to understand the Knossian society that made use of this objects and therefore it is essential to establish a new category in this analysis, besides the categories of imports and imitations and of equal importance. This new category will be the objects of the uncertain provenance (i.e. Near Eastern or local). By the term 'local objects' I mostly mean objects that probably were made at Knossos. This, however, does not exclude products produced elsewhere in Crete. Nonetheless, sometimes it is impossible to know where an object was produced, even within Crete. This category was created not in order to avoid further investigation on the provenance of those objects but on the contrary, I believe that it will allow us to examine under new light various issues concerning this kind of products.

The safest category of items whose provenance is most secure is without a doubt the pottery. As in most cases, petrographic analysis can provide with some evidence on the provenance of the objects. However, there is an issue that needs to be explored further and this is the way that pots are perceived by the archaeologist. A BoR juglet is at the same time a Cyprus-Phoenician juglet and a BoR lekythos, according to the scholar who conducts the investigation.[123] This issue is linked to question 3 above; the main difference, though, is that the agent responsible for answering is the archaeologist and not the pot or the ancient society. As it can be seen in the next section, there is a series of different issues concerning chronologies, objects and pottery, where the power of the names and the subjectivity of the archaeologists have become extremely important.

iv. The problem of Names: Implications on chronology and terminology

> "Names have sense and each name has a unique sense attached to it"[124]

It has been observed that in some primitive societies the sense of a name approaches the status of an institution.[125] The unique sense or power that a name may hold is to be seen in other societies apart from the Kayan tribe in Borneo that Miller studied.[126] An example of such a 'society' can be that of the archaeologists and historians who gave names to the period investigated in this book (1100-600 BC). This is a period full of names which regard the chronological sequence, and sometimes overlap or even contradict each other. By giving a name to a certain period, there is always the potential problem (or effect) of transmitting the properties of the name to the period as well. The periodization of the Greek past is a minefield of potential problems.

---

[123] See Schreiber 2003.
[124] Luntley 1984, 65.
[125] Miller 1927, 585.
[126] Ibid.

In Crete, the names that have been employed since the initial discoveries of Evans and Hogarth to describe this period are more than one: the first name that was used in order to describe the EIA finds from Knossos was "*Greek Age*"[127] or simply "*Geometric*".[128] The term 'Greek' was used by Evans to distinguish between the 'unique' BA Non-Hellenic, Minoan civilisation from the later historical periods of Crete. It is not very clear why, but this name has become extremely popular among most of the British working in the Knossos region and even in core books of EIA archaeology at Knossos.[129] Coldstream[130] had even felt the need to explain his personal preference for the use of term 'Early Greek Knossos' instead of 'Early Iron Age Knossos'. A reason for this might have been a possible line of archaeological tradition after Evans and Hogarth that British archaeologists respected. A notable exception is Pendlebury,[131] who avoids the use of the term and instead uses the more reasonable for this period 'Post-Minoan' and then 'Geometric' for the succeeding period. Coldstream has also used the term 'Dorian' Knossos.[132] Thus, he links the chronological sequence with the alleged invasion or migration of the Dorians at the end of the BA. Brock, on the other hand, in his study on the EIA tombs at Knossos claimed that there is nothing connecting "*the Protogeometric culture*" with the Dorians.[133]

Sub-Minoan is another name that was used (in the same fashion as Sub-Mycenaean in the Greek mainland) for the first part of the EIA (1100-970 BC) in Crete and is applied in pottery style analysis. It can be very hard distinguishing archaeologically SM culture from Minoan especially when interments from these two periods are found inside the same chamber tombs. As the prefix 'Sub' implies, scholars have understood it either as less important than the glorious Minoan/BA past or simply as a transitional period before the arrival of the PG style and pots from Athens.[134] Myers[135] considers the SM as part of the BA and more specifically as part of the Post-Palatial period (Myers et al 1992, 33). Snodgrass,[136] on the other hand, has pointed out that SM (just like Sub-Mycenaean) should belong to the Iron Age since iron is in wider use. In general, the SM does not seem to be very different from the previous LM IIIC period at Knossos.

---

[127] Evans 1921, 404.
[128] Hogarth 1899-1900.
[129] Namely: *Fortetsa: Early Greek Tombs near Knossos* (Brock 1957) and *KNC: Early Greek Tombs* (Coldstream and Catling, 1996).
[130] Coldstream 2006, 581.
[131] Pendlebury 1963, 303.
[132] Coldstream 1984b.
[133] Brock 1957, 217.
[134] Chaniotis 2011, 422.
[135] Myers *et al* 1992, 33.
[136] Snodgrass 2000, xxiv.

'Dark Age' was another name which was used for describing the first part of the EIA Knossos.[137] Probably this term was employed in the same way that it was given to the Greek mainland after the collapse of the palaces in Peloponnese (1200-1150 BC) and central Greece. Naming a period as a Dark Age suggests a period of decadence from a previous 'Golden' age, a period of isolation from the rest of the world, poverty and even absolute illiteracy.[138] This term has been extensively used in the past to describe this period since Crete was treated as part of the Mycenaean world.[139] It must be admitted, though, that Desborough had already observed that the island of Crete did not share many similarities with the rest of the Aegean.[140]

There has been a critique on the issue of the Dark Age in Greece in general, led by archaeologists outside Cambridge. The objection is that a period with such features never existed in any region of the Aegean.[141] Other scholars insist more on the diversity of the regions. For example, the defenceless Knossos and the mountainous Kavousi in Crete have few things in common. Otters do not reject the term Dark Age entirely.[142] All scholars, seem to agree that Knossos is a special case. Apart from the destruction of the Palace which happened much earlier than that of the palaces of the mainland, there is nothing suggesting that Knossos entered any kind of Dark Age.

In this way, it is difficult to apply this term to Knossos, since there is no evidence of absolute destruction. In contrast, multiple burials persist (though the rite of cremation is gradually becoming dominant), tombs continue to receive similar offerings and contacts with the rest of Eastern Mediterranean do survive. Chaniotis[143] claims that both terms, i.e. 'Sub-Minoan' and 'Dark Ages' are ideological constructs that should be abandoned. I believe that the term EIA seems the fittest term mainly because introduces Crete to a wider Mediterranean network, without isolating it the island or attaching it to the Greek mainland.

Whitley[144] has also pointed out that the names which were applied to the Iron Age pottery sequences in Crete and were identical to the mainland names were probably not the most appropriate. He maintains that they were selected in

---

[137] Jones 2000, 11.
[138] Kotsonas 2016a, 241-242.
[139] Desborough1964; Snodgrass 2000, 2; Coldstream 1968; Morris 1987, 10-14; Whitley 1991, 6-9.
[140] Desborough 1964, 166.
[141] Papadopoulos 1993 194-7; 1996, 253-255.
[142] Dickinson 1994; 2006, 8.
[143] Ibid.
[144] Whitley 1998, 611.

order to build a strong connection of 'Greekness' with the mainland while downplaying Knossos' links with the Levant.[145] A step towards the opposite direction is the use of the term 'Proto-Orientalizing'[146] and 'Early Cretan Orientalizing'[147] instead of PGB[148] style. Scholars have supported that Oriental influences on pottery decoration on Knossos occurred at least two centuries earlier than in the rest of Greece and owned a lot to Near Eastern metalwork, as it did to PG and G styles.[149] Kotsonas,[150] while accepting the influence of Cypriot motifs on the local pots, maintains that this influence is not inspired by pottery but from artefacts made of metal and ivory. He explains the Oriental influence was only one among the four currents that formed the PGB style[151] and that this style emerged in Knossos and spread to north-central Crete.[152]

A term that has been used extensively in the present book is 'Near Eastern'. This term might seem a bit general and there are other, more traditional, terms such as 'Oriental' that could be used instead. However, for the present research, the use of the term 'Near Eastern' in a geographical sense is much more useful because it embraces different areas of the Eastern Mediterranean. As Near East, I mean mostly the Phoenician coast, Cyprus and Egypt, because sometimes it is impossible to distinguish, for example, whether a statuette of an Egyptian goddess originates from Egypt or it is a Phoenician imitation. I exclude Asia Minor on account of the very strong connections to the coastal cities with the Aegean Islands and the Greek mainland.

One could argue that Cyprus also had strong connections with the Aegean because of the presence of Greek pottery on the island and the possible migration of Greek-speaking people after 1200 BC. However, I believe that the role of the Cypriots and their relations with the Syrian and Phoenician coasts has been underestimated a lot by Greek archaeologists. Additionally, the Cypriot pottery reaching Crete during EIA has much more in common in style with the Phoenician world than with the Aegean. Moreover, Cyprus apart from a production centre was a 'transhipment' point of material moving from Near East to Crete.[153] Furthermore, in Cyprus, one traces evidence of different traditions, which are also reflected on the imports coming to Crete. Therefore,

---

[145] Ibid.
[146] Andreadaki-Vlasaki 1990, 99; Morris, S. 1997, 58.
[147] Whitley 1998, 611.
[148] Brock 1957, 142-145.
[149] Ibid.
[150] Kotsonas 2008, 37-38.
[151] Ibid., 38.
[152] Ibid., 38-39 and Whitley 2016, 412-415 for different discussions on the PGB and the O styles and periods of Knossos.
[153] Hoffman 1997, 21.

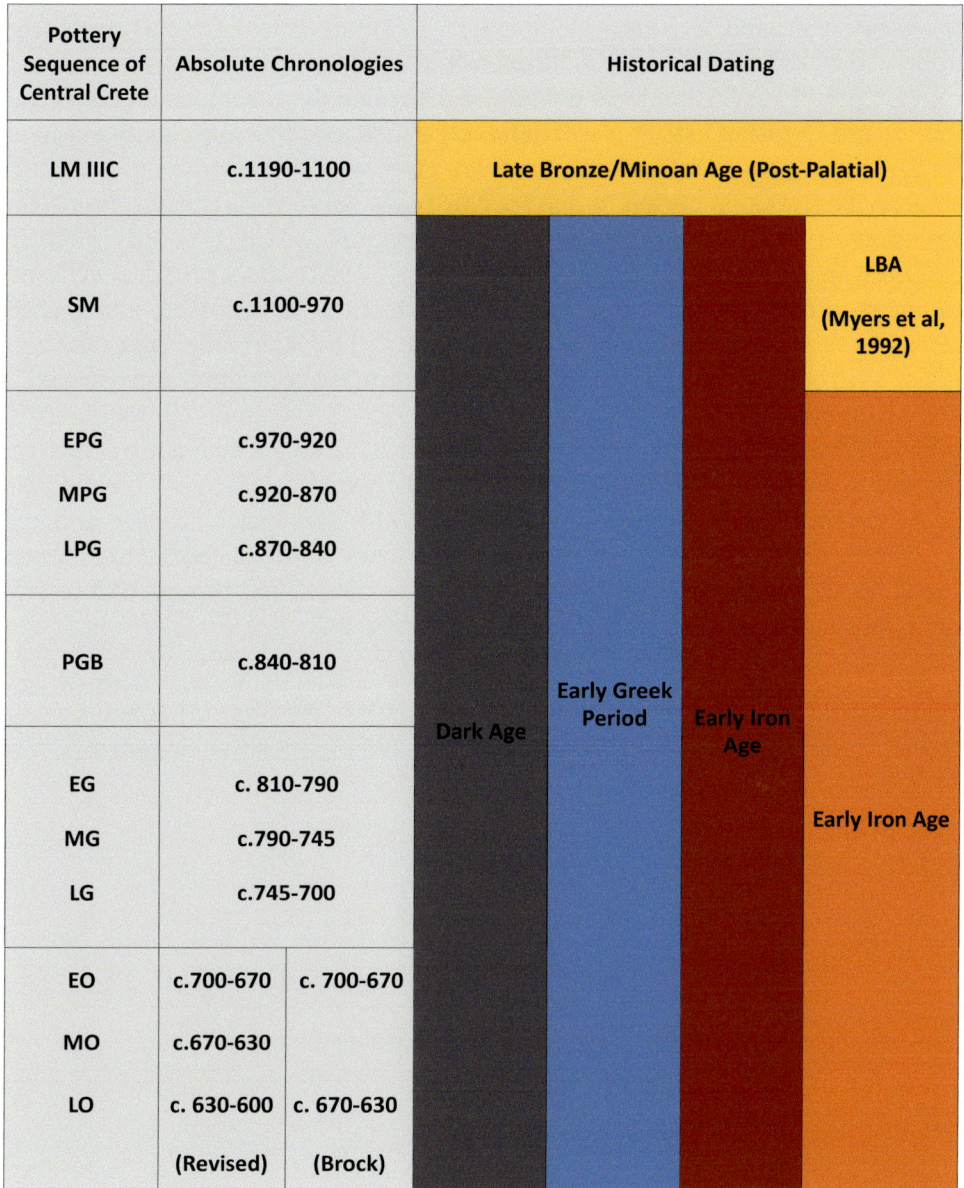

TABLE 1: A BASIC CHRONOLOGICAL SEQUENCE OF KNOSSOS BASED ON COLDSTREAM (1996; 2001) AND ON DIFFERENT VIEWS OF HISTORICAL DATING.

the term 'Near Eastern' can be used as a loose general geographical term for describing Egypt, Cyprus and the North Syrian and Phoenician coast.

All these terms and their combination can frustrate any student of archaeology, especially when one attempts to correlate the chronology of Crete with that of the Greek mainland, Cyprus and Phoenicia. The main reason for this confusing approach is that chronology has been built over the last two hundred years not only on pottery style and local pottery sequence analysis but also on historical names and Egyptian lists. It is worth having a look into the complexity entailed for an investigation when many names are employed at the same time in order to describe the same period in one specific place. As regards the chronological sequence, I followed Coldstream's[154] suggestions, which are only slightly different from Brock's[155] proposed chronology. Coldstream's proposal is based on more recent evidence derived from excavations at Knossos, along with Snodgrass's proposal concerning central Crete.[156] The main difference between Brock's chronology and the ones revised after him is about the O and especially the MO phase. Brock proposed a two-phase system (EO and LO). Moignard[157] after studying a specific Tomb (KNC, Tomb 285) suggested a three-phase, including the MO which was adopted by Coldstream.[158] Kotsonas[159] claims that there is a transitional stage between EO and LO for some specific vases and not a different phase. I think this is correct and more evidence is needed in order to break the O in three different phases. It must be made clear though that in any case, no evidence comes from the tombs after 630 BC.

---

[154] Coldstream 1968; 1996a, 2001.
[155] Brock 1957.
[156] Snodgrass 1971, 135.
[157] Moignard 1996, 461-462.
[158] Coldstream 2001, 72.
[159] Kotsonas 2008, 35.

Chapter 2: Would you like your tomb with or without dromos? Tombs and Society in EIA Knossos

i. Tomb Typology

Before the detailed overview of the Knossian cemeteries, it is essential to have a look at the different types of tombs, which in many cases coexisted within the same cemeteries or clusters of tombs. The most common type of tomb for the EIA Knossos is the chamber tomb, as was also the case in the LBA. The chamber is approached by a dromos (i.e. entrance passage). The chamber is entered through a *stomion*, a low rectangular opening, much smaller than the chamber and the dromos.[160] *"There is usually a step down from the dromos to the chamber. The descent usually begins some way back from the entrance, as it were in a cutting in the dromos, the edges of the cutting being in line with the sides of the door. The entrance was sealed by a wall of stones or by a large stone slabs, or by a combination of both"*.[161] An example of a rather typical EIA tomb, but with a narrower than the usual *stomion*, can be seen below:

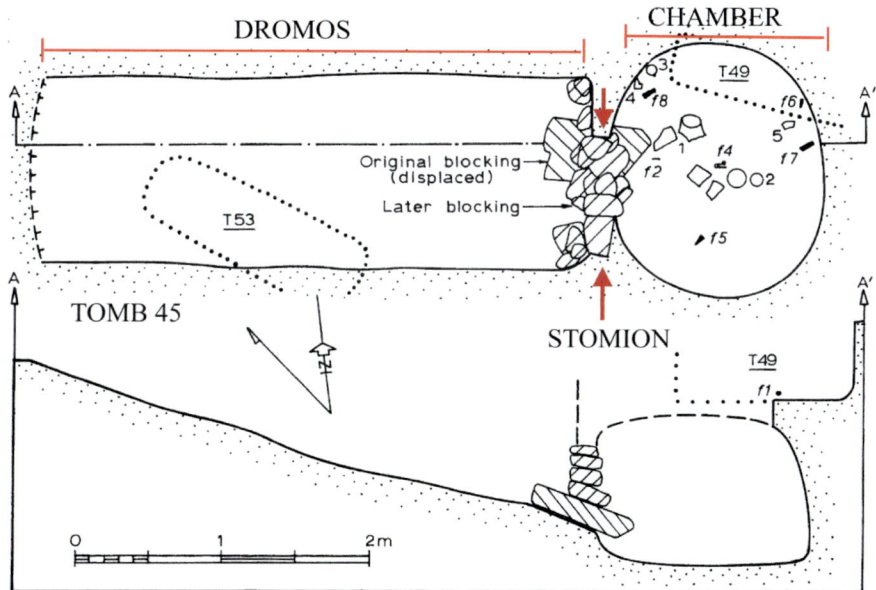

Figure 3: Terminology of the chamber tomb (Tomb 45, Med. Faculty, Coldstream and Catling 1996, figure 24). Reproduced with permission of the British School at Athens.

---

[160] Brock 1957, 2.
[161] Ibid.

28 KNOSSOS AND THE NEAR EAST

Pit-caves were also found at Knossos.¹⁶² Arthur Evans was the first archaeologist who excavated pit-caves (or pit-cave graves) at Knossos in the LM III cemetery at Zafer Papoura and gave the name to this structure.¹⁶³ The size of the chamber and the recovered finds point that pit-caves were tombs constructed only for single burials. Most of the scholars claim that pit-cave is a simpler form of burial structure in comparison to the chamber tombs, a cheaper substitute.¹⁶⁴ They tend to emphasize the practical aspect of the access to the chamber of the pit-cave. For them it seems that a pit-cave is a chamber tomb that lacks its dromos. The reason for the absence of dromos can be practical, a labour-saving version of the chamber tomb.¹⁶⁵ However, what seems to be practical or cheaper for archaeologists was not necessarily considered practical or cheap for past societies. Cavanagh¹⁶⁶ is right when he infers that the difference between chamber tombs and pit-caves, must have been something more than a mere practical decision. Pit-tombs, large circular pits, are similar to pit-caves but due to the bad state of preservation of the tomb, is not certain the prior existence of a chamber.

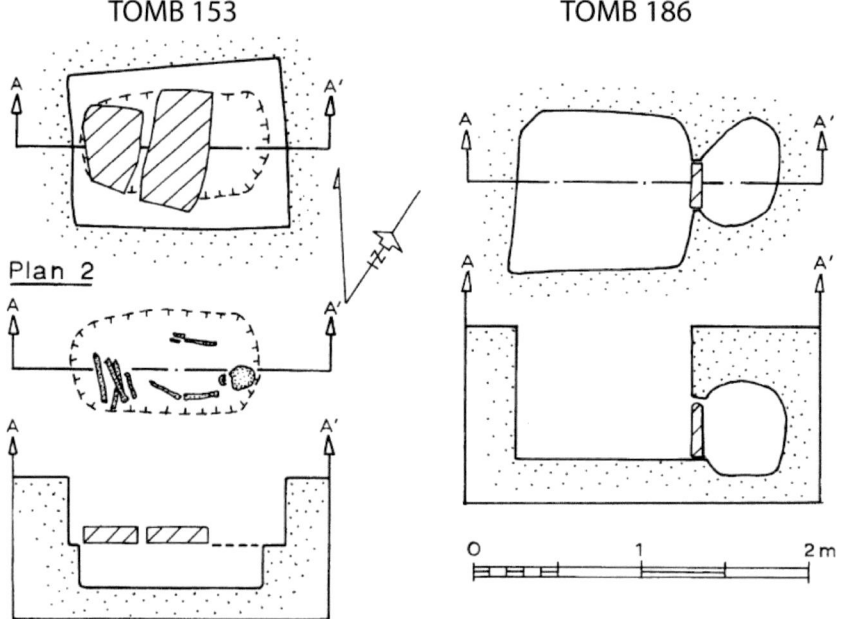

FIGURE 4: A SHAFT GRAVE AND A PIT-CAVE GRAVE, (TOMBS 153 AND 186 KMF RESPECTIVELY, COLDSTREAM AND CATLING 1996, FIGURE 43). REPRODUCED WITH PERMISSION OF THE BRITISH SCHOOL AT ATHENS.

---

¹⁶² See Tomb 186, in figure 4.
¹⁶³ Evans 1906, 104, Dickinson 1983, 57.
¹⁶⁴ Miller 2011, 56; Lewartowski 2000, 55.
¹⁶⁵ Dickinson 1983, 57.
¹⁶⁶ Cavanagh 1996, 658.

In addition, a few shaft graves[167] were discovered. While pit-caves were used for both inhumation and cremation in the BA and EIA respectively, shaft graves were exclusively used for inhumation. Both types were largely a SM phenomenon[168] and both share a BA past. Few pithos burials, which normally are inhumations in pithoi (but not always) found in pits outside chamber tombs. There are also some amorphous large pits which some of them are associated with earlier tombs.[169] For the purpose of the contextual study, tombs which cannot be clearly distinguished from the chamber tombs will be placed into the same group of analysis.

ii. History of Discoveries and Spatial Distribution of Tombs and Cemeteries

Tombs are grouped with other tombs in bigger or smaller clusters and occasionally in extended cemeteries. This might reflect certain aspects of the social and political relations between the EIA Knossians or it can be related with the terrain and quality of the soil for the construction of a tomb. It is not easy to distinguish when a cluster of tombs can be called a cemetery. Before however proceeding to further analysis one should first approach the subject from the point of view of the historiography of the discoveries combined with the spatial distribution and location of the tombs. In the following map, one can see all the locations of the EIA Knossian burial grounds and throughout the discussion there will be a reference to this map.

As early as 1900, the very same period when Evans was revealing the first fragmented frescoes from the BA Palace, David Hogarth, investigated burial structures. Hogarth's primary aim was to discover the tombs associated with the Minoan hierarchy.[170] In other words, he was after the tombs of the Minoan Kings (if one can use this term) and Princes. What he discovered was an extension of the Minoan settlement further south and in the north, on the Kephala Ridge (Map 3), with a series of chamber tombs, dated to the 'Mycenaean' and the 'Geometric' Periods.[171] This was a group of six tombs of which he wrote a preliminary archaeological report.[172] Coldstream,[173] based on Hogarth's short report and some notes made by Welch,[174] concerning pottery, attempted to match these notes with the surviving pottery, located in the archaeological

---

[167] See Tomb 153 in figure 4.
[168] Ibid., 651.
[169] Ibid., 653.
[170] Hogarth, 1899-1900, 81-1; Coldstream 2002, 202.
[171] Hogarth, 1899-1900, 82-85.
[172] Ibid.
[173] Coldstream 2002.
[174] Welch 1899-1900, 85-92.

Figure 5: Map 3: The location of EIA tombs.

museum of Heraklion, in order to write a more detailed analysis. He suspected however that the construction of the tombs was of the Minoan period.[175] Based

---

[175] Coldstream 2002, 216.

on the evidence from the pottery and the contexts, he dated these tombs from the SM to the transition between the LG and the EO.[176]

Apart from Hogarth, Evans himself excavated a group of two EIA tombs on the Kephala Ridge in 1907 and twenty years later two more were excavated by Payne in the same area.[177] None of them has been fully published and we only know that they are dated from the PG to the O.[178] As in the case of the tombs excavated by Hogarth, the dating of the construction of the chamber tombs is normally based on the discovered context of the chambers. One cannot be certain if the burial structure is of SM date or earlier. A discovery which supports the theory of the reuse of BA tombs in the same area of the Kephala Ridge took place in 1958. There, a chamber tomb was excavated and found to be a tomb of a single burial dated to the MPG by Coldstream.[179] However, the construction of the tomb, its long dromos with walls leaning inwards and the square chamber were dated to LM III.[180] Another argument for the secondary use of most of the aforementioned tombs in the EIA is that all of them are located along what probably was a Minoan 'Via Appia' leading from the Palace to the Minoan Royal tombs of Isopata and the BA Harbour.[181] Furthermore, between those tombs, Hogarth and Payne excavated two LM chamber tombs.[182]

Another burial ground lies 1.5 km west of those tombs and north-west of the BA Palace in a suburb of Heraklion, known as Ayios Ioannis (Map 3). There, a cemetery with at least 14 chamber tombs containing burials from the SM to the LPG[183] was discovered in different periods and circumstances. Six of them were excavated by Hutchinson, four by Dunbabin and one by Petros.[184] Two more were destroyed and another was disturbed during the Second World War.[185] Boardman studied and published eight tombs.[186] Only these eight tombs are included in the present contextual study, since the remaining tombs have not been fully published and the material recovered from them was either lost or misplaced during the war.

---

[176] Ibid.
[177] Hood and Smyth 1981.
[178] Ibid.
[179] Coldstream 1963, 38.
[180] Ibid.
[181] Coldstream 2002, 214.
[182] Hood and Smyth 1981, 37.
[183] Boardman 1960, 143.
[184] Hood and Smyth 1981, 34.
[185] Ibid.
[186] Boardman 1960, 128.

Just north of the cemetery of Ayios Ioannis, outside the region 'supervised' by the British School, there is Atsalenio, another suburb of Heraklion (Map 3). There, a considerable number of EIA tombs have been discovered by the Greek archaeological authorities, but only two were fully published by Davaras.[187] One more is reported by Platon in 1958 and four (three of them badly damaged) were excavated by the local archaeological service, in 1979.[188] Davaras[189] considers that the tombs he excavated, along with unpublished ones, belonged to a cemetery that must have been the northernmost of the Knossos cemeteries. Coldstream and Catling,[190] on the other hand, maintain that those tombs, including the ones from Ayios Ioannis, were not the burial grounds for the people that lived in the central settlement of Knossos. The problem with the suburbs of Atsalenio, Mastaba and Katsaba is that they are now parts of the city of Heraklion, where not many things are about its Iron Age past.

Boardman[191] addresses the problem regarding the distance of these tombs from the main settlement of Knossos. He suggests that, if all those tombs were constructed during the BA, then during the EIA they might have been used people from the main settlement of Knossos to reuse them.[192] A discovery which might confirm Boardman's hypothesis is a chamber tomb discovered in Ayios Ioannis, east of the aforementioned cemetery of Ayios Ioannis and west of the tombs discovered by Hogarth at Kephala Ridge. This chamber was excavated by Hawkes in 1959, and dates to the LM II (dated from pottery and bronze finds). The construction of the tomb (square chamber, long dromos) also dates it to the LM II period.[193] However, it contained at least two SM burials of a man and a woman.[194]

Further south, in a previously rural area, which was known by the name of Teke and now as Ambelokipi, is where most of the EIA tombs of Knossos were found (Map 3, Map 4). The distance of this area from the BA Palace varies from 500 to about 1500 meters. In the excavations which have taken place in the past 100 years, archaeologists have discovered at least 150 tombs. All these tombs are grouped in small clusters but most probably constitute part of the same cemetery (Map 4). The northernmost group of this extended cemetery is at

---

[187] Davaras 1968, 133-146.
[188] Kourou and Karetsou 1998.
[189] Davaras 1968, 142.
[190] Coldstream and Catling 1996, 714.
[191] Boardman 1960, 143.
[192] Ibid.
[193] Hood and Coldstream 1968, 209.
[194] Ibid.

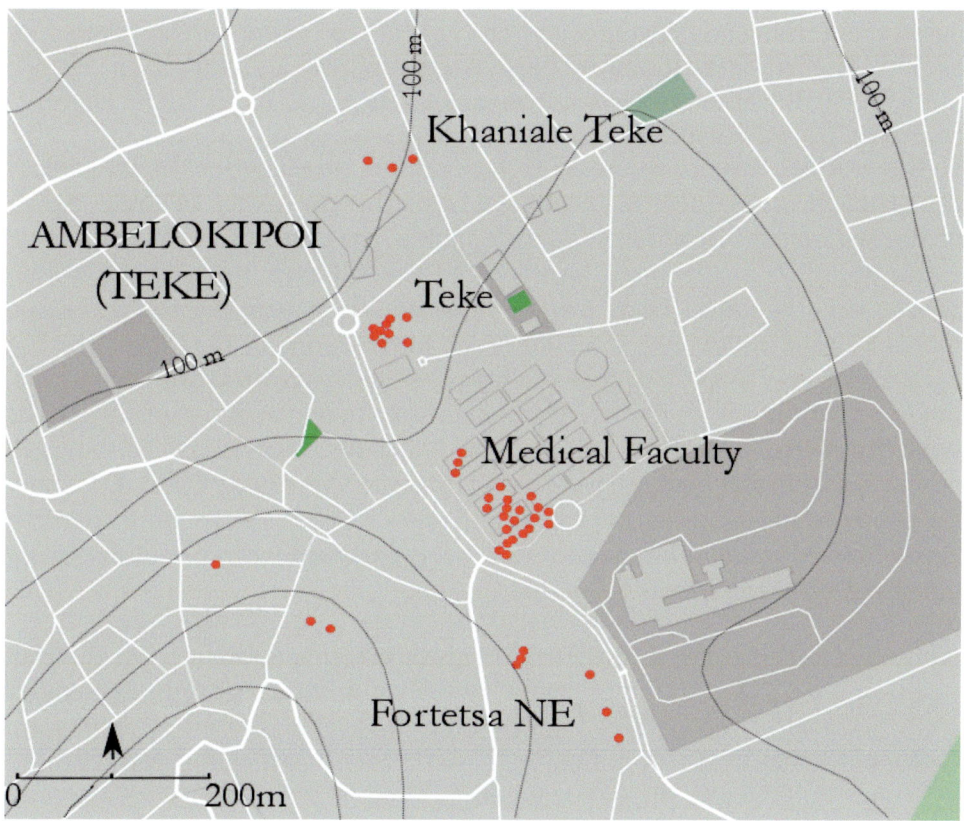

FIGURE 6: MAP 4: THE BURIAL SITES WITHIN KNC.

the Khaniale Teke district, which was excavated by Hutchinson in 1940.[195] He found a tholos tomb constructed probably in LBA[196] and two chamber tombs with rectangular chambers. According to evidence of pottery, the contexts of all three tombs date from the PGB to the EO.[197]

At about 100 meters south from the Khaniale Teke tombs lies a group of at least thirteen tombs, known as the Teke Tombs (Map 4). The first of them were discovered during the war: In 1943, soldiers of Wehrmacht, attempting to construct an anti-aircraft shelter, accidently discovered the dromoi of two chamber tombs.[198] Nikolaos Platon, the then director of the local archaeological service, after negotiating with the German officers about the finds of the excavation, managed to excavate the two tombs and, on the basis of the finds,

---
[195] Hutchinson and Boardman 1954; Boardman 1967.
[196] Kotsonas 2006, 150; Hutchinson and Boardman 1954, 222.
[197] Hutchinson and Boardman 1954, 220; Boardman 1967, 59.
[198] Coldstream and Catling 1996, 9.

dated them from the PG to the O.[199] The rest of the tombs were excavated by Sackett, Popham and Howell in 1975-76, during a rescue excavation.[200] Once more, the dating of the tombs was the same as for those excavated by Platon.

To the east lies the site where in 1978 began the planning for the immediate construction of the new Medical Faculty of the University of Crete, north of the Venizeleion Hospital (Map 4). This was the reason for a major rescue excavation.[201] The agreement between the Greek authorities and the British School was still active. Many British scholars (which were not typical rescue archaeologists) conducted, in about seven months, one of the biggest rescue excavations ever made in Greece.[202] This site became known as the KMF. There, at least 310 tombs from the EIA, the Hellenistic, Roman and Byzantine periods were discovered and excavated. At least 70 chamber tombs and 20 tombs of other types (pit, shaft graves) were dated from the SM period to the LO.[203] There were many different groups of tombs and types within this cemetery and both rites of cremation and inhumation had been practised with the former being dominant.[204]

A hundred meters to the south, there is a group of tombs with the name Fortetsa (Map 4), which was examined again by British archaeologists in September 1967.[205] Traces of ten chamber tombs were discovered and all of them were thoroughly looted.[206] At the same site, at least three other tombs were discovered by Payne and Blakway in 1933. Hood discovered in 1953 three more chamber tombs, all of them looted. One contained a G pot, the other inhumations with bronze pins and the last one was empty.[207] The tombs discovered in 1967 were named 'Fortetsa 1967' and those found by Payne were also named Fortetsa, because they are located between Teke and the village of Fortetsa (but much closer to Teke though). Payne's discoveries were included in the Fortetsa publication of Brock.[208] In the present book, these two Fortetsa groups will be called Fortetsa NE (North-East of Fortetsa) in order not to be confused with another cemetery south-east (SE) of the Fortetsa village (see below).

---

[199] Hood and Smyth 1981, 36.
[200] Coldstream and Catling 1996, 1-3.
[201] Ibid.
[202] Whitley 1998, 101.
[203] Coldstream and Catling, 1996.
[204] Cavanagh 1996, 652-675.
[205] Coldstream and Catling 1996, 284.
[206] Ibid.
[207] Hood and Smyth 1981, 38.
[208] Brock 1957.

Coldstream and Catling maintain that the Fortetsa NE tombs were the southernmost limit of an extended cemetery which contained the Teke tombs cemetery, the KMF cemetery and the Fortetsa NE cemetery.[209] It is probably for this reason that they included all these sites in the publication with the name 'Knossos North Cemetery' (KNC). These sites are located north of the BA Palace and essentially north of the main (if not single) EIA urban nucleus.

Coldstream excavated another chamber tomb in the Teke area, in a garden of a modern house in 1959.[210] At least two chamber tombs were probably located nearby. Payne probably excavated them in 1927.[211] All these tombs which are not published, as well as the Khaniale Teke tombs, are not included in the KNC publication but judging from their position they were part of it. Coldstream and Catling[212] also admit, based on unpublished reports that the northern limit of the cemetery might have extended even beyond the Khaniale Teke group. There are more tombs discovered by the Greek authorities in the North Cemetery. Thirty-two tombs were discovered by the local archaeological service in 2010 (two chamber tombs and the rest of them are either simple pits for pots or small irregular shafts that contain pots).[213] Seven chamber tombs were excavated and six more were traced in the same area.[214] None of them has been fully published.

South-east of the Fortetsa village lies another cemetery, which was published by Brock in 1957 and excavated by Greek and British archaeologists from 1933 to 1935 (Map 3, Map 5). The Fortetsa SE, as this cemetery is called in the present book, is located on the lower western slopes of the Monasteriako Kephali Hill (also known as Acropolis Hill), which rises above the villa Ariadne west of the Palace.[215] Its distance from the Palace and the EIA settlement is less than a kilometre. In this area, N. Platon, first as an assistant and then as a director of the local archaeological service conducted the first rescue excavation in 1933 and discovered two chamber tombs.[216] Following the agreement between the Greek authorities and the British School of Archaeology, his investigation continued by Payne, Blakeway and Brock in two successive archaeological campaigns from 1933 to 1935. A total of 17 tombs were excavated. Due to the sudden death of Payne and Blakeway, Brock carried out the study and published the material alone. Brock divided the cemetery into three different groups of

---

[209] Coldstream and Catling 1996, 285.
[210] Hood and Smyth 1981, 37.
[211] Ibid.
[212] Coldstream and Catling 1996, 714.
[213] Rousaki and Anagnostaki 2012, 230-235.
[214] Gramamtikaki 1993, 448-450; Kourou and Grammatikaki 1998.
[215] Brock 1957, 1.
[216] Marinatos 1933, 304.

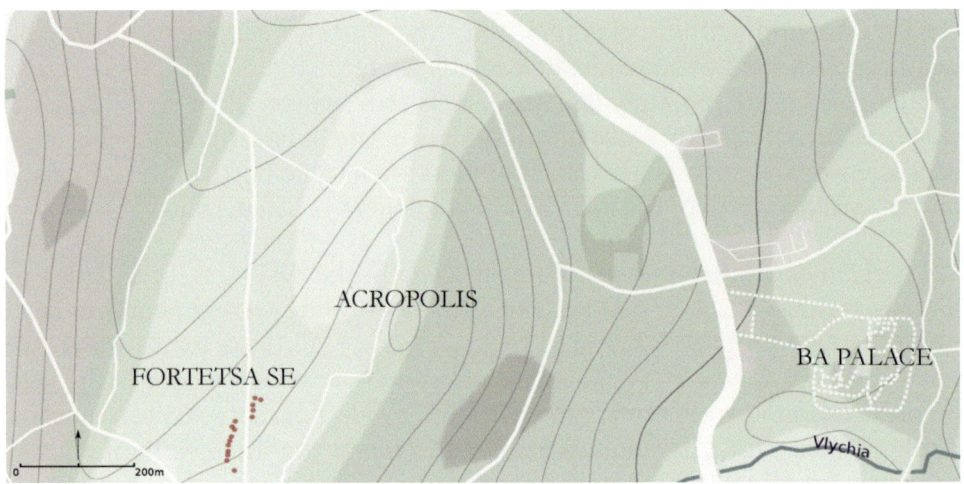

FIGURE 7 MAP 5: FORTETSA SE TOMBS.

tombs according to their location. After a meticulous study of thousands of pots, he managed to establish a chronology of the EIA Knossos and central Crete. His proposed chronological sequence has been slightly modified ever since.[217] In the same publication, Brock[218] included the three tombs which Payne and Blakeway excavated in 1933 in Fortetsa NE site.

To the south-west of Fortetsa SE, no other tombs have been located. To the south-east, on the other hand, there is a chamber tomb on the north slopes of the Lower Gypsades Hill excavated in 1975 and published by Coldstream.[219] In the nearby area, on the southern slopes of the hill, there are probably some other chamber tombs excavated or plundered during World War II by the Germans or the locals[220] These tombs suggest the existence of a cemetery in this area in the EIA. Coldstream believed that this was probably the southernmost cemetery of the EIA Knossos.[221] It must be stressed though that a LM chamber tomb cemetery was also discovered a bit further, on the Upper Ghypsades.[222] Perhaps there was a reuse of some of these tombs after the BA (Map 3). In chamber tomb VII, which is probably the latest tomb of the cemetery, one iron knife was found in a (LM IIIB 2?) larnax along with a group of SM vases. Also, in tomb VIa a stirrup jar was discovered. Three skeletons were found in these tombs.

---

[217] Whitley 1998, 612.
[218] Brock 1957.
[219] Coldstream *et al* 1981, 142-165.
[220] Hood and Smyth 1981, 59; Coldstream *et al* 1981, 142-165.
[221] Coldstream and Catling 1996, 714; Coldstream 2006, 586.
[222] Hood *et al* 1958-59, 194-262.

Catling[223] places tombs VIa and VII in the SM, however, the excavators do not say that these are indeed SM burials and the fact all the burials in the tombs and the cemetery are inhumations makes the distinction even harder.[224] Coldstream does not place these two tombs in the wholly post-Minoan Tombs.[225] At the same time, though, he dates these successive burials to the SM.[226] There is also a possibility that these burials belong to a transitional period before the coming of the SM and the presence of a few SM vases is not convincing evidence for a much later use. The deposition of iron knives is not conclusive evidence for SM use either because these bimetallic knives had been circulating in the Eastern Mediterranean since the 12th century BC.[227]

A Minoan cemetery that was reused by the EIA Knossians was the Mavro Spilio (i.e. a big artificial cave which contained chamber tombs). It is located to the east of the Palace at a distance less than 500 m (Map 3). All the chamber tombs excavated by Evans and Fordsyke[228] in 1926-27 were either of MM or LM date. In three of them, Forsdyke discovered many *"Geometric"* pots right above the Minoan grave deposits and some of the 'infant bones' contained therein.[229] Coldstream studied the remaining pots that he found in the Heraklion museum.[230] He dated the pottery to the EO and interpreted these burials as some of the last made in Knossos before 630 BC when evidence for burial activity stops only to resume in the Hellenistic period.[231] He suggested that the decision for the reuse of Minoan tombs in Ghypsades and in Mavro Spilio was prompted *"by the pressure on space in the densely stuffed chambers...in the older plots, especially in the North Cemetery"*.[232]

Finally, there is some information about some tombs of the EIA Period supposedly discovered within the area of the EIA settlement. The first case was an O cremation urn (polychrome pithos) discovered by Evans during a sounding in the modern village of Knossos, but no tomb was found.[233] A rather similar case was that of a LPG bell crater containing eleven miniature pots suitable for child burial. This crater was discovered by a workman again in the modern village at a distance no greater than 200 meters to the north-west. Evans had discovered

---
[223] Catling 1996d, 307-309.
[224] Hood *et al* 1953-4, 208-10, 226.
[225] Coldstream 2000a, 295 n. 75.
[226] Ibid.
[227] Dickinson 2006, 146.
[228] Forsdyke 1926-27.
[229] Coldstream 2000a, 291-294; Hood and Smyth 1981, 53; Forsdyke 1926-27, 243-296.
[230] Coldstream 2000a, 291-294.
[231] Ibid., 295.
[232] Ibid.
[233] Ibid.

the cremation urn in the same area. Coldstream[234] conducted an excavation but found nothing like a burial ground.

The third case of a supposed 'intramural' burial is located outside the northern entrance to the Palace where Evans found LG potsherds and an oval-shaped construction resembling a tomb. Mackenzie, on the other hand, interpreted the construction as an oven.[235] Coldstream did not find G pottery from this spot in the museum and some more recent excavations also brought to light an oven in the same location, confirming Mackenzie's theory.[236] So far nothing conclusive has been found suggesting intramural burials in EIA. If the theory that Knossians did not bury their dead within their city is correct (there are no serious arguments against it), then the limits of the cemeteries which are peripheral to the main settlement may define the border of the city.[237] If this is correct, then the Fortetsa SE cemetery is also located on the borders of the main settlement, contrary to previous arguments.

In general, the term cemetery will not be used for all the groups of tombs in this study. In fact, as already mentioned, it is hard to define when a group of tombs makes a cluster and how many clusters make a cemetery. It has been calculated in the site of Medical faculty that normally six tombs compose a cluster.[238] I would suggest that at least two clusters of tombs are required in order to have a cemetery. However, this view would make the various groups of tombs at Fortetsa SE a different cemetery from the KMF. So, the distance between the various clusters must also be very significant. The location of the clusters is also another important matter: The suitability of land must have been very crucial in order to choose a burial site. The presence of BA tombs could also indicate a site suitable for burials.[239] I would add that there was a motive for not choosing to use a specific burial site.[240] This is namely the competition between the various elites of Knossos even from the beginning of the EIA and especially after the LPG. However, at the same time, one should also bear in mind that the extension of most of the EIA burial sites is strictly dictated by the rescue excavations conducted there and not by systematic investigation.

In summary, the contextual study of this book includes the following burial grounds:

---

[234] Ibid., 295 n. 77.
[235] Coldstream 2000a, 295, n.79.
[236] Ibid.
[237] See below in the 'Settlement' section.
[238] Cavanagh 1996, 600.
[239] Ibid., 657.
[240] See Chapter 4.

1. The burial sites north of Knossos BA Palace, including the Khaniale Teke, the Teke, the KMF and the Fortetsa NE tombs. Together, these sites probably compose the KNC (Map 3, Map 4), which was the main cemetery of the city, with the KMF site being the densest.
2. The tombs at Ayios Ioannis, which form a cemetery on their own. These probably belong to the main settlement despite the considerable distance from it.
3. The two Atsalenio tombs excavated by Davaras,[241] which might have been the northernmost cemetery of the settlement. However, due to the absence of more published archaeological data, this is only a working hypothesis.[242]
4. The Fortetsa SE tombs, because, as the surveys have shown,[243] they are attached to the settlement. However, it is a different cemetery from KNC.
5. The tombs at Kephala Ridge, because they form a group of tombs which contains SM burials as early as the earliest ones of the North Cemetery. It remains to be seen whether these tombs belong to the same cemetery as well (the area between the KNC and the Kephala Ridge tombs has not been excavated due to intensive agriculture).
6. The two reused LM III tombs at Upper Gypsades Hill, which contain SM burials.
7. The Lower Ghypsades Hill Tomb, because it is the only published tomb south of Knossos in an area very close to the EIA settlement.
8. The three tombs from the LM cemetery at Mavro Spilio, which were reused in the LG Period.

All these fully published tombs will be examined in order the contextual study to be as accurate as possible. Hogarth's tombs from the Kephala Ridge and Evans' from Mavro Spilio are also used because there are secondary detailed studies of Coldstream.[244] Those which are not selected are the ones north of Atsalenio[245] for two main reasons: firstly, it is not certain whether they belonged to Knossos or to a coastal site that would serve Knossos as its port. The existence of a port on the north coast of Knossos is very probable. In the Minoan times, it was Poros (Modern Heraklion) and during the EIA the volume of imports from the mainland and the East suggests the existence of a port with suitable facilities for receiving large quantities of goods. Secondly, most of these tombs are excavated but not published. For example, the full excavated material from the Kourou and Karetsou publication[246] has not been published

---

[241] Davaras 1968.
[242] Kotsonas et al 2012.
[243] See the 'Settlement' section in this chapter.
[244] Coldstream 2000a, 2002.
[245] Lebessi (1970, 270-297) made a full publication of a chamber tomb (LPG-EO) at Mastaba.
[246] Kourou and Karetsou 1998.

despite the discovery of a Phoenician cippus. The same stands for a tomb at Ambelokipoi where an anthropomorphic cippus was discovered.[247] Similar cippi have also been discovered at the cemetery of Eleutherna.[248] These tombs will not be included.

All the fully published tombs dated to the EIA are presented in Appendix I. The first column contains the inventory name of the tomb as used by the excavator. Only a tomb at the Lower Gypsades Hill, one at Teke and another tomb at Ayios Ioannis, did not have an inventory name because they were isolated discoveries. The second column contains the type of the tomb or grave and the third one the site where the tomb was discovered. In the fourth one can see the dating of each tomb. In the reused LM tombs and larnax graves I have noted only the EIA use. In the following two columns, there is information on how many cremations and imitations were discovered in each tomb. In the ninth column, there is information about the main publication of the tomb.

As one can see in the list of tombs of Appendix I, there are 166 fully published tombs which are located around Knossos and were in use the EIA. At least 111 of them were found disturbed and in some cases completely looted, eroded, or destroyed. The rest of them have been found either intact or having suffered minor disturbances due to extensive reuse (i.e. successive burials), partial looting, roof collapse, or bulldozing activities before the rescue excavations.[249] In any case, the vast majority of the context and finds of the rest 49 tombs has been preserved. Table 2, Graph 1 illustrates all the types of tombs and graves which were in use at Knossos during the EIA.

At least 118 out of the 166 tombs at Knossos are chamber tombs. This represents a percentage of about 71 % and reveals that this type of tomb was the most popular for the Knossians buried in these cemeteries. In chamber tombs, burials (inurned cremations in the vast majority) were placed in the chamber: *"When the floor space was filled up, a second tier of urns was placed on top of the first"*.[250] Not infrequently, burials were also discovered in the dromos. Additionally, burials could be found in niches and side-chambers attached -probably after the initial construction - to the main chamber and/or dromos. Most of the burials found in these deposits have been characterised as successive burials and are of a later date than those of the main chamber.

---

[247] Grammatikaki and Kourou 1998.
[248] Stampolidis 1990; 2004; Stampolidis and Kotsonas 2006.
[249] For the state of preservation of each tomb see Appendix 2.
[250] Brock 1957, 3.

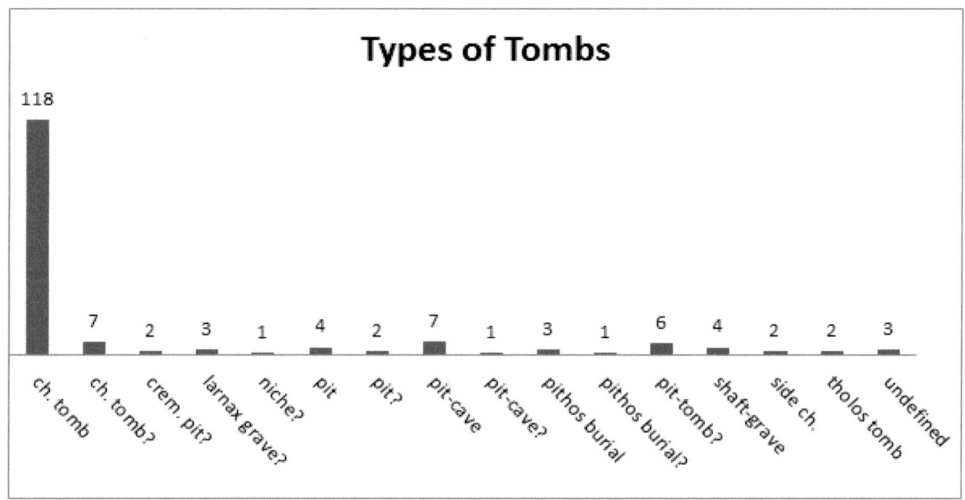

TABLE 2: GRAPH 1: NUMBERS OF TOMBS PER TYPE.

In other cases, however, burials have also been discovered inside the main chamber, while other burials have carefully been relocated inside or outside the chamber. Such an example is Tomb 218 at the KMF site, where one LPG jug was found on top of a PG urn.[251] There are other examples where all burials have been found together in a very chaotic state caused by looting in Antiquity, this, for example, is the case of Tomb 283 at the KMF site.[252] It seems that niches were opened only when the main chamber could not receive more funereal urns and grave goods.[253] This happens mostly in the LG and O.[254] Even if the niches and side-chambers do not constitute part of the initial construction of the tomb, they still should be considered as parts of the burial monument. This was the intention of the people who created and used them for more than one generation, architecturally and symbolically. It should be noted, however, that niches cut in chamber tombs were considered an old practice by the EIA. It has been observed in LM tombs as well.[255]

iii. Funerary Rites and Rituals in Knossian Context

As far as the various rites and rituals are concerned, the burial practices in Knossos are a mixture of old and new elements.[256] Coldstream describes the

---

[251] Coldstream and Catling 1996, 201.
[252] Coldstream and Catling 1996, 230-1.
[253] Brock 1957, 3.
[254] Cavanagh 1996, 653.
[255] Ibid, 658.
[256] Coldstream 2003, 48.

cremation rite in Crete, where the cremated remains were placed in a necked pithos (or amphora, or bell crater), with (or without) painted decoration.[257] The bones were wrapped in cloth.[258] There are also cases where both inhumations and cremations were discovered in the same tomb. Most of these tombs are of SM date (Tombs 45, 98, 112 at KMF and F67/5 at Fortetsa NE), but there are also examples from the entire PG (Tombs L and at Fortetsa NE and Tomb VIII at Ayios Ioannis). The later cremation burials seem to treat the inhumations with respect and so it seems very hard to believe, at least in the case of Knossos, that there was a deep ideological or religious differentiation between the people who practised these two rites. As Catling[259] notes the only site that has revealed cremations during the SM is the KMF and the Fortetsa NE, both of which belong to the main cemetery. Apart from these two sites, all the SM tombs held only inhumations.

Coldstream also indicates the presence of small pots inside the urn and drinking vessels in the tombs.[260] While in EIA Athens the drinking vessels were smashed in the pyre, at Knossos the drinking cups were placed by the urn probably intact.[261] A variety of other vases, such as perfumed oil flasks, were also placed in many tombs.[262] Other offerings were also found, such as jewellery, weapons, domestic equipment, oboloi, tripods, fire-dogs, copper, faience and stone vessels, tools, cosmetic items, horse-bits, figurines and a game piece.[263]

It is worth comparing the Knossian cemeteries with the ones on the mainland. The major difference is that the vast majority of the tombs in the Knossos area were used for multiple burials while in post-Mycenaean Greece the main practice was the single burial. Brock sees similarities between Knossos and contemporary cemeteries in Cyprus, like the ones at Lapithos and Kourion.[264] The practice of multiple burials was favoured in Crete, but it was more a general phenomenon in EM and MM.[265] In sum: a Knossian chamber tomb in the MM was used for multiple (at least more than two) inhumations, in the LM for one or maximum two inhumations, while in the EIA again for multiple burials (but now cremations).

---

[257] Ibid.
[258] Cavanagh 1996, 666.
[259] Catling, 1996c, 643.
[260] Coldstream 2003, 48.
[261] Ibid.
[262] Cavanagh 1996, 670.
[263] Ibid.
[264] Brock 1957, 217.
[265] Snodgrass 2000, 164.

In Mycenaean Greece collective burials were the norm for the chamber tombs and single burial for the shaft graves. In SM Athens, the Pompeion cemetery in the Kerameikos area is a single burial cist-tomb cemetery. The same is observed in Lefkandi.[266] Finally, in one of the most important SM cemeteries of Attica, at Perati, which begun its function in LHIII,[267] most of the tombs held single burials, while others which had been reused held a maximum of three. The vast majority of the 159 tombs held inhumations, while only in ten tombs they have been discovered cremations. All the cremations were found in chamber tombs together with inhumations. Additionally, there is also evidence for urns containing double cremations.[268]

The reason that EIA Knossians continued to use chamber tombs can be tradition, conservatism, or connection to a 'glorious' past. Another explanation can be that multiple burials normally require more space than a single burial. The construction of a chamber tomb, featuring a chamber, a dromos and in some cases niches (in both dromos and chamber), can provide considerable space for more than one burial.[269] However, the main difference, in form is that the Iron Age chambers tend to be smaller than the ones of the BA. A reason for this reduction can be the change of the rite, from inhumations to cremations, with the latter requiring less space.[270] Cavanagh admits that the presence of inhumations inside the earliest EIA tombs indicates that the reduction of the size might not be related to the change of the rite.[271]

It is also worth mentioning that, according to Brock, no distinctive visible markers were found above the chamber tombs to indicate their position.[272] If this is true, two distinct reasons can be inferred regarding the burials. The first is that those BA tombs were re-discovered by accident during EIA by the later generations which simply reused them since in this way they could have avoided digging a new tomb. Making a chamber tomb is not an easy task even on the soft limestone of Knossos area, *Kouskouras*, as Cretans call it. The second is that no tomb marker was needed because the successive generations knew very well who was buried and where, so they chose to bury deliberately their dead next to the old burials. The only thing they had to do was either to re-open the tomb or build a new one next to it.

---

[266] Dickinson 1996, 184.
[267] Iakovidis 1969, 29-31.
[268] Lemos 2002, 186; Paidousis and Sbarounis 1975, 129-159.
[269] Cavanagh 1996, 675.
[270] Ibid.
[271] Ibid.
[272] Brock 1957, 4.

I believe that the second approach is more persuasive even if it cannot be applied in all cases, especially when there is a considerable interval between the primary and the secondary burials. In this case, one should probably choose the first approach. Wallace sees a relation between two different types of groups or, as she puts it, two different levels of kin represented in the burial patterns, one inside the tomb with multiple burials and the other beyond or around the tomb in the cluster.[273] From the distribution of the chamber tombs in the cemeteries, it is evident that they are separated into different smaller groups (or clusters). This is obvious in the case of Fortetsa SE, where Brock split the tombs into three different groups. A less obvious distinction can be seen in the KMF and Teke sites. There, however, with the aid of statistical analysis, Cavanagh made a very interesting study. He observed that the tombs are grouped in rows of four to six and sometimes other tombs are added outside the main alignments.[274] The concentration and possible relationship between different tombs will be explored further in Chapter 4 since it is essential for the study and analysis of the distribution of the Near Eastern imports and their imitations. It is important to say, though, that no less than 139 tombs and seven out of nine sites are located north of the Knossos EIA settlement. This close concentration of different cemeteries verifies once more the area where Knossians had chosen to have their main burial grounds, away from the world of the living.

iv. Who Used the Cemeteries?

As far as the number of burials in the KNC publication is concerned, it has been calculated that inside the tombs there were between 422 to 671 inurned burials.[275] The higher estimation proposed by Cavanagh[276] depends on the assumption that other shapes were used as ossuaries. My calculation for the KNC by counting the pithoi and other attested funerary urns gives 466 inurned burials.[277] If one adds to Cavanagh's estimation the inhumations and the single

---

[273] Wallace 2010, 297.
[274] Cavanagh 1996, 657.
[275] Cavanagh 1996, 660.
[276] Ibid., 659.
[277] It is not certain that all pithoi contained cremations. Payne (1927-28, 228) believes that in PG and G most of the pithoi found in the tombs were used as cinerary urns. In the O, however, there were some pithoi used as duplicates or companion-pieces of the cremation pithoi (Ibid.). Brock (1957, 101, n.2) mentions that not all pithoi from Tomb P (Fortetsa SE) contained burials. He admits, however that the tomb was disturbed (Ibid., 101). Moignard (1996, 426) agrees with Payne for the O. This however may be the result of various unfortunate incidents during the reopening of the tomb for the successive burials. One cannot overrule the assumption that during the O, more people had the right to formal burial in the Knossian Cemeteries. On the other hand, at Khaniale Teke (Hutchinson and Boardman 1954, 222) and at KNC (Cavanagh 1996, 659) the entire amount of pithoi was used for the calculation of the burials.

graves (pits, shafts, etc), then the number ranges from 445 to 694. I believe it is safe to set the number somewhere in the middle, at about 570 burials.[278] The 21 inhumations and 340 cremation burials from the remaining tombs around Knossos (my calculation), included in Appendix 2, could be added to this figure. The total amount would be around 931 burials for the entire EIA in Knossos from the fully published tombs.

The number does not look particularly high for such a long period and probably does not represent the amount of population at any given phase. Additionally, there is a similar situation in other sites on the Greek mainland (Athens, Argos), where a limited number of burials seems to be more an indication that a specific part of society had exclusive access to the tombs, as many authors have observed6.[279] In other words, regarding a number of burials discovered in the tombs at the Teke, KMF and Fortetsa NE sites (i.e. the KNC publication), there must have been some kind of restriction and not everyone had the right to be buried in these sites.[280] Cavanagh links the social concerning hierarchy and the right to burial in a specific place.[281]

He also observed, as Morris had argued for Athens, that during the 8th century there is a rise in the number of burials.[282] According to these two authors, this increase was much more related to a change of customs that opened the access to the cemeteries than a rise in the population.[283] Thus, it becomes clear that there was probably a divide between the people who could be buried in the cemeteries and those who could not. Certainly, the same divide may have also been present before the 8th century. Furthermore, Morris[284] believes that at the beginning of the EIA only the group of "*agathoi*"[285] had the right to formal burial not only in Athens but also in Knossos.

Instead of agathoi the term 'elite' may also be used but always with caution, since different elites and ruling classes, such as aristocrats, agathoi and/or big men, may exist at the same time. This has been inferred for Athens and its

---

[278] Cavanagh 1996, 660.
[279] Morris 1987; Whitley 1991; Cavanagh 1996; Dickinson 2006.
[280] Cavanagh 1996, 664.
[281] Ibid., 675.
[282] Cavanagh 1996, 664; Morris 1987.
[283] Snodgrass (1980, 21) was the first to mention the selectivity in burial practices as possible explanation for the shortfall in burials in Greece between 1100 and 800, but he finally declined it.
[284] Morris 1991, 1987, 198.
[285] The *agathoi* (singular *agathos,* which in Greek means "the good one") were, according to Morris, a considerable part of the population which in Athens ranged from 25 to 50% of the total population. Morris (1987, 94-5) believes that the *agathoi* were the *elite* and that this group was subdivided in a small ruling class and the non-governing *elite*.

cemeteries.²⁸⁶ The diversity of the EIA societies must never be underestimated. Dickinson,²⁸⁷ who is rather sceptical about Morris' model of restriction of burial rights in Athens, is much keener on accepting Morris' interpretation in the case of Knossos. The reason is the limited number of burials in relation to the elaborate rites and burial constructions.²⁸⁸ Additionally, the fact that the Knossian cemeteries are much better documented than those of Athens. Overall one may observe:

- Limited/restricted number of burials
- Construction and size of complex burial structures (Chamber tombs, pit-caves)
- Rite of cremation, as manifestation of lavish ritual
- Imports from many parts of the Mediterranean
- Local golden, silver, ivory, bronze objects/grave goods

If one combines the data, then it looks that the vast majority of the tombs, apart from some cist tombs, found looted, must have belonged to the wealthiest or strongest part of Knossian society. This view, however, cannot necessarily give a satisfactory answer on the identity of the people buried there, or on the order in which the dead were grouped into the same tomb. It is not certain either whether all the elite members had the same burials rights or even whether there were further privileges for some of them.

For many scholars, the explanation is very straightforward: Coldstream²⁸⁹ implies that the chamber tombs were the resting place of families and in many cases, were used for more than one generation. Brock²⁹⁰ also talks about families that used the tombs for successive generations. Catling²⁹¹ also maintains the same view, although he prefers the term 'group' as a more neutral alternative to the term 'family'. An argument in favour of the use of tombs by families is that the mortuary evidence has shown that in the SM all ages, both sexes and children are represented.²⁹² After the SM, the same occurs with the cremation rite.²⁹³ There is only one notable exception: the remains of infants and very young children are absent.²⁹⁴

---

²⁸⁶ Whitley 1991, 197.
²⁸⁷ Dickinson 2006, 175.
²⁸⁸ Ibid.
²⁸⁹ Coldstream *et al* 1981, 143.
²⁹⁰ Brock 1957, 41.
²⁹¹ Catlin 1996c, 641.
²⁹² Musgrave 1996, 691.
²⁹³ Ibid., 690-692.
²⁹⁴ Ibid.

However, the assumption that a family possesses a tomb and uses it for many generations cannot explain the limited number of burials in most of the tombs. On the contrary, it rather reveals that not all in all the cases could the members of one family, or clan, be buried in the same tomb. Cavanagh,[295] who also supports the theory of the family tombs, suggests that a tomb might have been inherited from a father only to a single heir and thus eventually after a few generations the lineage would cease to exist. On the other hand, an argument against the family character of the tombs is that even in SM there were Knossians buried outside the KNC in locations such as the Lower Ghypsades Hill and Fortetsa SE, and the Kephala Ridge. In all these cemeteries, the finds are almost identical to those of the KNC.

Archaeologists have interpreted the existence of other cemeteries not so much in relation to the possible existence of other settlements, but to different ethnic or political groups, tribes or families who did not want to associate themselves to the main cemetery and to what this could symbolise.[296] This suggestion is based on the old theory of division between post-Minoan, post-Mycenaean and Dorian groups, who hypothetically coexisted (or fought against each other) in EIA at Knossos.[297] This view might look outdated but politically speaking, the EIA must have been a very unstable period indeed as the contemporary defensive settlement at Karphi and Kavousi might imply. For this reason, perhaps different social and political status and family relationships and customs could be reflected in the tombs and burial rites.

However, there is a contradiction in Coldstream and Catling[298] since the existence of different political or social groups buried in other cemeteries might signify that a possible political diversity in Knossos was much stronger than family bonds and lineages. As an extremely remote ethnological example, one could mention the civil wars of the 20th century in Spain (1936-39) and Greece (1946-49), where literarily brothers killed brothers and whole families were eliminated mainly due to political and social reasons. Therefore, the Knossian cemeteries might not have been the resting places of families but of different elite groups who were establishing or displaying their status according to the cemetery where they were buried.

Whitley was initially rather sceptical of the 'family' tomb idea and what he calls 'family groups' in collective tombs.[299] He felt that the evidence, especially from

---

[295] Cavanagh 1996, 666.
[296] Coldstream and Catling 1996, 715; Snodgrass 1996, 596.
[297] Prent 2005; Catling 1996, 643.
[298] Coldstream and Catling 1996, 715.
[299] Whitley 1998, 613.

the North Cemetery, has not been studied in relation to other interpretations apart from the obvious 'family' idea. For example, he pointed out that all sexes and ages are represented in the cemetery but he also noticed that there was not an even representation within an individual tomb.[300] Additionally, because a large amount of arms found in some tombs, he suggested, following Sallares view,[301] that these tombs were not for families but for a particular age or sex grades. However, Whitley seems to finally accept the view of the family tombs.[302]

Kotsonas[303] doubts that the chamber tombs at Knossos were the resting place for families. He questions the correlation between pots (rising number or urns in the 9th century) and demography (equal to an increase of population) and he believes that the rise in the number of urns cannot be matched with the increasing number of nuclear or even extended families.[304] He argues that classes, ages and sexes must have been more important than close kin relationships and refers to Tomb A1K1 at Eleutherna, where mostly males are represented.[305]

A combination of two or more different hypotheses might also be a further explanation. For example, different elite groups could have been buried in different cemeteries and their relatives or followers could have also been buried in the same or neighbouring tombs. The existence of different groups of tombs according to sex or age would require much more detailed analysis of the anthropological evidence but remains plausible especially for the tombs which contain large numbers of burials.

The hypothesis that different clusters of tombs in the Knossian cemeteries may represent different political groups (or elites) which competed to each other might be supported from another archaeological study: a similar case can be seeing in the Greek mainland back in the Mycenaean Period. Mee and Cavanagh[306] in their investigation of the spatial distribution of the Mycenaean tombs within the same cemeteries argue that there is a specific pattern for the creation of the clusters.[307] They initially accept a kind of a pattern based on kinship relations but later they claim that the main reason for the different clustering is small-scale political alliances. One of their basic arguments is that the limited amount of the tombs cannot represent the population of each

---

[300] Ibid.
[301] Ibid.; Sallares 1991, 184–185.
[302] Whitley 2009, 613.
[303] Kotsonas 2011a 129-138.
[304] Ibid., 133.
[305] Ibid., 130.
[306] Mee and Cavanagh 1990.
[307] Ibid., 242.

settlement, not even its elite. Another interesting point that they make after a cluster analysis in the cemeteries of Mycenae and Prosymna is that in the case of the different groups of tombs, the richest tombs are not clustered together.[308] As they maintain even in the peripheral groups rich and poor tombs are closely associated. This simply means that the cemeteries were not arranged according to wealth with the richer tombs cluster together but probably according to other political relationships.[309]

At Knossos, even if most of the tombs are in the North Cemetery, the rest of the tombs have proportionately produced much more burials. The 18 chamber tombs of Fortetsa SE have produced 202 burials, while the 79 tombs of KNC about 570. This is a very rough calculation and some tombs contain much more burials than others, but if we divided the number of burials with the number of the tombs in each of these two cemeteries, the average for all periods of inurned burials per tomb is 11.22 for Fortetsa SE and 7.21 for North Cemetery respectively. This discrepancy is because many (but not all) of the North Cemetery tombs were very damaged and looted. However, there is also the possibility that the tombs outside the North Cemetery were successively used for a longer period or without interruption. The people who used the Fortetsa SE cemetery might have also sought to preserve the connection with the old chamber tombs rather than to create new ones, as the Knossians of the North Cemetery might have done. This may reveal a difference in the ideology and political behaviour of each group.

Such ideology can be for example a need for continuity and connection to the past for emotional or political reasons. This need can be seen in Tomb P at Fortetsa SE, where more than 80 pithoi have been squashed in the same tomb. Most of them were used as cinerary urns. Additionally, in the chamber tomb at Lower Gypsades, 35 estimated burials[310] were found. The period of use ranges from LPG to LO for Tomb P and from PGB to LO for the tomb at Lower Gypsades. Both tombs were relatively undisturbed. At the same time, one should not underestimate the BA past of Knossos and the possibility that many of the Minoan customs and traditions were inherited to the Iron Age Knossians. The way cemeteries were formed and grouped in the LM period was not very different from the way they were formed in the EIA and chamber tombs were also grouped in clusters.

---

[308] Ibid., 234.
[309] Ibid., 232-234.
[310] As already explained, the calculation of cremations is made by counting the pithoi (which are the typical cremation urns of the area), even if they were found empty.

A custom that could explain the absence of a large number of tombs and burials is what happens nowadays not only in Crete but all over Greece. In modern Greece, where inhumation is the dominant if not the sole burial rite,[311] after the decomposition of the body inside the coffin, the bones are collected in a wooden box and kept in an osteophylakion (i.e. ossuary). Finally, if the empty tomb belongs to the family, it will be used by its members; otherwise, other people would be buried there. There is one case at the North Cemetery where a similar but not identical process was detected. In Tomb E at the Teke Cemetery dated in LPG, one of the funerary urns contained non-cremated human bones of a young girl. The excavator of the tomb believes that the body had been left to decompose first and then the bones were placed in the urn.[312] The non-cremated bones of a young man were found outside the crater, in the same chamber. Musgrave believes that the decomposition of the bodies took place inside Tomb E and the bones were not brought from elsewhere.[313] This could also mean, in the case of the young female that both her primary and secondary burial occurred in the same place and the chamber tomb opened twice for the ritual of the secondary burial (i.e. the deposition of the bones inside the urn).

Archaeologists discovered in Knossos very few burial pits, used either for cremation or inhumation.[314] A simple pit containing the remains of a person is not a very recognisable archaeological feature and sometimes archaeologists tend to oversight them: my personal experience comes from an excavation in Attica at the old banks of Kifissos River.[315] This is an area with soft limestone like the *Kouskouras* of Knossos, (i.e. a sedimentary rock). *Kimilia*, once excavated it can be rapidly transformed from a very humid sand-like soil into a more stable almost solid rock. Occasionally this transformation can be very confusing because one may think that he or she has reached the bedrock, but more burials, especially simple pits can be located at a lower level. Its stratigraphy can also be tricky; is very hard sometimes to distinguish different deposits inside the soft limestone's yellowish colour. Mechanical clearance by excavators such as the ones employed in KNC can make things even worse regarding the stratigraphy of the soft limestone.

---

[311] The Greek Orthodox Church strongly opposes the idea of cremation for dogmatic reasons and anyone wishing to be buried in this way is cremated abroad, normally in Bulgaria. The urn with the cremated bones may finally enter the family tomb but without a proper religious service. There is an ongoing debate on this matter in Greek society, even nowadays that cremation is permitted by law.
[312] Sackett and Musgrave 1976, 128.
[313] Ibid.
[314] See Appendix I for these graves.
[315] This unpbished resque excavation of an EIA cemetery took place from 2006 to 2010 in Kifissos Avenue, Aigaleo near the intersection with *Hiera Odos*. *Kouskouras* in the area of Attica is known as *Kimilia* (chalk).

FIGURE 8: HERAKLION HOSPITAL AT KNOSSOS, BELOW THE FENCE IS KOUSKOURAS THE SOFT YELLOW LIMESTONE, WHICH WAS IDEAL FOR THE CONSTRUCTION OF THE CHAMBER-TOMB (PHOTOGRAPH BY THE AUTHOR).

Finally, with the following case study, I wish to demonstrate that for the expansion of the Knossian cemeteries is not necessarily related to the rise or fall of the population. One would expect that a rise in the number the burials would signify a rise in the construction of tombs. I shall test this hypothesis in the KNC as studied by Cavanagh (i.e. the KMF, Teke and Fortetsa/67 sites). In the following graphs, one can see an estimation of the rise of burials per period, as studied by Cavanagh.[316]

The British scholar calculated[317] that there was a sharp rise in the number of burials in the 8th century (EG) by simply counting the number of urns per period. In another calculation based on the number of cremations divided by the estimated duration of the period, Cavanagh calculated that the maximum rise on the burials per year was at the end of the 9th century (PGB-EG). At the same time, if one calculates the number of new tombs (of all kinds) per period for the same time, one will get the following results shown in Table 5, Graph 4.

At a first glance, one can see that the fluctuations of the numbers of burials as described by Cavanagh do not exactly match with the construction of new tombs per period. There is a rise in the construction of tombs in PG and then another one in G. In fact, in the PGB, when the number of cremations rose

---

[316] Cavanagh 1996, 661-2.
[317] Ibid.

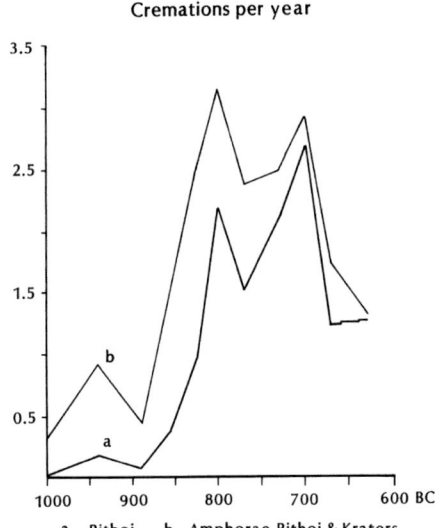

TABLE 3: GRAPH 2: MAXIMUM AND MINIMUM OF CREMATION URNS (CAVANAGH 1996, 661). REPRODUCED WITH PERMISSION OF THE BRITISH SCHOOL AT ATHENS.

TABLE 4: GRAPH 3: CREMATIONS PER YEAR (CAVANAGH 1996, 662). REPRODUCED WITH PERMISSION OF THE BRITISH SCHOOL AT ATHENS.

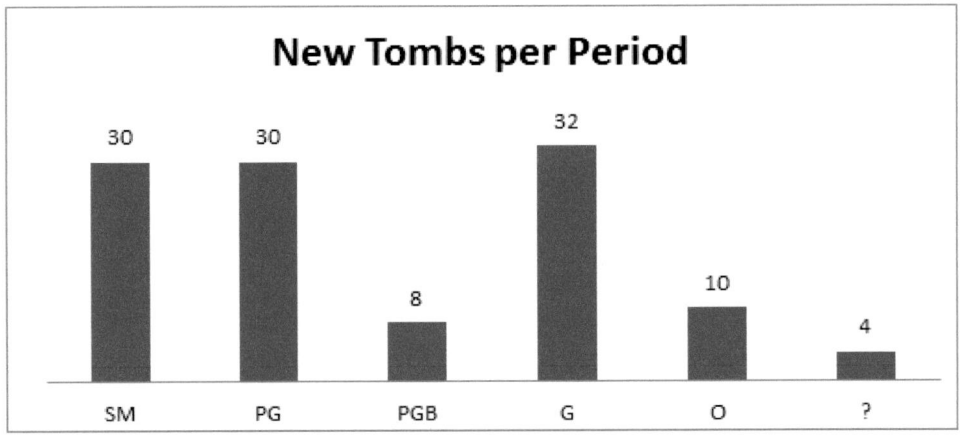

TABLE 5: GRAPH 4: CONSTRUCTION OF NEW TOMBS PER PERIOD.

sharply, only eight tombs were constructed. On the other hand, one should bear in mind that PGB is a much shorter period. It is more interesting to see the fluctuations in the appearance of new tombs within the PG and G in Table 6, Graph 5 and Table 7, Graph 6.

From these two more detailed graphs, it becomes obvious that the rise in the number of burials did not occur at the same time with the rise in the construction of tombs. I believe that this is a clear sign that the creation of new tombs and possibly new plots of tombs within the same cemetery is necessarily related to

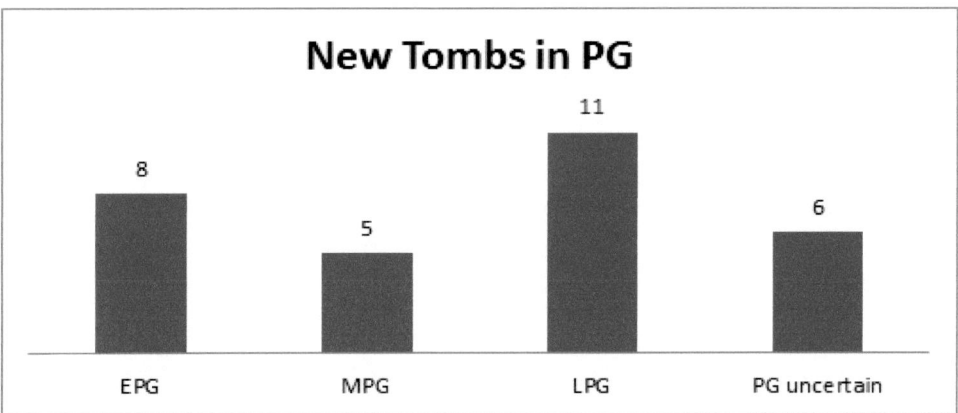

TABLE 6: GRAPH 5: CONSTRUCTION OF NEW TOMBS DURING THE PG PERIOD.

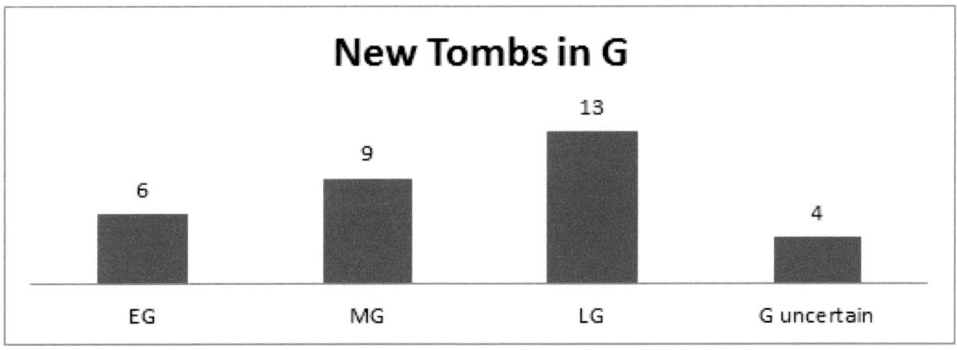

TABLE 7: GRAPH 6: CONSTRUCTION OF NEW TOMBS DURING THE G PERIOD.

increase in population. It might reflect some tension between the people who already had the right to be buried in the cemetery, or that people outside the main elite group sought more privileges. The construction of new tombs might mean new (or more) elite members.

v. EIA Cemeteries and BA Tradition

The Knossian EIA covers more than four centuries and in such a long period one would expect to see various shifts in the way the dead were buried. Regarding the earlier period, it has already been explained that the EIA cemeteries are located near BA tombs and/or cemeteries. In fact, in some cases, there is EIA reuse of BA tombs, immediately above LM burials. The tomb at Ayios Ioannis is the most obvious example where two skeletons of the SM were discovered immediately above LM burials.[318]

---

[318] Hood and Coldstream 1968.

It seems that the sites that which are not used before the SM are: Fortetsa SE,[319] the KMF, Teke and the Fortetsa NE tombs. The most detailed analysis is provided by Cavanagh.[320] The author is using a series of cluster analyses and comparisons between BA chamber tombs and the chamber tombs at the KMF. The result of this analysis is that there is a great possibility that all the chamber tombs in the KNC publication were constructed after the end of the BA and mainly reflected the EIA rites and customs.[321] His main argument is that the size of the chamber tombs is much smaller than that of the BA ones, especially as far as the size of the chamber is concerned.

At the same time, there are tombs in his analysis, which could be of an earlier construction date. For example, from the KMF site, Tomb 283 and five more tombs (75, 207, 82, 219, 106) might be reused BA tombs, as suggested by the size of the chamber and their narrow stomia. However, Cavanagh[322] rejects this possibility and assigns them a later date, arguing that EIA Knossians simply imitated older constructions in order to embrace a 'glorious' past. Coldstream and Catling maintain in the KNC publication that from the aforementioned cluster, only Tomb 75 could have been a BA construction.[323] Catling[324] however in the section on SM burials of the same publication firmly states that *"...it was a virgin site, where no previous burials had been made. I do not believe that any of the chamber tombs were opened before the SM period"*.[325]

Despite Cavanagh's and Catling's rejection, and apart from the size of the tombs, there is further evidence pointing to the possibility of a BA phase at KMF, such as the existence of fragments of larnakes inside the chamber tombs and sometimes the use of such larnakes as coffins for EIA inhumations. All the 16 larnakes found are dated to the LM III A-B period.[326] One could argue that EIA Knossians discovered these clay coffins in their attempt to dig their new tombs and simply reused them for their own burials, thus making a symbolic connection to the Minoan past. It is also reasonable to assume that those larnakes were found on the same sites where the chamber tombs were constructed. Catling does not accept this argument and suggests that those larnakes were brought from elsewhere (failing to specify where from) and used

---

[319] Brock 1957.
[320] Cavanagh 1996.
[321] Ibid., 657.
[322] Ibid., 655.
[323] Coldstream and Catling 1996, 719.
[324] Catling 1996c, 639.
[325] Ibid.
[326] Only one might be an EIA imitation (Coldstream 1998, 58).

in the PGB by the Knossians as a manifestation of continuity with the past.[327] Without any doubt, the context where most of the larnakes were found inside of chamber tombs and the stratigraphy certainly suggest a secondary EIA use.

It seems that Coldstream[328] was not entirely satisfied with the aforementioned interpretation of the KNC publication made by him and Catling[329] for an EIA construction of the KMF tombs. Shortly after the KNC publication, he changed his view and argued for the reuse of BA tombs in this area and thus for a LM phase of the KNC cemetery.[330] He says that this new approach must be understood as supplementary to the main publication of the KNC.[331] He uses the cluster[332] analysis of Cavanagh, in order to argue for a series of bigger than the usual size chamber tombs.[333] He considers those tombs genuinely Minoan and not an EIA imitation as Cavanagh thought. The LM larnakes used in later burials in the same cemetery were initially discovered, according to Coldstream in those tombs.[334]

In order to combine a new SM phase and the Bronze Tombs, Coldstream formulated the following hypothesis: The North Cemetery (in this case the KMF and the Teke sites) were also cemeteries in the BA Period probably until LM IIIA-B, as the evidence from the larnakes and the few large tombs suggest. Then, there is a gap for about 90 years (i.e. the whole LM IIIC period). After this 'caesura', the SM phase begins in the cemetery with a series of pit-cave and chamber tombs.[335] Then, according to Coldstream, another 'caesura', though less sharp, occurred in the mid-9th century, even though there is burial activity in this period.[336] At the same time, in the PGB period, all those bigger than usual chamber tombs came into use together with the use of LM larnakes for the burial of children, in a period when cremation was the main funeral rite.

In my opinion, Coldstream's approach is correct and this is supported by further evidence: It is worth mentioning Tomb 294. One of the interpretations of the evidence that the excavator uses for the history of the tomb is the following: first, there was a LM tomb with two larnakes, which was discovered by the constructors of the chamber tomb and whose context was reused inside

---

[327] Catling 1996c, 639; Cavanagh 1996, 656.
[328] Coldstream 1998.
[329] Coldstream and Catling 1996, 719.
[330] Coldstream 1996b, 236-62; 1998, 58-61.
[331] Coldstream 1998, 58 n. 1.
[332] He also adds tomb Q at Teke site a possible BA construction (Colstream 1998, 59).
[333] These are the tombs of Cavanagh's (1996) cluster analysis.of tombs (286, 75, 207, 82, 219, 106).
[334] Coldstream 1998, 59.
[335] Ibid.
[336] Ibid.

the new tomb for EIA burials.[337] This is the only tomb where the excavators seem to admit that the larnakes were probably found in situ in the EIA. If the interpretation of the evidence is correct, then this is proof that there was Minoan burial activity in the KMF, as well.

Another important aspect is that the KNC publication does not include all the tombs discovered in this area. There are at least three tombs (and a few more not published) such as Tombs L, TFT, Π, which are located within the KNC, and it is not certain whether they were constructed before or after the end of the BA. Cavanagh[338] includes Tomb TFT in the tombs that could have been constructed in the BA in his cluster analysis, but then he rejects the idea due to the asymmetric stomion of the tomb. Further, regarding the larnax graves and the shafts found empty in the KMF cemetery, it is not very clear that they belong to the EIA. Even if their dimensions are smaller than the average size of the tombs belonging to the BA, a LM date cannot be easily rejected. One must forget the five tombs discovered at Venizeleion Hospital (Next to KNF site) by Hood that they were attributed to LM warriors.[339]

A tomb that has not been recently considered to be a BA construction was Tomb P at Fortetsa SE. In the only general plan available from this cemetery tomb is one of the largest chamber tombs but unfortunately, its dimensions are not known.[340] More than 80 pithoi were discovered in this tomb. If pithoi can be an indication of the number of cremations found in a tomb,[341] this makes tomb P the one with the highest number of burials in the entire Knossian BA.[342] In this case, its size must have been much larger than the average EIA chamber tombs. A larnax and a M potsherd were discovered near the dromos of this tomb.[343] The LM larnax was found south of the dromos and parallel to it.[344] Brock is not negative that this tomb could have been constructed in the BA.[345]

There is also the case of the Khaniale Teke group, which also belongs to the extended area of the North Cemetery. Tomb II at Khaniale Teke, excavated by

---

[337] Coldstream and Catling 1996, 276.
[338] Cavanagh 1996, 656.
[339] Hood *et al* 1958-9, 246-255.
[340] Broke 1957, xii.
[341] Cavanagh 1996, 659, n. 1495.
[342] Brock (1957, 101, n.2) mentions that not all pithoi from Tomb P contained burials. This however may be, as already suggested, the result of various unfortunate incidents during the reopening of the tomb for the successive burials.
[343] Ibid., 3, n. 2,
[344] Ibid., 98.
[345] Ibid., 4-5, 216.

Hutchinson,[346] is a tholos tomb constructed in the LM and reused from the end of PG. Catling and Coldstream,[347] in their attempt to prove that most of the tombs, if not all of them, are of an EIA date, do not disregard the possibility that even the Tholos Tomb II at Khaniale Teke might be an EIA imitation of a BA tomb. However, due to the solid construction of this tomb, this argument does not sound very convincing.[348] The other two tombs from the same group, which have a rectangular chamber, also suggest a LM date of construction. Despite the EIA context, larnax fragments are again present.[349]

Suming up the evidence one can say that the stratigraphy of tomb 294 suggests a BA phase in the KMF. It is probably only at its very core (i.e. only the tomb clusters around pit-cave complex 200-202) that a SM cemetery was established in a relatively clear from older tombs area. It is also important to underline that SM Knossians did not destroy the older cemeteries like the one at Zafer Papoura for example. This also might be another interesting bond with the past. Another important aspect that suggests further connections between the BA and the EIA cemeteries is the combination of various burial types within the same group of tombs. Chamber tombs are not the only kind of tomb that existed in the Bronze and Iron Ages at Knossos. One must not rule out the possibility that some other forms of burial pre-existed on the same burial sites before the EIA. As explained in the beginning of the chapter chamber tombs, pit-caves and shaft graves coexisted in the same cemeteries in the EIA cemeteries. This is not, however, a post-BA innovation. In the LM IIIA and perhaps even earlier these burial types were also in use at least in one of the main Knossian cemeteries.

I would like to pay attention to the pit-caves since this burial type plays a major role in the SM period at Knossos. A total of 18 pit-caves (tombs 6, 7, 10, 37, 41, 43, 45, 48, 51, 55, 64, 64, 70, 71, 76) were excavated by Evans[350] at Zafer Papouta cemetery, all of them dated in LM IIIA.[351] The cemetery is located about 800 meters north of the Palace of Minos. In the summer of 1926, Evans conducted excavations at Mavro Spilio cemetery, at about 800 meters east of the Palace. Forsdyke assisted him in the following season. One of the tombs (XI) that were described by Fosdyke as irregular shaft[352] could have been according to a pit-cave.[353] No date is given but the cemetery was in use from MM to LM IIIA. In 1952, during the rescue excavations

---

[346] Hutchinson and Boardman 1954.
[347] Catling and Coldstream 1996, 719.
[348] Ibid.
[349] Hutchinson 1954, 215; Boardman 1967, 70.
[350] Evans 1906.
[351] Catling 1996c, 643.
[352] Ibid., 271.
[353] Miller 2011, 56.

for the construction of Venizeleion, Hood discovered a structure (tomb IV) that if it was indeed a tomb it might have been a pit-cave, but the excavator was not certain. The next possible example of pit-cave comes from the Upper Gypsades MM-LM III cemetery. There, the same excavator[354] identified a destroyed and looted shaft as a possible pit-cave (tomb XVII). In 1960 four tombs were excavated east of Kairatos River opposite the Temple Tomb. The first was a chamber tomb while the other three were pit-caves.[355] The first was plundered, in the other, a LM vase was found, while the third had been used for three successive burials. All inhumations were placed in wooden coffins. Apart of the initial publication, no other information is available for these tombs.

In the KMF eight tombs (2, 98, 121, 186, 200, 201, 202, 208) were discovered. Probably there were more pit-caves in the KMF of which their shape was altered later (Tomb 229 is a strong candidate) but also in other sites. For example, the pit-tombs at Ayios Ioannis probably were just another form of pit-cave.[356] The pit-caves that share more common elements are those discovered at Zafer Papoura and at KMF. Their structure is identical with those at KMF being smaller than those at Zafer Papoura. This is something that has been observed also in the EIA chamber tombs since most of them are much smaller than those of the BA. In the case of Zafer Papoura the 18% of the tombs are pit-caves and at KMF the ca. 13%. It is again evident that BA and EIA had many things in common regarding death and a link between the pit-caves of different periods cannot be denied.[357]

vi. Additional Archaeological Evidence

As stated in the introduction, I consider the addition of archaeological evidence from contexts other than cemeteries very important for the present investigation. This can offer deeper knowledge of the Knossian society and the way the world of the dead (if I may use this expression), interacted with the world of the living. For this reason, I offer below an overview of the archaeological evidence for the settlement and for the sanctuaries.

a. From the BA palace to the EIA settlement

The evidence for an EIA settlement at Knossos is a *"meagre filling in a massive sandwich between the Late Minoan town...and the Roman colony above, whose massive foundations have disturbed the Greek strata almost to the point of obliteration"*.[358] The Palace of Minos was deserted before the end of the BA

---

[354] Hood *et al* 1958-9, 220.
[355] Hood 1960, 266.
[356] Catling 1996d, 308.
[357] Catling 1996c, 644.
[358] Coldstream 2006, 586.

and part of it probably became a sanctuary area.³⁵⁹ Traces of occupation have also been discovered within the Palace area.³⁶⁰ The main centre of occupation developed west and north of the Palace site.³⁶¹ A major difference has been observed in the archaeological record of Knossos, and to other sites in Crete: The Knossians continued to live in a place that was very hard to defend. Knossos is in a valley and its non-defensive position did not change after the end of the BA, while other contemporary sites in the island were in places that are much easier to defend.³⁶² There are settlements on the picks of mountains, such as Kastro, Karphi and Kavousi that share all the characteristics of defensive, or refuge settlements. Nowicki³⁶³ comparing Knossos with the refuge settlements argues for the continuity of life in Knossos since the BA. This might imply that the EIA Knossians did not need protection because they controlled the entire valley up to the shore. Following this line of thought, one could suggest that the inhabitants of Knossos could pose a threat to the other inhabitants of the island who were forced to seek refuge in the mountains. There is a possibility that the hill west of the Palace might have been used as a defensive Acropolis during this period. However, apart from the apparently natural defensive position of the hill, only a few G potsherds and a fragment of an early Doric capital were found at this site.³⁶⁴ This might suggest that a sanctuary may have existed there.³⁶⁵ It must be stressed, nevertheless, that no evidence for any kind of fortification has been found on the hill dating to this early period.

EIA pottery was also discovered further to the north of the Palace inside wells and it is likely that there was an extension of the settlement at the LG period towards the north. The result of the stratigraphic soundings and excavations (i.e. concentration of potsherds), when grouped to a plan of central Knossos, enclose an extensive area of 1,200 m² within which many other sites have produced Early Greek pottery.³⁶⁶ This can give an idea about the possible extension of the settlement but is more an assumption based on potsherds discovered in this area and, in many cases, not found in stratified levels or in closed deposits, as Coldstream admits.³⁶⁷ Further proof is needed as far as pottery is concerned. The stratified pottery should be examined in relation to the architectural remains. Two apsidal houses dated to LM IIIC, discovered by Warren in an excavation behind the Stratigraphic Museum.³⁶⁸ The excavator viewed the two structures

---

[359] Hood and Smith 1981, 16.
[360] Coldstream and Macdonald 1992, 244.
[361] Hood and Smith 1981, 16.
[362] Myers *et al* 1992, 38.
[363] Nowicki 2000, 25; 2000.
[364] Hood and Smith 1981, 16.
[365] Ibid.
[366] Coldstream 2000a, 260-261, fig. 1.
[367] Ibid., 263.
[368] Coldstream 2006, 581; Warren 1983, 69-71.

as distinct to the local Minoan architecture and interpreted them as a sign of the arrival of foreigners from the Mycenaean mainland.[369] Warren identified four SM building phases (walls) with no apparent disruption from the previous LM IIIC period[370]

Apart from the walls, a considerable amount of pottery was discovered in stratified pit deposits of the same site and it is possible to demonstrate an uninterrupted sequence of pottery from LM IIIC to the SM.[371] More specifically, domestic SM pottery was found over an area of c. 800 m² extending from the Stratigraphic Museum to the west border of the Palace of Minos.[372] There is also a considerable amount of recovered material (pottery) from the PG to the O period without any apparent interruption from other locations within the central area.

Domestic pottery (storage vessels and cooking pots) was found at levels above the Unexplored Mansion ranging from the LBA to the EPG.[373] In the soundings, north and south of the royal road, remains of two walls belonging probably to a post-Minoan house have been discovered.[374] In addition, stratified pottery extending from the SM to the G was found within the levels of the house. G pottery was recovered from at least fifteen well deposits at the hospital area.[375]

In the south-west border of the Palace, EIA levels were discovered (stratified SM and EPG pottery and, after a gap, EO pottery) within a LM II-III house. Part of it was used again for housing in the succeeding periods .[376] From the EO, more evidence for houses and terraces was discovered along with a path and a pottery kiln. This discovery next to the Palace lead the excavators to the conclusion that, apart from the Palace itself, the surrounding area was not necessarily a tabu for the later Greeks who probably lived within it.[377]

Under the Roman Villa of Dionysos, there was probably a settlement nucleus, as two different succeeding levels from the PG have been located along with traces of walls from the second-level.[378] In earlier test trenches (1935-6) in the Roman Villa, Hutchinson discovered G walls and pottery. The walls had the same

---

[369] Ibid.
[370] Warren 1983, 76-87.
[371] Ibid.
[372] Coldstream 2000a, 297.
[373] Popham 1992, 65.
[374] Coldstream 1972, 64.
[375] Ibid.
[376] Coldstream and Macdonald 1997, 243.
[377] Ibid.
[378] Coldstream and Hatzaki 2003, 286.

orientation as the abovementioned PG walls. The discovery of a PG house at a relative distance (c. 300 m to the north) from the contemporary settlement was a surprise for the excavators since they believed that that the main settlement had not expanded to the north before the 8th century.[379] Archaeologists regarded the existence and the location of the house as an isolated phenomenon.

As already mentioned, Coldstream interprets the findspots of recovered SM material as the nucleus of the EIA town of Knossos.[380] In addition, he interprets the expansion of the latter city as a reverse process of the Aristotelian model regarding the birth of the Greek cities of the mainland. Many mainland cities were created by the unification of small hamlets.[381] Coldstream based his claim on the evidence from tombs outside the settlement and on the pottery sequence and walls in a wider area, However, other archaeologists who have worked at the greater Knossos region and outside the main area, which falls outside the responsibility of the British School, have maintained the position that there were hamlets or farmsteads outside Knossos during the EIA.[382] This view is supported by a relatively small amount of G potsherds discovered on the hills of Kallithea and Ayios Ioannis as well as on the Acropolis Hill that overlooks the BA Palace from the west.[383]

Another argument supporting the idea of the existence of small hamlets is that near the hills, they were tombs[384] that might have formed small groups or cemeteries at quite a distance from the main settlement. However, no traces of walls or other signs of habitation have been discovered apart from wells. Such wells were detected in the Venizeleion[385] area, north of the main settlement, and plain pottery was discovered at a distance much closer than the hills. Regarding these well deposits, Sjögren[386] argues that the domestic pottery found in an area with no traces of building structures probably served the people attending the funeral rites. Her argument is since most of the pots recovered from the wells are hydriai and globular jugs. Pots associated with the preparation of food are lacking.[387] One cannot exclude though that, even if pots for the preparation of the food had been found, those could have had been used for feasting as part of the funeral process. The main concept behind the theory of small hamlets

---

[379] Ibid., 299.
[380] Coldstream 2006, 297.
[381] Ibid.
[382] Alexiou 1950, 296.
[383] Hood and Smith 1981, 18.
[384] For a detailed analysis see next section.
[385] This was the sanatorium which was built immediately north of the Palace area in 1953.
[386] Sjögren 2003, 31.
[387] Ibid.; Coldstream 1972, 81-84.

coming together to form a city is probably that a group of tombs or a bigger cemetery must have been within a short walking distance from the settlement, as it was common at that time on the Greek mainland.[388]

However, this is a theory which cannot be supported without the presence of domestic evidence in areas that have been thoroughly investigated and no other traces of domestic activity have been found. At the same time, the supporters of the two different views (one settlement or many hamlets) do not explain the motivation for placing a cemetery at a shorter or longer distance from the settlement. Coldstream[389] mentions the possibility that the remote tombs were not related to a settlement but to ancestral land owned by families living in the nuclear town. The Knossians of the main settlement might have wished to be buried there and not at the main cemetery.[390] It is not clear, though if there was any attempt by the Knossians to control their land and their inherited property. This for example has been observed in the relationship between urn cemeteries and settlements in the almost contemporary (1400-1000 BC) Southern England.[391] In any case, it would have been very strange if the 'small-settlement' theory proposed by Coldstream was able to maintain the North Cemetery whose extension was much more extended than that of the settlement itself.

The most recent major investigation concerning the size of the settlement of Knossos has been carried out from 2005 to 2008 by the Knossos Urban Landscape Project (KULP)[392] The purpose of this project was to understand the nature of the settlement of Knossos. This was a joint effort by the British School and the local Ephorate. There is no final publication yet, but from the preliminary articles published so far and the conferences, it can be said that the view on the Knossos EIA settlement might change drastically in the near future. 1,500 out of 355,000 of the recovered potsherds date to the EIA. Based on preliminary results, the members of the project claim that the EIA settlement was much larger than Coldstream claimed.[393] They maintain that the Acropolis Hill was incorporated in the settlement. They also believe that the cemetery of Fortetsa SE on its western slope was the limit of the settlement.[394] Towards the north, the city extended almost as far as the southernmost tombs of KNC. The northern

---

[388] Coldstream 2006, 582.
[389] Coldstream 2000a, 260; 1981, 144.
[390] Ibid.
[391] Bradley 1981, 102; Goody 1962.
[392] Whitelaw *et al* 2008.
[393] Kotsonas *et al* 2012; Whitelaw *et al* 2008; Bennet *et al* 2006.
[394] Bennet *et al* 2006, 107.

slopes of the Gypsades Hills were the southern limit of Knossos settlement. The western bank of Kairatos River was probably its eastern limit.[395]

This means that the city did stretch almost as far as its peripheral cemeteries. In this case, it could be likely that that the way that cemeteries placed around Knossos might reflect different elites living within the main settlement but in different areas. In other words, each elite could have its separated satellite cemetery. I use the word 'elite' for all the cemeteries because it does not seem to be at first glance any a sharp social difference between the various cemeteries. This could also explain the location of the Fortetsa SE cemetery. In the following map, one can see the different suggestions regarding the size of the EIA settlement of Knossos. The extended settlement is the one proposed by the KULP[396] and the smaller urban nucleus is the one proposed by Coldstream.[397]

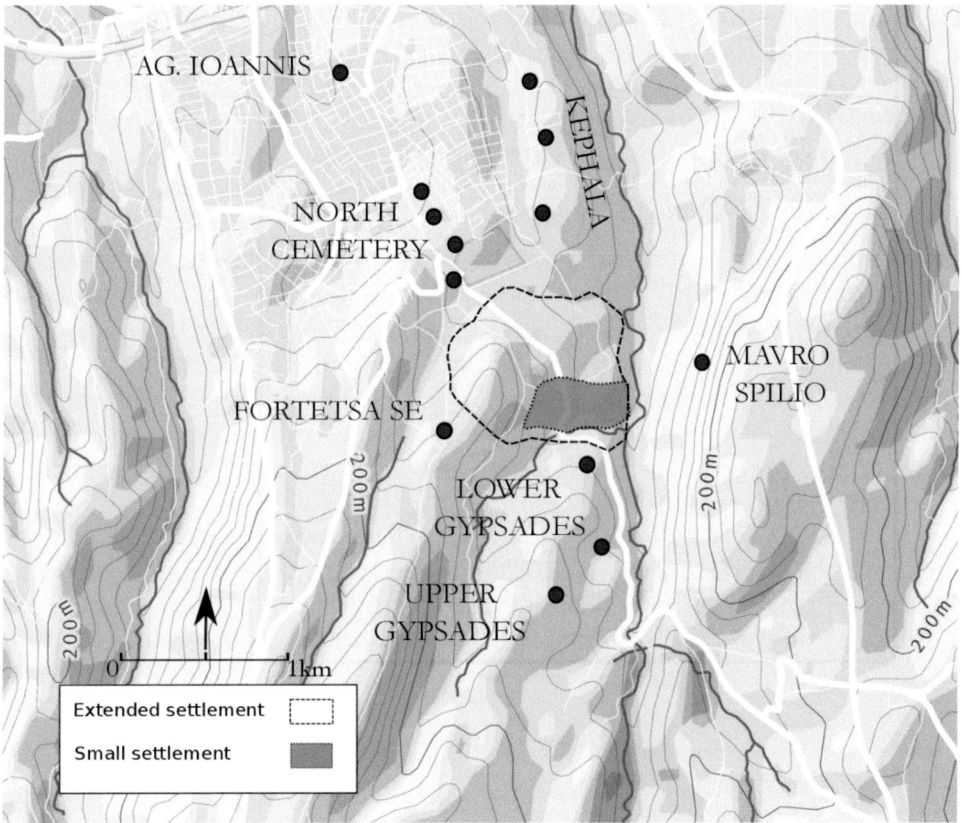

FIGURE 9: MAP 6: THE SETTLEMENT OF KNOSSOS.

---

[395] Kotsonas *et al* 2012, 222.
[396] Kotsonas *et al* 2012.
[397] Coldstream 2000a.

Finally, one should add that north of Knossos where the modern capital of Crete is now located, it is very hard, due to the expansion of the modern city, to know if the tombs discovered there were related to hamlets or even to a site which served Knossos as a port. Coldstream believes that probably must have been hamlets there. Importantly, domestic pottery was discovered in Heraklion in rescue excavations conducted by the local archaeological service.[398]

b. Cult activity

It has been even more difficult to find archaeological proof for cult activity in Knossos than archaeological evidence associated with the settlement. One may observe that for the excavators of Knossos since Evans, three are the most important aspects for the period followed the end of the BA. The first aspect is the preservation of the Palace structure from later building activity. This could indicate an open-air cult.[399] The second is that the EIA divine presence in Knossos, which in general is connected to a vegetation/nature goddess, is related to Demeter, her mother Rhea and her daughter Persephone[400] and thus to the arrival of new people, namely the Dorians.[401] The third aspect is related to the nature of these female deities: It has been suggested that all of them were related to beliefs concerning the afterlife[402] and probably to funerary activities.

One could observe that the first aspect is based on archaeological evidence (either on its presence in its absence) and the second on the traditional historical explanation of invasion and migration. It looks like in Knossos the archaeologists attempted at the same time to highlight the continuity of the site since the LBA (i.e. Minoan vegetation goddess) and to explain the changes in the archaeological contexts in association with the Mycenaeans and Dorians, who supposedly invaded at different periods.[403] The third aspect is mostly related to the interpretation of the archaeological evidence.

As far as the first aspect is concerned, almost nothing was built upon the Palace and most of its area until the 5th century BC. In the Classical Period, Knossians using Minoan building material built a structure which was probably a temple.[404] Additionally, Diodorus Siculus[405] mentions the sacred grove of Rhea,

---

[398] Coldstream and Catling 1996, 714.
[399] Evans 1928, 7.
[400] Coldstream *et al* 1981, 95.
[401] Coldstream 2006, 582.
[402] Prent 2009, 238.
[403] Coldstream 2006, 581-596.
[404] Hood and Smith 1981, 16; Coldstream 2006, 582; 2000, 286.
[405] Diodorus Siculus 5.66.

the mother of the Gods[406] and Evans[407] believed that the Palace area had been transformed to the sacred grove where Rhea was venerated. This could mean that not only the 5th-century sanctuary but also the earlier open cult was dedicated to Rhea. Pendlebury[408] interpreted this absence of building activity at the Palace after the LBA as a tabu of the later Greeks with apparent religious significance. Cult activity has also been observed upon the ruins of other Cretan Palaces.[409] Open-air worship seems to have been a common practice at the end of the BA in Crete.[410] Votive drinking vessels and miniature pots, all dating from the early 5th century BC and onwards, were found in the south-west corner of the Central Court, adjacent to this supposed temple.[411] This temple could indicate the sacredness of the place in earlier times.[412] Before the construction of this structure, in an area without later domestic building activity, there are some traces of open-air worship during the EIA in the South-West corner of the Central Court. Most of these finds are elusive since the PG and G potsherds mentioned by Hartley are either missing or misplaced.[413] On the contrary, part of a LG animal figurine illustrated by Hartley and a MG bird askos found by Kalokairinos do indicate cult activity.[414]

The second aspect regarding cult activity is related to the discovery, made by Evans[415] of a small shrine structure south of the Palace in the Spring Chamber dating to the SM. What was first discovered was an earlier deposit of conical cups containing carbonised olive stones, which imply a vegetation cult dating to the LM I.[416] The second deposit was composed of SM vessels and a hut-urn or house-model with a figure inside which was interpreted by Evans as a Minoan goddess.[417] The figure had the hands raised in the same way as the images of the LM IIIB. However, its context and the overall style of the vessel are of a much later date. A SM date seems to be the most appropriate.[418] Evans[419] gave a date of LM IIIB. According to Prent[420] the suburban location of the sanctuary

---

[406] Coldsrteam 2006, 582; Evans 1928, 5-7.
[407] Evans 1928, 5-7.
[408] Pendlebury 1963, 305.
[409] Coldstream 2000a, 296; Foley 1988, 145-147; Klein 1997, 247-322.
[410] D'Agata 2001, 351-3.
[411] Coldstream 2000a, 283.
[412] Coldstream 2006, 582.
[413] Coldstream 2000a, 286.
[414] Ibid.
[415] Evans 1928, 123-139.
[416] Coldstream 1973, 181; Alexiou 1958, 206; Evans 1928, 134.
[417] Evans 1928, 128-129.
[418] Alexiou 1958, 206; Coldsrteam 1973, 181.
[419] Evans 1928, 134.
[420] Prent 2005, 618.

and the scarcity of the objects suggest that during the LM IIIC-SM this cult was not of primary importance and that the goddess venerated there only by a few Knossians. Thus, the communities of different cultural or ethnic background were involved in the cult activities practised in the older settlements such as Knossos and in the new defensive settlements such as Karphi.[421] While there is no conclusive evidence for this claim, one wonders whether within the settlement of Knossos participation in different cult activities might signify a social or political division between the Knossians.

Coldstream maintains that after the spring was blocked up by particles of gypsum around 1000 BC, the cult was transported or revived about fifty meters further south in the Lower Gypsades Hill.[422] One can find there, evidence at least by the eighth century BC for a cult dedicated to Demeter:[423] A 5th-century temple of Demeter was also discovered there with votive terracotta figurines of humans and animals.[424] The earliest pottery deposit and the construction of a terrace wall are dated to the 8th century. There are some PG potsherds. It is not impossible then to consider a cult/religious continuity from the SM and onwards.[425] According to Coldstream[426] and Desborough,[427] the SM cult in the Spring Chamber and certainly the cult of Demeter suggest the existence of a strong Dorian society which had adopted some forms of Minoan iconography and perhaps its religious practices as well. This can also be seen on a PG Pithos found in chamber tomb 107, depicting two sitting figures on a wheeled platform with trees and birds.[428] The explanation based on the Dorian presence and a subsequent invasion have been criticised as old ideas maintain their hold on new facts.[429]

The third aspect of this section is related to the representation of these female deities and their worship during the entire EIA. From the PGB the female deities with the upraised hands begin to appear in funerary context at Knossos. They are painted on a crater[430] in Tomb P at Fortetsa SE and on two cremation pithoi at tombs 107 and 114 of KMF respectively.[431] In one of these scenes, the goddess

---

[421] Ibid.
[422] Coldsream 2006, 584; D'Agata 2006, 406.
[423] Coldsream 2006, 584.
[424] Coldstream 1973, 180–1.
[425] Coldstream 1973, Coldstream *et al* 1981; D' Agata 2006, 407.
[426] Coldstream 1973, 180-181.
[427] Desborough 1964, 180.
[428] D'Agata 2006, 407; Coldstream and Catling 1996, 316.
[429] Whitley 1998, 613
[430] Crater 1420, Tomb P (Brock 1957, 123).
[431] Pithos 283.11, Tomb 283 and pithos 107.114, Tomb 107 (Coldstream 1984b, 95-98, Colstream and Catling 1996, 148, 230).

lowers her arms and she probably departs, on her wheeled platform, to a trip that symbolises the coming of winter, or death or both.[432] Coldstream saw in the representation of female deities in PGB cremation pithoi and kraters, the transformation of the omnipotent Mother goddess of the Minoan tradition into a *"vegetation goddess compelled to spend the winter months in the House of Hades"*.[433] Coldstream[434] and Prent[435] think that Persephone could be this nature goddess because she is connected both to nature and the afterlife as the spouse of Hades.

If one excludes the traditional explanation related to the Dorian invasion, then one could see female nature goddesses prevail in the former Palace and their cult is expanded in the Spring Chamber and even further in the Gypsades hill. They also seem to prevail in the burial sites. It seems that these goddesses were related to certain aspects of death, as Persephone did in the Classical period in Knossos. In this case, one can see that apart from lavish burial rituals related to social competition, death had an important role to play in all the cult activities of the Knossians.

vii. Conclusion

Concluding this chapter and at the same time the first part of the book, one may express some further thoughts and proceed to a summary of the evidence discussed so far: During the SM, inhumation was the dominant burial rite outside the nucleus of KMF. From PG and onwards, cremation became the dominant rite, normally in urns but sometimes also without urns. Although new cemeteries appear, a strong connection with the Minoan past can be seen in the reuse of Minoan symbols and objects. Without downplaying the importance of the existence of BA tombs in these new cemeteries, the strongest link with the past is the construction of new chamber tombs. A difference is that, in EIA, chambers are smaller in size. BA tombs were reused for EIA burials in more than one case, in most of the peripheral cemeteries. The alignment of the tombs in the cemeteries is also like the alignments in the BA past. It is also obvious that the past was very important to them and the most obvious argument in favour of that is the respect is shown to the ruined BA Palace and the way that BA dead discovered by EIA Knossians were treated.

Chamber tombs, which are the commonest type of burial construction, are normally placed in groups of up to six within the same cemetery, revealing an

---
[432] Coldstream 1984b, 98, figure 2.
[433] Colstream 1984b, 101.
[434] Ibid.
[435] Prent 2009, 238.

interconnection related either to kin relations or to class, age or sex groups. In any case, these cemeteries probably represent the tombs of the elite, given the luxury grave goods contained and the fact that the absolute number of burials is too limited to represent the entire EIA Knossian at Knossos. The right to burial in these cemeteries must have been restricted, a practice not unknown in other contemporary sites of the Aegean. Overall, one can see a strong sense of community among the EIA Knossians and the cemeteries are the manifestation thereof. All the peripheral cemeteries were probably at the borders of an expanded EIA settlement. As the evidence from cult activity suggests there must have been a strong connection with the BA past but also there were some religious affinities with the Greek mainland. The female deities prevail not only in the cult activities of the settlement but also in the burial context.

Chapter 3: The Near Eastern Connection: The Finds and their Contexts

i. Revisiting the Evidence

As already mentioned in the introduction, an important part of the analysis is a descriptive examination of the evidence in a catalogue. This presentation is essential for understanding the distribution of the imported material and of their imitations in the tombs. There are three categories of objects:

- Imports
- Imports or local imitations
- Local imitations

The first category includes the Near Eastern imports of any kind. The second category of evidence includes all the objects which are not certain whether they are imports or local imitations. It is very interesting to examine the distribution of such objects in relation to the genuine Near Eastern imports. In the third category, I include all the finds which are imitations of Near Eastern objects and whose imported prototypes were also found in Knossos, in most of the cases.

At the same time, a definition is needed of what exactly I mean by the term 'imitation' and which of these imitations will be included in the catalogue: since the vast majority of the imitations are pots, I will include only those pots which imitate both Near Eastern shapes and motifs and even in they are 'freer' versions or more evolved adaptations. The reason for including only the above category of pots is that I focus on a narrower set of data directly linked to imports rather than to the local repertoire.

Another reason for not including all pots that simply bear a distant similarity to Near Eastern features is the fact that the influence of Near Eastern pots in general and Cypriot pots to the local ceramics is immense. From the beginning of the PGB there are too many elements in local pottery shapes such as eyes painted in oinochoe lips, figurative scenes in belly craters or the 'comb' motive.[436] For example I will not include in the catalogue the Praisos lekythos. This juglet is an amalgam of Attic geometric, local and Near Eastern features. Its shape and decoration depart from the focus of the book (Near Eastern shapes and decorations).

---

[436] Coldstream 1979, 259.

This effort is also made in order understand the difference between EIA Knossians who were willing to accept and use imports, especially in funeral rituals and rites, and those who were against this practice (or simply could not afford it). Therefore, the catalogue will be divided based on the cemeteries. Since context has been defined as the major factor in this book, the categorisation of the finds will be primarily made according to the tomb in which they have been discovered and not according to their material or function. In the following pages, one can see all the available information regarding the imports, their imitations and the context and where they have been found. After the presentation of the evidence of each tomb, there will also be a few comments concerning the tomb and/or the artefacts, where appropriate. The cases of isolated tombs such as the one discovered at Lower Gypsades will be also assessed.

As far as the dating is concerned, I have attempted to combine the dates of each object to the context of the tomb. Imports are dated according to their style/type since some of them predate the rest of the objects found in the tombs. When the dating of an import cannot be established, then a dating is suggested in accordance with the context of the tomb which is also given. Regarding the terminology of the shapes of the pots in the catalogue, I primarily use their Greek names: Lekythos for juglet, oinochoe for trefoil-lipped jug and trefoil-lipped alabastron or alabastron-aryballos for sack-shaped juglet. For the imitations of Cypriot pottery, in the case of lekythoi, I use Coldstream's typology for the LPG-EG[437] and for the rest (i.e. the Creto-Cypriot lekythos) mostly Brock's.[438] The only modification to Brock's typology is the substitution of the word 'original' with the word 'freer adaptation' that Coldstream uses. The imitations and adaptations of Cypriot oinochoe follow Coldstream's typology up until LG, and Brock's for the entire O.

---

[437] Coldstream 1996a, 353-5.
[438] Brock 1957, 158-9.

ii. The Catalogue

First Location: North Cemetery
First site: KMF (Main site of the Cemetery)

Tomb 1: (Ch. Tomb) Undisturbed, MG-EO? Coldstream and Catling 1996, 56[439]
Local imitations
• Lekythos (1.1) Creto-Cypriot class E (iii)a, EO
Coldstream and Catling 1996, 57; Brock 1957, 158.[440]

Tomb 13: (Ch. Tomb) Undisturbed, PGB-EG. Coldstream and Catling 1996, 60
Imports
• Faience handle of bowl (13.2) Egypt or Near East, EO
Webb 1996, 606.
Local imitations
• Oinochoe (13.26) type E (i), imitation of Cypriot Black slip I-II, LPG-EG
Coldstream 1979, 257-8; 1996a, 354, 346-7; 2000b, 468; Brock 1957, 158.

Tomb 14: (Ch. Tomb) Disturbed, G-LO. Coldstream and Catling 1996, 63
Imports
• Glass bead (14.f8) Assyria? LG-E
• Glass bead (14.10) Assyria? LG-EO
Webb 1996, 602.
Local imitations
• Lekythos (14.18) enlarged version of Cypriot, class E (ii)b, LG-EO
• Lekythos (14.30) Creto-Cypriot class E (iii)a, EO
Coldstream 1996a, 354.

Tomb 19: (Ch. Tomb) Undisturbed, LG-EO. Coldstream and Catling 1996, 70
Local imitations
• Lekythos (19.20) Creto-Cypriot class E (iii) LG-EO
• Lekythos (19.21) Creto-Cypriot class E (iii)a LG
Coldstream 1984c, 135; Coldstream 1996a, 71-72; He places them in class E (iii), but I believe that due to the presence of chevrons in the 19.21, it can also be categorised as E (iii)a according to Brock's typology (1957, 158).

---

[439] Reference to the final publication of each tomb and its catalogue of finds.
[440] References to the particular study of the object.

Tomb 24: (Ch. Tomb) Disturbed, SM-EPG. Coldstream and Catling 1996, 72
Imports or local imitations
• Obelos441 (24.2) Cyprus or local, EPG-MG
Snodgrass 1996, 590.

Tomb 26: (Ch. Tomb?) Disturbed, SM-LO* Coldstream and Catling 1996, 75
Imports
• Faience rim of a bowl (26.9) Egypt or Near East, EO
Webb 1996, 607.

Tomb 48: (Ch. Tomb) Disturbed, SM-LO* Coldstream and Catling 1996, 91
Imports
• Blue scarab (48.4) Egypt, EO
Webb 1996, 604.

Tomb 56: (Ch. tomb) Undisturbed, SM-LO* Coldstream and Catling 1996, 94
Imports
• Lekythos (56.10) Red Slip II, Phoenicia, after 700 BC
Coldstream 1996, 408-9; Schreiber 2003, 298.

Tomb 60: (Ch. Tomb) Disturbed? Coldstream and Catling 1996, 100
Local imitations
• Oinochoe (60.22) close imitation of Cypriot BoR II, LG
Coldstream 1984c, 128; Coldstream 1996a, 353; Kotsonas 2012, 170; 2011a, 142.

Tomb 61: (Ch. Tomb) Disturbed, SM-LO/Coldstream and Catling 1996, 104
Local imitations
• Lekythos (61.1) exact copy of BoR, LG
• Alabastron (61.2) class G(i), LG-EO
Coldstream 1984c, 132; Coldstream and Catling 1996, 104 and 353.

Tomb 63: (Cremation Pit?) Disturbed, PGB-MG. Coldstream and Catling 1996, 104
Local imitations
• Oinochoe (63.2) type E (i), imitation of Cypriot Black slip I-II, PGB-MG
Coldstream 1979, 132; 1996a, 346-7, 2000b, 468.

Tomb 75: (Ch. Tomb) Undisturbed, EG-LO. Coldstream and Catling 1996, 107
Imports
• Glass bead (75.109) Near East? LG-EO
Webb 1996, 601.

---

[441] The only obelos fragment not included is from tomb 247, because it is the sole find of an absolutely destroyed tomb and its context was uncertain.
*Not continues use.

Imports or local imitations
- Obeloi (at least two 75.f20+) Cyprus or local imitation, LG
- Obelos (one? 75.f47+) Cyprus or local imitation, uncertain date
- Obeloi (two?75.f85+) Cyprus or local imitation, uncertain date

Boardman 1971, 5-8; Karageorghis 1977, 168-72; Snodgrass 1996, 590.

Local imitations
- Lekythos freer imitation of Cypriot BoR juglet (75.43) MG

Coldstream 1984c, 133.

Tomb 78: (pithos burial) Undisturbed, LG-EO. Coldstream and Catling 1996, 123

Imports
- Egyptian Blue Scarab (78.3) Egypt? Levant? LG-EO
- Egyptian Blue Scarab (78.4) Egypt? Levant? LG-EO
- Egyptian Blue Scarab (78.9) Egypt? Levant? LG-EO
- Egyptian Blue Scarab (78.10): Egypt? Levant? LG-EO
- Faience figurine-Nefertum (78.8) Levant? Rhodes? Cyprus? LG-EO
- Faience figurine-Ptah Embryon (78.20) Levant? Egypt? LG-EO
- Faience figurine-Nefertum (78.24) Levant? Rhodes? Cyprus? LG-EO
- Faience bead (78.28) Near East, LG-EO

Webb 1996, 604-6; Hoffman 1997, 48; Jones 2000, 229.[442]

Tomb 100: (Ch. Tomb) Disturbed. EPG-EG. Coldstream and Catling 1996, 132

Imports
- Faience bead (100.16) Phoenicia, PGB
- Faience bead (100.27) Phoenicia, PGB
- Faience disc beads and dentalium shell (100.28) Near East, PGB
- Faience base of couchant lion vase (100.41) Levant, c. 750 BC
- Bronze Lotus-handled jug (100.31) Egypt? Phoenicia? PGB-EG

For Faience: Webb 1996, 600, 606. *For bronze jug:* Catling 1984, 87, Matthäus 1988, 90; Catling 1996a, 563, 568-9.

Imports or *local imitations*
- Obeloi (at least two: 100.f2a+) Cyprus or local imitations, LPG
- Bronze rod tripod (100.f4+) Cyprus or local imitation, 10th c.

For obeloi: Boardman 1971, 5-8; Karageorghis 1977, 168-72; Snodgrass 1996, 590- *For tripod:* Catling 1984, 87, Matthäus 1988; Catling 1996a, 563, 568-9, Papasavvas 2001, 170-174, 248-249.

---

[442] Hoffman and Jones have catalogued these objects as belonging to tomb 112, because this pithos was found into the dromos of tomb 112. Moreover, Catling (1978-9, 50) in a preliminary publication registered them as objects of tomb 78.

Tomb 104: (Side Chamber) Disturbed PGB-LG. Coldstream and Catling 1996, 139[443]
Imports
- Two-handled Lekythos (104.8) BoR I, Cyprus, 850-750
- Lekythos (104.123) BoR II, Cyprus, late 8th c. BC

Local imitations
- Oinochoe (104.35) type E (i), imitation of Cypriot Black slip I-II, PGB-EO

Coldstream 1977, 257-8; 1984c, 128; 1996a, 407; 2000b 468; Jones 2000, 226-7; Schreiber 2003, 295.

Tomb 106: (Ch. Tomb) Disturbed, EG-LO. Coldstream and Catling 1996, 145
Imports
- Lekythos (106.39) Bich. III, Cyprus, 850-750 BC

Coldstream 1984c, 127; Hoffman 1997, 84; Jones 2000, 228; Schreiber 2003, 294.

Local imitations
- Lekythos (106.5) Creto-Cypriot class E (iii)a, EO
- Oinochoe (106.16), Creto-Cypriot class, close imitations, LG-EO
- Lekythos (106.21), Creto-Cypriot type E (iii)b, EO

Coldstream and Catling 1996, 146-8.

Tomb 107: (Ch. Tomb) Disturbed, PGB-LO. Coldstream and Catling 1996, 148
Imports
- Lekythos/ Round mouthed jug (107.80) Bich., Phoenicia, late 9th c. BC
- Oinochoe (107.199) BoR II, Cyprus, early 8th c. BC
- Lekythos (107.201) BoR II, Cyprus, early 8th c. BC
- Glass bead (107.14) Assyria? LG-EO
- Glass beads various (107.47) Levant, EO

For the pots: Coldstream 1984c, 123,128, 131; Coldstream 1996a, 407-8; Hoffman 1997, 67, 79, 81; Jones 2000, 225-7; Schreiber 2003, 294-8. *For glass beads*: Webb 1996, 603.

Imports or *Local imitations*
- Obelos (one 107.f22+) Cyprus or local imitation, O

Snodgrass 1996, 590-1; Boardman 1971, 5-8; Karageorghis 1977, 168-72; Hoffman 1997, 141-6.

Local imitations
- Lekythos (107.33) Creto-Cypriot E (iii)b, LG-EO
- Lekythos (107.34) Creto-Cypriot E (iii)b, LG-EO
- Lekythos (107.43) Creto-Cypriot E (iii)b, EO
- Lekythos (107.53) Creto-Cypriot E (iii)b, EO
- Lekythos (107.75) Creto-Cypriot E (iii)b, EO
- Lekythos (107.87) Creto-Cypriot E (iii)b, EO

---

[443] See Coldstream and Catling 1996, 138-140 for the problematic stratigraphic relationship between tombs 104 and 134.

- Lekythos (107.190) Creto-Cypriot E (iii)b, EO
- Lekythos (107.204) Creto-Cypriot E (iii), EO
- Alabastron (107.37), EO

Coldstream 1984c, 127; 1996a, 354; Moignard 1996, 442; Schreiber 2003, 299-7.

Tomb 125: (Ch. Tomb) Disturbed, MG. Coldstream and Catling 1996, 166
Imports
- Lekythos (125.16) BoR I, Cyprus, 850-750 BC
- Glass Bead (125.1) Assyria? MG

Coldstream 1984c, 132; Coldstream 1996a, 407. *For the glass bead*: Webb 1996, 602.

Tomb 134: (Pit-tomb?) Disturbed, LPG-EO. Coldstream and Catling 1996, 174
Imports
- Lekythos (134.33) BoR I, Cyprus, 850-750 BC

Coldstream 1984c, 129; 1996a, 407; Hoffman 1997, 73; Jones 2000, 226; Schreiber 2003, 295.

Local imitations
- Lekythos (134.3) Freer adaptation of BoR, MG
- Lekythos (134.28) Freer adaptation of BoR, MG

Coldstream 1996a, 354.

Tomb 175: (Ch. Tomb) Disturbed, EPG-O. Coldstream and Catling 1996, 184
Imports
- Oinochoe (175.52) BoR II, Cyprus, early 8th c. BC

Coldstream 1984c, 128; 1996a, 406; Hoffman 1997, 81; Jones 2000, 227; Schreiber 2003, 295.

Local imitations
- Lekythos (175.60) Exact copy of Cypriot BoR, MG-LG
- Alabastron (175.14) EO

Coldstream 1984c, 132; 1996a, 353; Moignard 1996, 442.

Tomb 200: (Pit-cave) Undisturbed, SM. Coldstream and Catling 1996, 191
Imports
- Gold necklace of 81 beads (200.8) Cyprus, SM
- Ivory comb (200.4) North Syria or Levant, SM

Catling 1996a, 530-2; Jones 2000, 223.

Tomb 201: (Pit-cave) Undisturbed, SM. Coldstream and Catling 1996, 193.[444]
Imports
- Bronze arrowhead (201.2) Levant or Cyprus, SM
- Bronze arrowhead (201.3) Levant or Cyprus, SM
- Bronze arrowhead (201.4) Levant or Cyprus, SM
- Bronze arrowhead (201.5) Levant or Cyprus, SM
- Bronze arrowhead (201.6) Levant or Cyprus, SM
- Bone inlays (201.14-15 frag.) Cyprus? SM
- Four-sided bronze stand (201.1) Cyprus or local, SM

For bronze and bone objects: Catling 1978-9, 46; 1996a, 519-21 and 533-34; Jones 2000, 223. The bronze stand is most probably a Cypriot import and one of the earliest examples found in an Aegean EIA burial context (Papasavvas 2001, 174-75).

Imports or *local imitations*
- Iron knife (201.9) Cyprus or local, SM

For iron: ibid 529-30. Waldbaum 1978, 325-49 and Hoffman 1997, 139-41 view this type of knifes as local.

Tomb 218: (Ch. Tomb) Undisturbed, LPG-O. Coldstream and Catling 1996, 200
Imports
- Iron Arrowhead (218.f19a) Cyprus, LG
- Iron Arrowhead (218.f21) Cyprus, SM

Snodgrass 1964, 154; 1996a, 585.

Imports or local imitations
- Obelos (at least one 218.f22+): Cyprus or local imitation, G?

Snodgrass 1996, 590-1; Boardman 1971, 5-8; Karageorhis 1977, 168-72; Hoffman 1997, 141-6. Hoffman considers it a local product (ibid).

Local imitations
- Lekythos (218.2) class E (ii) close imitation of BoR, EO
- Lekythos (218.41) close imitation BoR II, MG
- Lekythos (218.84) class E (ii) imitation of Cypriot, EO
- Lekythos (218.6) imitation of Cypriot, EO
- Lekythos (218.118) imitation of BoR, EO
- Lekythos (218.19) close imitation of Cypriot, EO
- Lekythos (218.120) freer imitation, EO
- Lekythos (218.88) freer imitation, EO
- Lekythos (218.16) freer imitation, EO
- Lekythos (218.4) imitation of Cypriot, MG-LG
- Lekythos (218.15) Creto-Cypriot class, EO
- Lekythos (218.11) Creto-Cypriot class E (iii)b, EO

Coldstream 1984c, 131-3; 1996a, 353-4; Schreiber 2003, 296-7.

---

[444] Coldstream (1996a, 346) assigns in tomb 202 an Oinochoe type E, imitation of Cypriot Blak slip I-II with the inventory number 202.102. Tomb 202 was empty and its SM date does not much with the PGB-EG Oinochoe.

Tomb 219: (Ch. Tomb) Disturbed, LPG-LO. Coldstream and Catling 1996, 210
Imports
• Oinochoe (219.43) Red Bich., Cyprus or Kos, LG
• Oinochoe (219.97) Red Bich.,Cyprus or Kos, LG
• Amphoriskos (219.22) BoR II, Cyprus, early 8th c. BC
• Lekythos (219.40) BoR I, Cyprus, late 9th c. BC
• Lekythos (219.98) BoR II, Cyprus, early 8th c. BC
• Faience vase of couchant lion (219.62) Levant, c. 750 BC
• Ivory handle: Frag. figurine of two-headed goddess (219.27) Syria, 9th-8th c. BC
• Ivory handle/Sleeve (219.35) Phoenicia, MG-LG
• Bronze Bowl with loop Handles and Lotus flowers (219.f85) Cyprus, LG
• Egyptian Blue bowl (219.83) Near East, LG
• Ivory inlay roundel (219.f16) Phoenicia, MG-LG
• Faience disc bead (219.6) Phoenicia, LPG
• Glass bead (219.38) Near East, LG-EO
• Glass beads (219.49) Near East, LG-EO
• Faience disc bead (219.39) Phoenicia, LPG-PGB
• Faience, four disc beads (219.82) Phoenicia, LPG-PGB
• Faience, ten disc beads (219.95) Phoenicia, LPG-PGB
• Glass beads (219.f18) Near East, LG-EO
• Glass Beads, three (219.24) Near East, LG-EO
For pots: Coldstream 1984c, 129-131; 1996a, 406-8; Hoffman 1997, 71-86; Jones 2000, 226; Schreiber 2003, 294-5 *for bronze*: Catling 1996a, 562, *for ivory*: Evely 1996, 630 *for Faience, glass and Egyptian blue*: Webb 1996, 600-6.

Imports or local imitations
• Fire-dogs (219.f56i) Cyprus or local, LG
• Fire-dogs (219.f56ii) Cyprus or local, LG
• Fire-dogs (219.f128) Cyprus or local, LG
• Fire-dogs (219.f128a) Cyprus or local, LG
• Fire-dogs (219.f128b) Cyprus or local, LG
• Fire-dogs (219.f130) Cyprus or local, LG
• Fire-dogs (219.f138) Cyprus or local, uncertain date
• Fire-dogs (219.f139) Cyprus or local, uncertain date
• Obeloi (at least two 219.f14+) Cyprus or local imitation, LG
• Obeloi (at least six 219.f36+) Cyprus or local imitation, LG
• Obeloi (at least two 219.f125+) Cyprus or local imitation, uncertain date
Snodgrass 1996, 590-1; Boardman 1971, 5-8; Karageorhis 1977, 168-72.

Local imitations
• Lekythos/, imitation of BoR (219.56), MG
• Lekythos/, Creto-Cypriot class E (iii)a (219.64), EO
Coldstream 1984c, 131; 1996a, 354 and 365; Schreiber 2003, 296.

Tomb 229: (Ch. Tomb) Undisturbed, MG-EO. Coldstream and Catling 1996, 225
Imports
• Oinochoe (229.11) WP, Cyprus, 750 BC
• Faience scarab in pot 6 (229.3) Near East, LG-EO
• Faience scarab in pot 6 (229.4) Near East, LG-EO
• Glass Bead (229.5) Near East? EO
For pot: Coldstream 1996a, 406; *for scarabs and bead*: Webb 1996, 600-4
Local imitations
• Lekythos (229.22) freer imitation of BoR Juglet, MG-LG
• Oinochoe (229.15) Creto-Cypriot shape, LG
• Lekythos (229.16) Creto-Cypriot class E(iii)b, EO
Coldstream 1984c, 133; 1996a, 354; Schreiber 2003, 295-6.

Tomb 283: (Ch. Tomb) Disturbed, PGB-LO. Coldstream and Catling 1996, 230
Imports
• Lekythos (283.50) Red slip, Phoenicia, 850-750 BC.
Coldstream 1984c, 132; 1996a, 409; Hoffman 1997, 68; (Jones 2000, 226); Schreiber 2003, 297.
Imports or *local imitations*
• Fire-dogs (283.f39) Cyprus or local imitation, Uncertain date
• Fire-dogs (283.f45+) Cyprus or local imitation, Uncertain date
• Obelos (at least one 283.f19+) Cyprus or local imitation, MG
• Obeloi (at least ten 283.f11+) Cyprus or local imitation, Uncertain date
Snodgrass 1996, 590-1; Boardman 1971, 5-8; Karageorghis 1977, 168-72.
Local imitations:
• Lekythos (283.24) close imitation of Cypriot Bich., MG-LG
• Lekythos (283.83) imitation of BoR, LG
• Lekythos (283.88) imitation of BoR, LG
• Lekythos (283.84) imitation of BoR, MG-LG
• Lekythos (283.15) Creto-Cypriot class E (iii)a, LG-EO
• Oinochoe (283.40) type E (i) imitation of Cypriot Black slip I-II, PGB-EO
Coldstream 1979, 257-8; 1984c, 127-132; 1996a, 352-4 and 368; 2000b 468; Schreiber 2003, 296-7.

Tomb 285: (Ch. Tomb) Undisturbed, LPG-LO. Coldstream and Catling 1996, 239
Imports
• Lekythos (285.45) BoR II, Cyprus, early 8th c. BC
• Lekythos (285.49) BoR II, Cyprus, early 8th c. BC
• Lekythos (285.52) BoR II, Cyprus, early 8th c. BC
• Lekythos (285.80) BoR II, Cyprus, early 8th c. BC
• Lekythos (285.85) BoR II, Cyprus, early 8th c. BC
• Lekythos (285.88) BoR I, Cyprus, 850-750 BC
• Lekythos (285.151) BoR II, Cyprus, early 8th c. BC
• Glass beads (285.16) Near East? EO
• Glass bead, four (285.19) Near East? MG

CHAPTER 3: THE NEAR EASTERN CONNECTION: THE FINDS AND THEIR CONTEXTS

- Glass beads (285.24) Near East? LPG
- Faience disc bead, nine (285.55) Near East, LPG
- Faience disc bead (285.70) Near East, LPG
- Faience disc bead (285.71) Near East, LPG
- Faience disc beads, sixteen (285.73) Near East, LPG

For pots: Coldstream 1984c, 129; 1996a, 407; Hoffman 1997, 74-75; Jones 2000, 227; Schreiber 2003, 294-5; *for glass and faience*: Webb 1996, 599-604.

Imports or *local imitations*
- Fire-dog (f57) Cyprus or local, PGB
- Fire-dog (f30) Cyprus or local, EO
- Fire-dog (f31/32) Cyprus or local, EO
- Fire-dog (f46/47) Cyprus or local, EO
- Fire-dog (f79) Cyprus or local, EO
- Obeloi (at least four 285.f27+) Cyprus or local imitation, EO
- Obeloi (at least ten 285.f43+) Cyprus or local imitation, EO
- Obeloi (at least eight 285.f48+) Cyprus or local imitation, 750-700 BC

Snodgrass 1996, 590-1; Boardman 1971, 5-8; Karageorghis 1977, 168-72.

Local Imitations
- Oinochoe (285.132) type E (i), imitation of Cypriot Black slip I-II, EPG-EG
- Oinochoe (285.145) type E (i), imitation of Cypriot Black slip I-II, EPB-EG

Coldstream 1996a, 346-7; 2000b, 468.

Tomb 292: (Ch. Tomb) Disturbed PGB-LO. Coldstream and Catling 1996, 257
Imports
- Oinochoe (292.211) Red Slip, Phoenicia, after 800 BC
- Oinochoe (292.80) Red Slip, Phoenicia, 800-770 BC
- Trefoil-lipped alabastron (292.96) BoR II, Cyprus, early 8th c. BC
- Oinochoe (292.94) BoR II, Cyprus, early 8th c. BC
- Two-handled lekythos (292.244) BoR II, Cyprus, early 8th c. BC
- Two-handled lekythos (292.245) BoR II, Cyprus, early 8th c. BC
- Lekythos (292.97) BoR II Cyprus, early 8th c. BC
- Lekythos (292.48) BoR II Cyprus, early 8th c. BC
- Lekythos (292.51) BoR II Cyprus, early 8th c. BC
- Lekythos (292.132) BoR II Cyprus, early 8th c. BC
- Lekythos (292.62) BoR I Cyprus, 850-750 BC
- Bronze Phiale (292.36, 292.46, 292.78) Levant? 750-700
- Glass Bead (292.12a) Assyria? LG-EO
- Glass Bead (292.15) Assyria? LG-EO
- Glass Bead (292.17) Near East, uncertain date
- Glass Beads (292.19) Assyria? LG-EO
- Glass Bead (292.21) Near East
- Glass, five ring-shaped beads (292.27): Assyria? LG-EO
- Glass Bead (292.33) Near East, LG-EO
- Glass Bead (292.34) Assyria? LG-EO
- Glass Bead (292.52) Assyria? LG-EO

- Glass Bead (292.53) Near East, LG-EO
- Glass vessel? (292.56) Mesopotamia? Levant? 8th c. BC
- Ivory hilt? (292.f49) Phoenicia or North Syria, EG-MG or MG-LG
- Bone handle/sleeve with lotus-bud (292.f61) Phoenicia or North Syria or local, EG-MG or MG-LG
- Bone handle/sleeve with chevron decoration (292.f79) Phoenicia or North Syria or local, EG-MG or MG-LG

For pots: Coldstream 1984c, 123; 1996a, 406-8; Hoffman 1997, 67, 75-77; Jones 2000, 227; Schreiber 2003, 294-7; *for bronze* Catling 1996a, 564; *for glass* Webb 1996, 600-3; *for ivory*: Evely 1996, 693-1. *For bone sleeves* Evely 1996, 630-1; Barnett 1975, 104-8.

Local imitations
- Lekythos (292.202) close imitation Cypriot Bich. III, MG-LG
- Oinochoe (292.76) freer imitation/hybrid of BoR, PGB-EG
- Oinochoe (292.92) freer imitation/hybrid of BoR, PGB-EG
- Oinochoe (292.104) freer imitation/hybrid BoR, PGB-EG
- Oinochoe (292.109) freer imitation/hybrid of BoR, PGB-EG
- Oinochoe (292.111) freer imitation/hybrid of BoR, PGB-EG
- Oinochoe (292.134) freer imitation/hybrid of BoR, PGB-EG
- Oinochoe (292.209) freer imitation/hybrid of BoR, PGB-EG
- Alabastron (292.35) freer imitation of Cypriot WP IV, EO
- Oinochoe (292.86) type E (i), imitation of Cypriot Black slip I-II, PGB-LO

Coldstream 1979, 57-8; 1984c, 133-4; 1996a, 353 and 346-7; 2000b, 468; Moingard 1996, 442; Schreiber 2003, 296.

Tomb 294: (Ch. Tomb) Disturbed MG-LO. Coldstream and Catling 1996, 274
Local imitation
- Lekythos (294.44) imitation of Cypriot BoR, MG
- Lekythos (294.45) Creto-Cypriot type E (iii)b, EO

Coldstream 1984c, 133; 1996a, 278.

Tomb 306: (Ch. Tomb) Disturbed LG-EO. Coldstream and Catling 1996, 279
Local imitations
- Lekythos (306.19) imitation of BoR, LG
- Lekythos (306.2) Creto-Cypriot class E (iii)b White on Dark, EO

Coldstream 1984c, 132; 1996a, 353; Moingard 1996, 441; Schreiber 2003, 296.

First Location: North Cemetery
Second site: Teke

Tomb A: (Ch. Tomb) Disturbed, PGB-LG? Coldstream and Catling 1996, 3
Imports
- Juglet, Bich. III (A.7) Cyprus? Near East? PGB-LG

Coldstream 1984c, 127; 1996a, 407; Hoffman 1997, 84; Jones 2000, 228; Schreiber 2003, 294-5. The dating of the juglet is proposed by its context.

Tomb G: (Ch. Tomb) Disturbed, MPG-EG. Coldstream and Catling 1996, 9
Imports
• Bronze Phiale mesomphalos (G.f1) Phoenicia, PGB-EG, context
• Bronze Lotus-handled jug (G.f5) Phoenicia, PGB-EG
Catling 1996a, 564-565
Local imitations
• Oinochoe (G27) type E (i), imitation of Cypriot Black slip I-II, PGB-EG
• Oinochoe (G28) type E (i), imitation of Cypriot Black slip I-II, PGB-EG
• Oinochoe (G29) type E (i), imitation of Cypriot Black slip I-II, PGB-EG
• Oinochoe (G30) type E (i), imitation of Cypriot Black slip I-II, PGB-EG
• Oinochoe (G31) type E (i), imitation of Cypriot Black slip I-II, PGB-EG
• Oinochoe (G32) type E (i), imitation of Cypriot Black slip I-II, PGB-EG
Coldstream 1979, 257-8; 1996a, 346; 2000b, 468.
Tomb H: (Ch. Tomb) Disturbed, MG-EO. Coldstream and Catling 1996, 23
Imports
• Two-handled Lekythos (H.15) BoR I, Cyprus, 850-750 BC
• Glass bead (H.f2) Assyria? LG-EO
Coldstream 1984c, 128; 407; Hoffman 1997, 72; Jones 2000, 226; Schreiber 2003, 295. *For the bead*: Webb 1996, 603.

Tomb J: (Ch. Tomb) Undisturbed, EPG-PGB. Coldstream and Catling 1996, 25
Imports
• Bronze semispherical bowl with inscription (J.1) Phoenicia, before 900 BC
Catling 1976-77, 12-13; 1996a, 563-4; Hoffman 1997, 28; Jones 2000, 223.
Tomb O: (Ch. Tomb) Undisturbed, PG-LG. Coldstream and Catling 1996, 38
Imports
• Glass bead (O.f18): Assyria? LG-EO?
Coldstream and Catling 1996, 52; Webb 1996, 602.
Tomb Q: (Ch. Tomb) Undisturbed, MPG-O. Coldstream and Catling 1996, 44
Imports
• Glass bead (Q.f18): Assyria? LG-EO?
Coldstream and Catling 1996, 52; Webb 1996, 602. Although Webb also mentions the glass bead (Q.f2), this bead does not appear in the inventory catalogue of tomb Q and therefore not included here.
Local imitations
• Oinochoe (Q.21) type E (i), imitation of Cypriot Black slip I-II, EPG-EO
Coldstream 1979, 257-8, 1996a, 346-7; 2002b, 468.

First Location: North Cemetery
Third Site: Khaniale Teke

Tomb II: (Tholos Tomb) Disturbed PGB-EO. Hutchinson & Boardman 1954, 57
Imports
• Lekythos (59) BoR I, Cyprus, 7th c. BC
• Lekythos B(60) BoR I, Cyprus, 7th c. BC
• Ivory crescent (6) Near East, c. 800 BC
• Steatite Scarab (22) Near East or Egypt, c. 800 BC, context
• Steatite Scarab (23) Near East or Egypt, c. 800 BC, context
• Silver dump, possibly from a silver Shekel (28) Phoenicia, c. 800 BC
• Gold dumps (11) Egypt, c. 800 BC.
• Gold dumps (12) Egypt, c. 800 BC.
• Gold dumps (27) Egypt, c. 800 BC.
• Ivory frag. of a handle palm-leaf finial (70) Phoenicia, 8th -7th c. BC, context
• Frag. of ostrich egg (80) Egypt or Phoenicia, 8th -7th c. BC, context
• Frag. of green faience bottle (79) Egypt or Phoenicia, 8th -7th c. BC, context
• Miniature faience segment beads (78) Egypt or Phoenicia, 7th c. BC, context
• Ivory disc head of bronze pin and eyes (71-73) Phoenicia or North Syria, 7th c. BC
• Biconical crystal beads (no number available) Mesopotamia? LO
• Fragments of faience: Egypt, LO context

For the pots: Boardman 1954, 225; Coldstream 1979, 261 n.31; Jones 2000, 242. Hoffman after examining these pots believes that '*they are close imitation of Cypriot vessels*' (1997, 69 n. 64). However, she does not say explicitly what kind of examination she did. The style of the pots, in any case, is BoR I. The objects 28, 11, 12, 27, 22, 23, 10, 25 were found in vase 104 (pyxis) together with jewellery of at least Near Eastern inspiration. Find 6 and also parts of 11, 12, 27 10, 25 were also found in oinochoe 57 (ibid). For the above objects and for the debate on the ethnicity of those buried in this tomb see: Boardman 1967, 57-75; Hoffman 1997, 191-245; Jones, 235-243; Kotsonas 2006, 151-2. Additionally, Hoffman believes that the eye inlays and the ivory pins were probably made in Crete by imported raw material (ibid, 193). The rest of the jewellery found in this tomb might constitute neither an import from the Near East, neither a direct copy. However, it must be underlined that the inlay technique employed for the manufacture and also some of the motifs place it in the Eastern tradition (Evely 1996, 632). The dating of the silver and gold dumps is based on the context.

Imports or *local Imitations*
• Bronze pomegranate pendant and stand (56-58+): Cyprus or Local? 7th c. BC
The bronze stand (56-58+) is either a Cypriot import (Catling 1996a, 568-9) or most probably a local product (Papasavvas 2001, 192; Hoffman 1997, 116-20; Matthäus (1988, 287-88).

Local Imitations
• Lekythos (58) Creto-Cypriot class E (iii)b variant, EO
• Lekythos (61) Creto-Cypriot class E (iii)b variant, EO
• Lekythos (62) Creto-Cypriot class E (iii)b variant, EO

- Lekythos (63) Creto-Cypriot class E (iii)b variant, EO
- Lekythos (64) Creto-Cypriot class E (iii)b variant, EO
- Lekythos (65) Creto-Cypriot class E (iii)b variant, EO

The dating of the pots is suggested by the present author and is based on Brock's typology (1957, 159). *For the clay stand*: Hutchinson and Boardman 1954, 226; Boardman 1967, 64; Coldstream 1996a, 368.

First Location: North Cemetery
Fourth Site: Fortetsa North-East

Tomb A: (Ch. Tomb) Disturbed, LPG-EO. Hood and Boardman 1961, 68
Imports
- Lekythos (15) BoR I, Cyprus, 850-750 BC

Hood and Boardman 1961, 74; Coldstream 1979, 261 n. 31; Hoffman 1997, 72; Jones 2000, 223.[445]

Tomb TFT: (Ch. Tomb) Undisturbed, PGB-EO. Brock 1957, 60
Imports
- Aryballos (669) Cyprus, 850-750 BC
- Aryballos (694) Cyprus, 850-750 BC
- Necklace, faience beads (726): Near East or Egypt, MG

For the pots: Brock 1957, 63-64 and 190; Coldstream 1984c, 131 n. 51; Hoffman 1997, 71-2; Jones 2000, 219, Schreiber 2003, 294.

Local imitations
- Aryballos (646) class E (i) close imitation of Cypriot type, MG
- Aryballos (701) Creto-Cypriot class E (iii)a, LG
- Aryballos (702) Creto-Cypriot class E (iii)a, LG
- Aryballos (687) Creto-Cypriot class E (iii)b, EO
- Aryballos (688) Creto-Cypriot class E (iii)b, EO
- Aryballos (717) Creto-Cypriot class E (iii)b, EO

Brock 1957, 64-5.

Tomb L: (Ch. Tomb) Undisturbed PG-PGB. Brock 1957, 31
Imports
- Gold diadem (336) Cyprus, mid-9th c. BC

Brock 1957, 34; Coldstream 1977, 49 n. 61; 1982, 267; Hoffman 1997, 52; Jones 2000, 217.

Tomb F67/4: (Ch. Tomb). Disturbed, LG-EO. Coldstream and Catling 1996, 286
Local imitations
- Lekythos (F67/4.12) imitation of Cypriot BoR, MG-LG
- Lekythos (F67/4.13) Creto-Cypriot type, E (iii)a, LG-EO
- Lekythos (F67/4.14) Creto-Cypriot type, E (iii)a, LG

Coldstream 1984c, 132; 1996a, 286; Brock 1957, 158.

---

[445] This item is included twice.

Second Location: Fortetsa South-East

Tomb II: (Ch. Tomb) Undisturbed, LPG-LO. Brock 1957, 84
Imports
• Faience bead of pin head (1113) Near East, LPG
• Cylindrical glass bead (1117) Near East, LPG
• Lyre player seal (1074) N. Syria? Phoenicia? 730-700 BC
• Scarab, white glaze (1076) Phoenicia, LO
• Scarab, white glaze (1077) Phoenicia, LO
• Scarab, glaze (1078) Phoenicia, LO
Brock 1957, 97 and 208; Hoffman 1997, 89-90 and 92; Jones 2000, 217 and 221.
Local imitations
• Lekythos (1048) Creto-Cypriot class E (iii)a, EO
• Lekythos (1049) Creto-Cypriot class E (iii)b, EO
• Lekythos (1052) Creto-Cypriot class E (iii)a, EO
• Alabastron-aryballos (984) G (ii), EO
• Alabastron-aryballos (985) G (ii) EO
• Alabastron-aryballos G (986) (ii) EO
• Alabastron-aryballos (1000) G (i) EO
• Alabastron-aryballos (1064) G (ii) EO
• Oinochoe class III.(iii) (974) LO
• Oinochoe type (1046), E, imitation of Cypriot Black slip I-II, PGB
Brock 1957, 156-9.

Tomb VI: (Ch. Tomb) Undisturbed, PG. Brock 1957, 11
Imports
• Faience bead (107) Near East/ Cyprus/ Egypt, EPG
• Faience ring (106 Phoenicia? EPG
• Large collection of paste beads (102) Near East/ Cyprus/ Egypt, EPG
• Faience ring (208) Egypt, EPG
Brock 1957, 15 and 208; Hoffman 1997, 39; Jones 2000, 216.
Imports or *local imitations*
• Obelos/pike (108) Cyprus or local imitation, EPG
• Obelos/spit (114) Cyprus or local imitation, EPG
Brock 1957, 202; Snodgrass 1996, 590-1; Boardman 1971, 5-8; Karageorghis 1977, 168-72 and Hoffman 1997, 141-6 who considers it local product.
Local Imitations
• Oinochoe (92) type E, imitation of Cypriot Black slip I-II, EPG
Brock 1957, 153, 157; Coldstream 1978, 258.

Tomb VII: (Ch. Tomb) Undisturbed. MPG-O/Brock 1957, 72
Imports
• Aryballos (842) Cyprus, 850-750 BC
Brock 1957,190; Coldstream 1984c, 127; 1996a, 4, 407; Hoffman 1997, 84; Jones 2000, 228; Schreiber 2003, 294-5.

Local imitations
• Lekythos (829) Creto-Cypriot class E (iii)a, LG
• Lekythos (833) Creto-Cypriot class E (iii)a, LG
• Lekythos (834) Creto-Cypriot class E (iii)a, LG
• Lekythos (816) Creto-Cypriot class E (iii)b, EO
Brock 1957, 74-75 and 158-9.
Tomb IX: (Ch. Tomb) Disturbed PG. Brock 1957, 29
Imports
• Figurine of Sekhment (264) Egypt/ Phoenicia, PG?
Brock 1957, 30 and 208; Hoffman 1997, 39; Jones 2000, 217.

Tomb X: (Ch. Tomb) Undisturbed, PGB-LG. Brock 1957, 41.
Imports
• Aryballos (489) Cyprus, 850-750 BC
• Trefoil mouth jug (425) Cyprus, 850-750 BC
Brock 1957, 46-49 and 190; Coldstream 1984c, 127; 1996a, 4, 407; Hoffman 1997, 73 and 83; Jones 2000, 219.
Local imitations
• Oinochoe (500) imitation of Cypriot type III (i) PGB
• Lekythos (453) imitation of Cypriot BoR E (i) MG
• Lekythos (527) imitation of Cypriot BoR E (i) MG
• Lekythos (410) larger imitation of Cypriot BoR E (ii) G
• Oinochoe (509) type E (i), imitation of Cypriot Black slip I-II, PGB
• Oinochoe/ type E (i), imitation of Cypriot Black slip I-II (473), PGB
Brock 1957, 44-50 and 157-158; Coldstream 1979, 258.

Tomb XI: (Ch. Tomb) Undisturbed, LPG? Brock 1957, 18
Imports
• Lead lion with heart-shaped ears (201) Syria, EPG
• Five spherical carnelian beads (194) Egypt? EPG
• Ivory pendant in form of bull's head (199) Near East , EPG
• Fragments of ivory pin head (204) Near East, EPG
• Necklace, flat blue paste beads (194) Near east/ Cyprus/ Egypt, EPG
Brock 1957, 22 and 208-9; Hoffman 1997, 66; Jones 2000, 216.
Imports or local imitations
• Obelos/pike (192) Cyprus or local imitation, EPG
• Obelos/pike (203) Cyprus or local imitation, EPG
• Bronze rod tripod (188) Cyprus? Local imitation?, 10th c. BC
Brock 1957, 202; Snodgrass 1996, 590-1; Boardman 1971, 5-8; Karageorghis 1977, 168-72 and Hoffman 1997, 141-6 who considers it local product. The bronze tripod stand as others is either a Cypriot import (Catling 1996a, 568-9), or most probably a local product (Papasavvas 2001, 172, 246; Hoffman 1997, 116-20; Matthäus 1988, 287-88).

Tomb F: (Ch. Tomb) Disturbed, PGB-EO. Brock 1957, 67
Imports
• Alabastron-aryballos (754) BoR, Cyprus, EO?
Brock 1957, 69 and 190; Coldstream 1979, 261; Hoffman 1997, 82; Jones 2000, 220.
Local imitations
• Oinochoe (745) III (ii), LG-EO
• Lekythos (765) Creto-Cypriot class E (iii)a, LG
Brock 1957, 68-9 and 158 and Coldstream 1979, 1984c for further discussion.

Tomb P:[446] (Ch. Tomb) Disturbed, LPG-LO. Brock 1957, 101
Imports
• Tall-necked aryballos (1251) WoR Phoenicia? LO
• Miniature neck amphora (1403) Phoenicia? EO
• Aryballos (1448) BoR II, Cyprus, LG?
• Aryballos (1262) BoR I Cyprus, LO
• Two-handled aryballos (1411) BoR II: Cyprus, LG
• Alabastron-aryballos (1458) BoR Cyprus LG
• Pyxis (1451) BoR II Cyprus, LG
• Bronze bowl (1559) Phoenicia, 800-750 BC
• Molded glass bowl (1567) Syria? 750 BC
• Necklace of flat faience beads (1166) Near East or East Greece, EPG
• Blue faience figurine flute player (1149) Egypt EO
• Bronze bowl with lotus-bud handles (1571) Egypt, 800 BC
• Bronze bowl with lotus-bud handles (1572) Egypt, 800 BC
• Bronze bowl (1559): Phoenicia, 800-750 BC
• Bronze pendant of naked female figure (1570) Luristan, PGB-LG
• Bronze relive bowl (2316) Phoenicia, 800 BC
• Faience aryballos (1557) North Syria, Rhodes, LO
• Faience aryballos (1558) North Syria, Rhodes, LO
For pottery: Brock 1957, 122-7 and 190; Coldstream 1984c, 129-31; Hoffman 1997, 70, 76-7 and 82-5; Jones 2000, 220; Schreiber 2003, 294-5 *for bronze and faience objects* Brock 1957, Hoffman 1997, 40; Jones 2000, 218 and 220-1. *For the aryballoi*: Brock 1957, 208. Hoffman believes that these faience aryballoi might be the first attempt in Crete for such a production (ibid, 42).
Imports or local imitations
• Obelos/spit (1613) Cyprus or local imitation, PGB
• Obelos/spit (1621-2) Cyprus or local imitation, PGB
• Obelos/spit (1630) Cyprus or local imitation, PGB
For the spits: Brock 1957, 202; Snodgrass 1996, 590-1; Boardman 1971, 5-8; Karageorghis 1977, 168-72 and Hoffman 1997, 141-6 who considers it local product.

---

[446] Tomb P includes the finds from tomb I, since the latter was a burial found in the dromos of P.

CHAPTER 3: THE NEAR EASTERN CONNECTION: THE FINDS AND THEIR CONTEXTS

Local imitations
- Alabastron-aryballos/ Sack-shaped Trefoil-lipped Juglet class G (i) (1388), EO
- Alabastron-aryballos/ Sack-shaped Trefoil-lipped Juglet class G (i) (1389), EO
- Oinochoe (1349) class III (i), LG-EO
- Oinochoe (1126) class III (ii), LG-EO
- Oinochoe (1300) class III (iii), LO
- Oinochoe (1265) class III (iii), LO
- Oinochoe (1310) class III (iii), LO
- Oinochoe (1195) class III (iii), LO
- Oinochoe (1191) class III (iii), LO
- Lekythos (1399) close imitation of BoR E (i), MG
- Lekythos (1432) larger imitation of BoR E (ii), G
- Lekythos (1407) larger imitation of BoR E (ii), G
- Lekythos (1535) larger imitation of BoR E (ii), G
- Lekythos (1315) Creto-Cypriot class E (iii)a variants, EO
- Lekythos (1395) Creto-Cypriot class E (iii)b, EO
- Lekythos (1455) Creto-Cypriot class E (iii)b, EO
- Lekythos (1456) Creto-Cypriot class E (iii)b, EO
- Lekythos (1498) Creto-Cypriot class E (iii)b, EO
- Lekythos (1504) Creto-Cypriot class E (iii)b, EO
- Lekythos (1509) Creto-Cypriot class E (iii)b, EO
- Lekythos (1510) Creto-Cypriot class E (iii)b, EO
- Lekythos (1339) Creto-Cypriot class E (iii)b variants, EO
- Lekythos (1324) Creto-Cypriot class E (iii)b variants, EO
- Lekythos (1357) Creto-Cypriot class E (iii)b WoB, EO
- Lekythos (1384) Creto-Cypriot class E (iii)b WoB, O

Brock 1957, 102-133 and 153-159. I included pot 1126 which was found in tomb I, since the latter is not a tomb but the dromos of tomb II. For further discussion see Coldstream 1979; 1984c.

Tomb P2: (Ch. Tomb) Disturbed LG-EO. Brock 1957, 77
Imports
- Oinochoe (876) BoR I? Cyprus, LG-EO
- Upper part of a blue faience figurine (924) Phoenicia, EO
- Blue faience alabastron (923) Phoenicia, EO

For the pot: Brock 1957, 79 and 190 Coldstream 1968, 320; Hoffman 1997, 81-2; Schreiber 2003, 295. *For the faience objects*: Both objects were found in pithos (923) apparently accompanying a cremation. Hoffman 1997, 41; Jones 2000, 228; both authors mention the possibility that the alabastron might be Rhodian products, but Hoffman admits that is not a strong possibility (ibid; 42).

Local imitations
- Alabastron-aryballos/ Sack-shaped Trefoil-lipped Juglet (865) class G (i), EO
- Oinochoe, class III (ii) (904), EO
- Lekythos (897) Creto-Cypriot class E (iii)a variants, EO
- Lekythos (896) Creto-Cypriot class E (iii)b variants, EO

- Lekythos (893) Creto-Cypriot class E (iii)b WoB, EO
- Lekythos (894) Creto-Cypriot class E (iii)b WoB, EO
- Lekythos (861) Creto-Cypriot class E (iv) O
- Lekythos (862) Creto-Cypriot class E (iv) O
- Lekythos (879) Creto-Cypriot class E (iv) O

Brock 1957, 102-133 and 156-159.

Third Location: Kephala Ridge

Tomb 3: (Ch. Tomb) Disturbed PGB-EO. Coldstream 2002, 206[447]
Imports or ***local Imitations***
- Bronze rod tripod, Cyprus or local imitation, c.800 BC

Hogarth 1899-1900, 83; Brock 1957, 22; Catling 1964, 198; Coldstream 2002, 209. These authors have viewed this object as an import which was two centuries old when it was placed in the tomb. On the other hand, Riis 1939, 6; Gjerstad 1948, 403; Matthäus 1985, 305; Hoffman 1997, 98 and Papasavvas 2001, 172-173, believe that it is a local imitation.

Tomb 6: (Tholos tomb) Disturbed, PG. Coldstream 2002, 45
Imports
- Disc, blue past beads, Egypt, LPG-PGB
- Gold tainia (diadem)? Cyprus? LPG

Coldstream (2002, 212 and 215) mentions a gold plain tainia from Hogarth's' diary as if it was identical with gold diadem (336) from tomb L Fortetsa NE.

Tomb V: (Ch. Tomb) Disturbed, PG-O. Coldstream 1963, 42
Imports
- Scarab, blue paste (V.4) Phoenicia, EO

Coldstream considers it a '*Levantine imitation rather than Egyptian*' (1963, 43). See also James 1961, 472; Skon-Jedele 1994, 1867; Jones 2000, 233.

Fourth Location: Ayios Ioannis

Tomb V: (Ch. Tomb) Disturbed, EPG-MPG. Boardman 1960, 128
Imports
- Faience beads (V.37) Egypt, EPG

Boardman 1960, 134.

Tomb -: (Ch. Tomb) Undisturbed, LM II-SM. Hood 1968, 205
Imports
- Pin with conical ivory head (B.5), Cyprus, SM

---

[447] Tombs 3 and 6 were excavated by Hogarth (1899-1900).

Hood and Coldstream 1968, 212-3 and 214-8; Hood 1973, 45; Jones 2000, 232. There is apparently a break between the two periods in which the tomb had been plundered or cleaned (Hood and Coldstream 1968, 207). This tomb apparently does not belong to the cemetery excavated by Boardman.

Fifth Location: Atsalenio

Tomb A: (Ch. Tomb) Disturbed, LPG-LO. Davaras 1968, 134
Imports
• Oinochoe (A.45) BoR II, Cyprus, LG
• Two-handled aryballos (A.56) BoR II, Cyprus, EO
Davaras 1968, 138-9, 143 and 141; Coldstream 1979, 261 n. 31; 1984c, 128, n. 40; Hoffman 1997, 78 and 80; Jones 2000, 240, 242.
Local imitations
• Aryballos (A.70) Creto-Cypriot class E (iii)b, EO
Davaras 1968, 140; Brock 1957, 159.

Tomb B: (Ch. Tomb) Disturbed, LPG-LO. Davaras 1968, 141-2
Local imitations
• Oinochoe (B.3) Creto-Cypriot class E (iii)b variants, EO
• Aryballos (B.23) Creto-Cypriot class E (iii)b, EO
Davaras 1968, 140; Brock 1957, 159. The dating of the oinochoe B.3 is suggested by the present author, based on Brock's analysis (ibid). Davaras (ibid, 141) notes 'O'.

Sixth Location: Upper Gypsades

Tomb VII: (Ch. Tomb) Disturbed, LM III (SM Use) Hood *et al* 1958-59, 205
Imports
• Iron Knife with two bronze rivets (VII.12) Cyprus or Levant, 11th c. BC
Hood *et al* 1958-59, 205; Sherratt 1994, 59-106; Hoffman 1997; 139-41. The early date and context of this knife makes it an import almost beyond any doubt.

Seventh Location: Lower Gypsades

Tomb -: (Ch. Tomb) Disturbed, PGB-LO. Coldstream *et al* 1981, 141
Imports
• Lekythos (54) Red Slip II, Cyprus, LG
• Oinochoe (77) BoR II, Cyprus, eatly 8th c. BC
• Blue paste scarab (122) Levant, MG
Coldstream 1979, 261, n. 31; 1981, 150-1, 153-4; Hoffman 1997, 81, 84; Jones 2000, 239. *For the scarab* Hoffman 1997, 88 Jones 2000, 237.
Local imitations
• Lekythos (22) Creto-Cypriot, class E (iii)b EO

- Lekythos (24) Creto-Cypriot, class E (iii)b MG
- Lekythos (25) Creto-Cypriot, class E (iii) LO
- Lekythos (106) Creto-Cypriot, class E (iii)b PGB
- Lekythos (107) Creto-Cypriot, class E (iii)b LG or EO
- Lekythos (108) Creto-Cypriot, class E (iii)a variants EO
- Lekythos (109) Creto-Cypriot, class E (iii)b EO
- Trefoil-lipped alabastron (27) Cypriot shape, class G (i) MG
- Oinochoe (111) class III (iii) LO
- Oinochoe (112) class III (iii) LO

Coldstream 1981, 146, 156; Brock 1957, 158-9. Coldstream (*ibid*) suggests that juglet (25) derives from class E (iii) and that is more sophisticated.

Eighth Location: Mavro spelio

Tomb 7: (Ch. Tomb) Disturbed, MM-LM Reused in LG-LO Coldstream 2000a[448]
Local imitations
- Lekythos (N19) Creto-Cypriot class E (iii), EO

Fordsyke 1926-7, 260; Coldstream 2000a, 295-295.

---

[448] Forsdske (1926-7) for the initial publication.

Chapter 4: Who gets the Imports and who the Imitations?

The analysis of the evidence is separated into three distinct levels. On the first-level, there is a series of discussions concerning the finds included in the catalogue of Chapter 3. These discussions are focused on the provenance, context and function of the finds. The second-level analysis focuses on the spatial distribution of the imports and their imitations in relation to the tombs. In other words, there is an attempt to understand the impact of these objects on the Knossian society. A cluster analysis of all the available evidence is the third and final stage of this study.

i. First-level Analysis: The Finds

The different debates and suggestions concerning the material, the shapes and the possible origins of the objects have already been briefly mentioned, in the catalogue. For this reason, in this analysis, I would like to proceed directly to following discussions:

a) The provenance of the imports in relation to their various places of origins.
b) The provenance of the objects which are either imports or imitations.
c) The significance of the imitations in relation to their prototypes: the pottery factor.

a. Provenance of the objects catalogued as imports

Although for the present book what is important is whether those imports were appreciated by the Knossians, the determination of provenance is necessary for understanding, with the aid of quantification, why Knossians used specific types of imported objects. I believe that there are some misunderstandings in the way that places of origin of the Near Eastern imports are presented in scholarship. Thus, one might understand whether Knossians were willing to accept and eventually copy any kind of object that reached the island of Crete from the East or whether they had had a specific taste only for a certain kind of imports.

Cyprus appears to be the place where most of the Near Eastern imports came from. This is no surprise since the vast majority of the pottery is of Cypriot origin and pottery is the most imported category during the EIA, even if it is not the most valuable. Clearly, luxury goods and prestige items made of precious metals and materials have also been found in the tombs. As shown

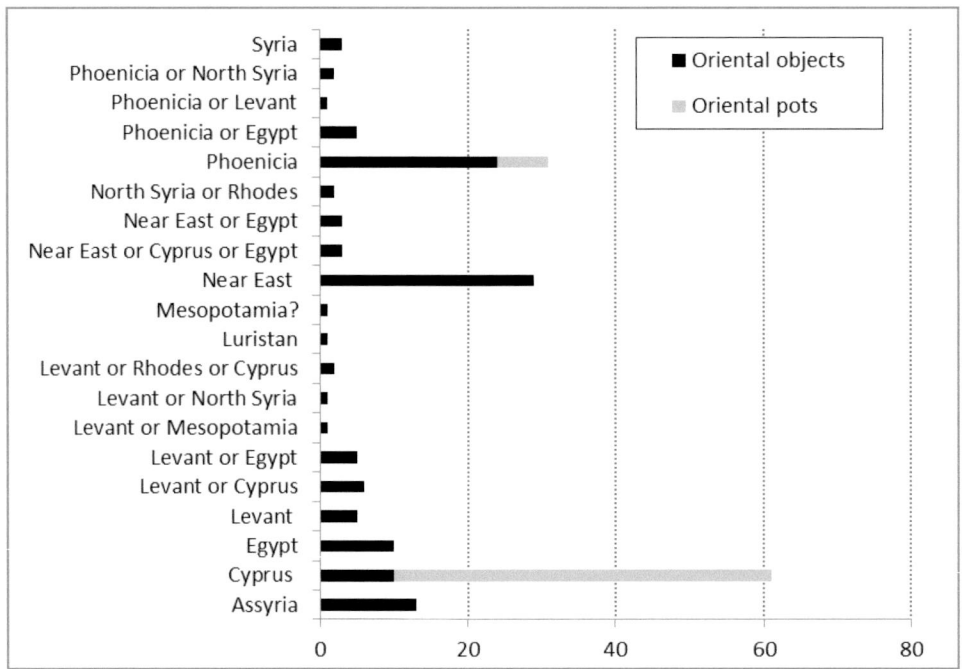

TABLE 8: GRAPH 7: PROVENANCE OF IMPORTS.

in the graph, the Near East and Phoenicia are the places where most of the non-pottery imports originate from. The graph illustrates quite clearly the first difficulty concerning the origin and character of the imports. In the case of Phoenicia, there is also the term Levant in order to describe the same place, or even to include Cyprus and coastal Syria. Catling[449] uses both terms in the KNC publication for the 'bronzes' he analyses, such as a hemispherical bowl (J.f1) at Tomb J and a mesomphalos phiale (G.f1) at Tomb G, Teke site. Others even use both terms for the same object as possible alternatives in their effort to assign an origin to it. Hoffman, for example, proposes as the place of origin for a faience bowl either *"Phoenicia or Levant"*.[450] She[451] even cites Boardman's words in order to justify why she does not believe that Phoenicia was the source of most of the Near Eastern imports in the Aegean in general.[452] I am not going to argue that Phoenicia and Levant are the same place politically, historically and geographically speaking, nor that the past investigations were not adequate. On the contrary, they were very precise on describing as well as possible the

---

[449] Catling 1996a, 564-5.
[450] Hoffman 1997, 43.
[451] Ibid., 15, n. 46.
[452] *"I use the word 'Levantine' deliberately because 'Phoenician' is over-precise and too loosely employed by scholars today"* (Boardman 1990, 10-11).

various origins of the objects. At the same time, though, one wonders how different Phoenicia and Levant can really be, especially in EIA terms, since the Phoenician cities did constitute the larger part of the Levant and Homer was more than aware of Phoenicians navigating in Crete.[453]

In order to approach the cultural traits on imported objects, one may assume that scholars have adopted the term 'Levant' when they were not certain about an object but could see the influence of Phoenician or North Syrians workshops. For example, the imitation of an Egyptian figurine of Ptah-Seker (78.f20) found in Tomb 78 at KMF. On the other hand, scholars use the term 'Phoenician' when they can compare directly an artefact with objects discovered in the Phoenicia cities. Such an example is the large bich. lekythos (107.80) from Tomb 107, KMF. As seen in the above graph, there are finds coming from Levant, from Phoenicia and from North Syria. Other imports come from the whole region of the Near East but not necessarily from Cyprus.

If, the bars in Graph 7, which refer to 'Phoenicia', 'Phoenicia or Levant', 'Levant' and 'Levant or Cyprus' merge into a single category/bar, then it becomes very clear that the area of Levant (i.e. where the ancient Phoenician cities still stand today) is one of the places with the greatest amount of imports to Knossos. If one bears in mind that many of the objects coming from the Near East are also related to the Phoenician manufacturing 'industry', then it is obvious that most of the imports are related to the Phoenician sphere of influence. In this sphere, one might or might not add the North Syrian agent, which probably is responsible for the figurative art on metallic objects.[454]

Regarding imported pottery, provenances most of the times does not appear to be a great problem, but in some special cases, though, even in pottery things are not always clear. For example, nowadays, archaeologists consider Cyprus as the home of the BoR pottery which produced in the island from the late 10th century BC and onwards.[455] On the other hand, the BoR pottery shares a distant relation to the Phoenician opposite coast. One must not forget that an alternative name of the BoR pottery in the past was 'Cypro-Phoenician' and BoR pots were imported to Phoenicia and imitated there.[456] Schreiber claims that the distant origin of the BoR pots, in general, must be in the Levant even before the beginning of the EIA[457] and for this reason probably prefers the term Cypro-Phoenician pottery. Iakovou rejects Schreiber's claim for the term Cypro-

---

[453] Homer *Odyssey* 15.415-433.
[454] Matthäus 1998.
[455] Bikai 1987, 37; Schreiber 2003.
[456] Schreiber 2003, 92-112.
[457] Ibid., 2-3.

Phoenician.⁴⁵⁸ A remote however association between the inspiration of the BoR pottery in Cyprus and certain traits, such the BoR technique, of the Phoenician mainland cannot be entirely dismissed.⁴⁵⁹

At the same time, not a single import of EIA figure-decorated Cypriot pot has been discovered and not a single Cypriot Black slip has been found in the Knossian cemeteries, even though their influences can be seen in many local pots. Not even one open-type vessel from Cyprus was discovered neither. In fact, only a single LG pithos from the Lower Gypsades Tomb⁴⁶⁰ was thought to be an import from Cyprus. However, Coldstream,⁴⁶¹ while accepting the Cypriot origin as a distant probability, agrees that the birds drawn on the pithos are more a common rediscovery in both islands of the LBA Aegean birds. In other words, Knossians, regarding juglets, had a tendency towards more 'eastern' appearance than Cypriot geometric styles. Another explanation could be that the people of Knossos did not need to use Cypriot pottery with geometric motifs, simply because Athens could provide them with geometric pots of unmatched quality. Imported Attic pottery is not part of this investigation, but it must be said that most of imported pottery discovered in the Knossian cemeteries comes from Attica.⁴⁶²

The BoR I and II juglets found in the Knossian cemeteries were all probably made in Cyprus and it is likely that Kouklia was at least one of the main production centres of those pots.⁴⁶³ Further, in the cluster analysis made by Liddy one of the groups revealed that BoR pots of the same production centre were found at Kouklia, Knossos and Al Mina.⁴⁶⁴ If this is true, then it seems that pots and other objects could have arrived at Knossos from various places apart from Cyprus. This possibility might reveal different commercial routes and merchants working under the same commercial network or independently and reaching Crete to trade their products. This also means that neither Cypriots nor Phoenicians were exclusively trading with Knossos, but there were more complex mechanisms involving Near Eastern people of many origins and Crete.

---

⁴⁵⁸ Iakovou 2004, 64-65.
⁴⁵⁹ Kotsonas 2008, 284; Bourogiannis 2012, 187; 2008.
⁴⁶⁰ Coldstream *et al* 1981, 145 no 2 pot.
⁴⁶¹ Coldstream (1979, 262; Colstream *et al* 1981, 145), while accepting the Cypriot origin as a distant probability, agrees that the birds drawn on the pithos are more a common rediscovery in both islands of the LBA Aegean birds.
⁴⁶² Coldstream 1996a, 393. Coldstream is referring to the KNC publication. However, the predominance of the Attic pots, among the imported pottery, can also be seen in Fortetsa SE (Brock 1957, 191).
⁴⁶³ Liddy 1996, 488-9.
⁴⁶⁴ Ibid.

Regarding chronology, the Phoenician pots reached Knossos at an earlier stage in LPG while the pots from Cyprus begin to arrive around the middle of the 8th century. The Phoenician pots, such as the bich. large lekythos (Tomb 107.80, KMF) and the red slip oinochoe (Tomb 292.80), probably came from various inland sites in the region of Tyre.[465] Coldstream considers Khirbet Selim as a possible place of origin and Tyre must be the place of origin for the rest of the Phoenician pots as well.[466] There is an uncertainty though regarding the two pots from Tomb P at Fortetsa SE. The tall-necked aryballos (1251) must have come from somewhere in Levant[467] while the provenance of the miniature neck amphora (1403) is less certain. One would expect that Cypriot and Phoenician pots would not help only determine absolute chronologies of the rest of the imports but also date the whole context of the tombs where these Near Eastern pots were found. Unfortunately, this does not work smoothly with Knossos cemeteries. First, the dating of the pots based on style analysis is not very helpful. Most of the pots are BoR slow-pouring vessels (juglets), the chronology of which is quite broad. In the next graph, one can see the quantities of the Near Eastern pottery in relation to their style.

As can be observed, most of the pots are juglets and the style of these juglets is either BoR I or II, with the latter being the widely represented. 71% of the pots are of BoR I and II style (26% and 45% respectively). The proposed absolute dating for BoR I pots range from 850 to 750 BC (Cypro-G III), while for BoR II

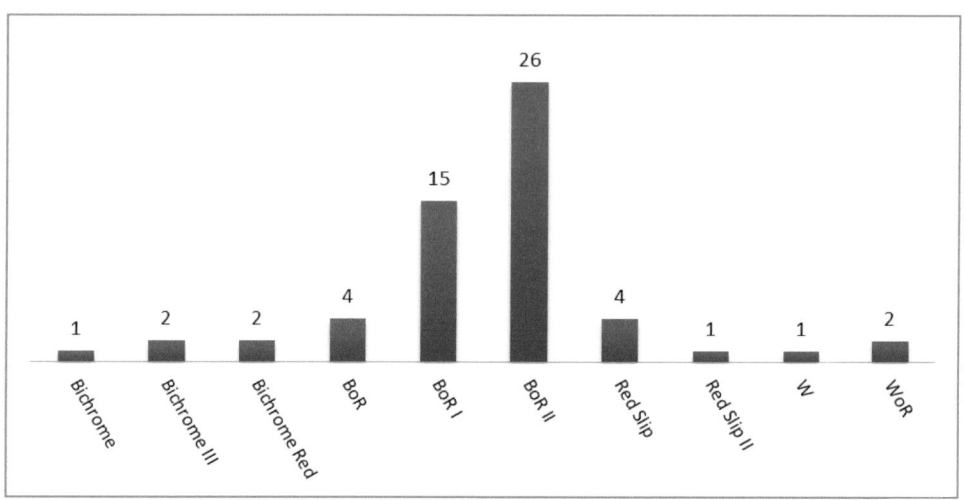

TABLE 9: GRAPH 8: POTTERY STYLE IN RELATION TO THE QUANTITIES FOUND AT THE KNOSSIAN CEMETERIES.

---

[465] Coldstream 1996a, 408.
[466] Ibid.; Chapman 1972; Bikai 1987.
[467] Hoffman 1997, 85; Falsone 1987, 191-2.

it ranges from 750 BC to 600 BC.[468] In terms of Cretan chronology, BoR I covers chronologically the period from the LPG to the MG/LG, while BoR II covers the period from the MG times and onwards. It is very clear that in the case of the BoR I juglets there are no safe conclusions to be drawn in terms of chronology. For this reason and whenever possible, a combination between the chronology of the context and the chronology of the style is suggested. This procedure can be applied to all the pots.

Certainly, in the MG/MG-LG the number of BoR II is much higher than any other import, while in the LG-EO, the presence of all kinds of faience objects and beads changes the picture. It is beyond doubt that the production of BoR imitations begun shortly after the arrival of the original pots at Knossos and that they do not imitate a distant shape, as in the case of Phoenician and Cypriot pilgrim flasks, with which local imitations share only a distant resemblance. The BoR style of pottery, in general, is not only the most successful import at Knossos but also the most successfully copied type of object.

Regarding the dating of the rest of the imports in relation to pots, precious objects such as the bronze arrowheads and at least one bronze four-sided stand (Tomb 200-202 KMF). These objects were among the first to have reached the island at the end of the BA, or the beginning of the EIA. All of them share the same provenance: Cyprus. While imported pottery seems to have reached its peak in MG, the rest of the objects have a more even presence during all the periods of the EIA beginning from the SM. The sharp rise in many objects during the LG-EO is due to the numerous objects made of faience and crystal beads

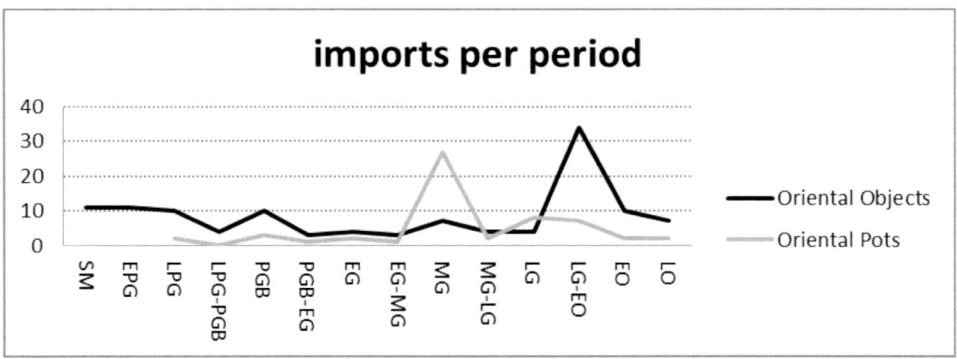

TABLE 10: GRAPH 9: NEAR EASTERN OBJECTS AND POTS PER PERIOD.

---

[468] I use the modified Gjerstad's (1948) chronology proposed by Demitriou (1978; n. 12) and Coldstream (1979; 1984c, 136). Certainly, there are other proposed chronological frameworks with Schreiber's (2003) being one of the latest with much higher dates.

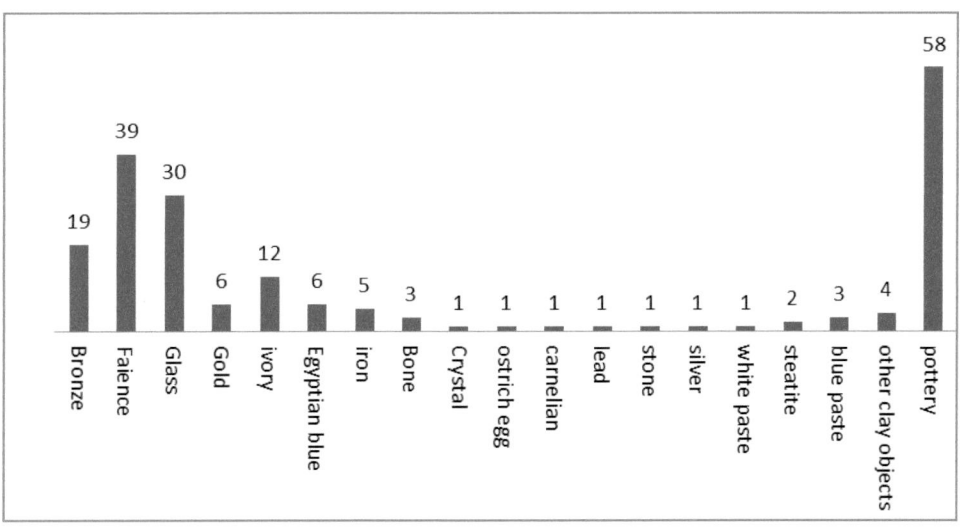

TABLE 11: GRAPH 10: MATERIAL OF IMPORTS.

such as necklaces, but beads can also be found individually in the tombs during this late period. The quantities of the objects in relation to their material are shown in Table 11, Graph 10.

Objects made of clay (pots mostly) represent the category found is the largest quantity, given that faience beads are counted as parts of groups (e.g. necklaces) and not as individual pieces. Seven out of the 58 pots discovered in Knossian Cemeteries come from Phoenicia and the rest from Cyprus (see catalogue). For the rest of the imports, one may observe that all the materials related to jewellery and amulets (faience, Egyptian Blue, white and blue paste and crystal beads) were found in large numbers in a much wider distribution of tombs than the rest of the materials and objects. This probably related to the small size of these objects. Hoffman[469] claims that their small size made their transportation easier and the fact they were found in cemeteries and sanctuaries (such as the Idaean Cave) suggests that they were used as prestige items.

However, one must not entirely overrule the possibility of religious connections. In some cases, for example, imported objects might have had a function identical to the rituals of the Phoenician homeland. Scarabs of Egyptian and Phoenician origin discovered in a MG cremation pithos (Lower Gypsades Hill tomb, catalogue no 122) and a LG-EO cremation pithos (Tomb 229, pithos catalogue no 229.6, KMF) and a pithos burial (Tomb 78, Medical faculty). These amulets probably share functions similar to the scarabs discovered inside

---

[469] Hoffman 1997, 248.

sealed cremation amphoras in the cemetery of Al-Bass in Tyre during about the same period.[470] Both at Knossos and Tyre, the scarabs were unburned and thus unaffected from the funeral pyre. In cremation pithoi and inhumation amphoras in Knossos were also found also faience figurines of Egyptian and Phoenician deities. The figurine of Sekhmet is such an example (Tomb IX catalogue no. 264, Fortetsa SE). The overall character of the use of such amulets might reveal that some religious and/or ritual processes were common (or at least not unknown) between Crete, Phoenicia and perhaps Egypt. This can provide evidence that the EIA Knossians did not have religious affinities only with the Greek mainland. Below one can see the photographs and drawings of scarab found at Khaniale Teke and in a cremation urn at the EIA cemetery of Al-Bass at Tyre.[471] There is a similarity in the shape of the scarabs and in the sitting figures, even if the Khaniale Teke scarab probably represents Maat and it is more simplified, while the second Horus.[472] Both scarabs are made of light brown steatite.

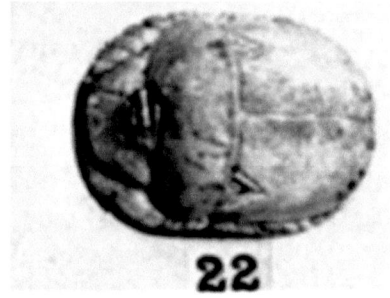

FIGURE 10: SCARAB FROM TOMB II, KHANIALE TEKE (HUTCHINSON 1954, FIGURE 3 AND PLATE 29). REPRODUCED WITH PERMISSION OF THE BRITISH SCHOOL AT ATHENS.

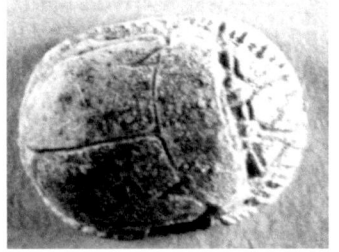

FIGURE 11: SCARAB FROM AL-BASS, TYRE (GAMER-WALLERT 2004, 407-408). REPRODUCED WITH PERMISSION OF PROFESSOR AUBET.

---

[470] Aubet 2004, 59; Gamer-Wallert 2004, 407-408.
[471] Gamer-Wallert 2004, 407-408.
[472] Ibid.

Imported bronzes have also been found. Certainly, the most famous of them is the bronze semispherical bowl from Tomb J (J.f1) at the Teke site, because of the Phoenician inscription it bears, its early date (before 900 BC) and the fact that it comes from *"an excellent closed PG context"*.[473] Sznycer[474] dated the inscription to c.900 BC, though it might have been much earlier. Cross[475] and Lipiński[476] think it was produced before 1000 BC. Again, this bowl must be a prestige item and most probably as an heirloom. Proposed translations of the inscription range from *"The cup of Shena, son of..."*[477] to *"Bowl which Tabni fashioned for Amon"*.[478] What seems rather limited is the presence of imported iron objects from the Near East, even though large amounts of iron weapons and tools were discovered in the tombs (mostly at the sites of the KMF and Fortetsa SE). One reason for this lack of Near Eastern tools and weapon must have been the possible presence of an independent iron manufacturing industry in Crete, which had gained its own mastery of iron production by 1050 BC.[479] A second reason might have been the fact that it is not certain whether a series of products made of bronze and iron are either imports or local imitations. This group of products is a separate category in the following section.

b. Provenance of the objects catalogued as imports or local imitations

In the previous section, I argued, without downplaying the role of Cyprus, that most of Near Eastern imports came to Knossos from what could be called the Phoenician sphere of influence. To this trait one should add a mix of Egyptian elements filtered by the Phoenician or North Syrian repertoire. Few SM prestigious imports from Cyprus are the only exception. The following category of objects is a very different character from the previous category. First, there is the problem that all the finds discussed here are characterised either as Cypriot or as close imitations of Cypriot imports produced in Crete. These objects are namely iron obeloi, fire-dogs, bronze rod tripods and four-sided stands. The debate about these objects continues even today. What is certain though is that these products are either of Cypriot or of Cretan manufacture unrelated to the Phoenician repertoire. Bronze stands, iron obeloi and fire-dogs are found in burial contexts not only in Knossos and other Cretan cemeteries but also on the Greek mainland (Argos) and certainly in Cyprus.[480]

---

[473] Catling 1996a, 564.
[474] Sznycer 1979, 92-93.
[475] Cross 1974.
[476] Lipiński 1983, 129-33.
[477] Hoffman, 122-3.
[478] Lipiński 2004, 182.
[479] Dickinson 2006, 146-150.
[480] Papasavvas 2001.

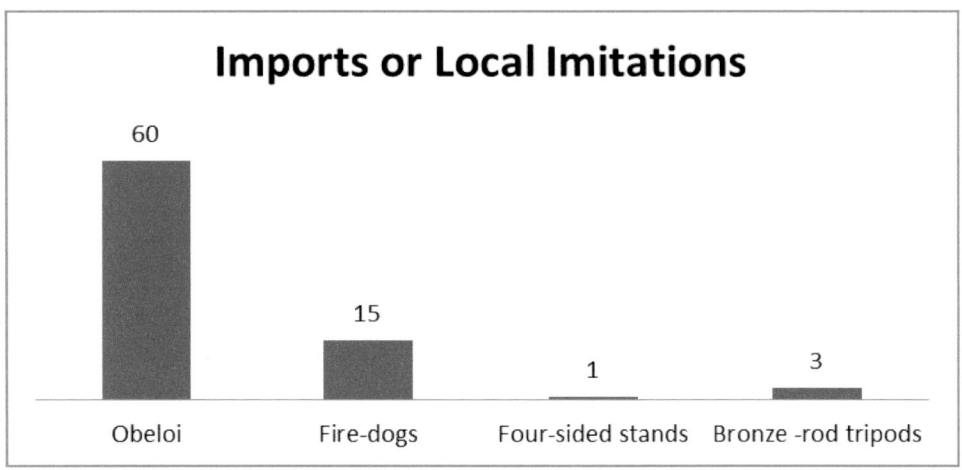

TABLE 12: GRAPH 11: NUMBERS OF IMPORTS OR LOCAL IMITATIONS.

All the 60 obeloi found in the KMF site and the few others discovered in Fortetsa SE seem to be associated with obeloi found in Cyprus, in sites like Kourion, Lapithos, Kition etc. with the earliest of them being made of bronze around 1000 BC[481] and perhaps earlier around 1050 BC, as some evidence from Paleopahos-Skales suggests.[482] Regarding the obeloi found at Fortetsa SE, they were initially registered as 'pikes' and 'pits'.[483] As one can observe in the following graph, the most numerous objects of this category are obeloi and this seems to be reasonable because they were probably placed in groups of six in each tomb and probably, but not always, in relation to fire-dogs.[484] Obeloi are associated with banqueting of aristocratic style.[485]

The same picture can be seen in other Cretan cemeteries. At a distance of a few kilometres south of the Knossos area, there is the EIA cemetery of Eltyna with chamber tombs dating from the PG to the G. The excavator thinks that this cemetery has much in common with the Knossian cemeteries and the area of Eltyna was probably controlled during this period by Knossos.[486] While this cemetery is not as big, or rich, as the Knossian ones, more than one hundred obeloi were found in the tombs, revealing that the use of these iron objects was neither exclusive to the Knossian elites nor so rare. The cemetery of Eltyna

---

[481] Karageorghis 1974, 169-170.
[482] Hoffman 1997, n. 106; Masson and Masson 1980, 411-13.
[483] See Karageorghis 1974. In the catalogue of the presented book I treated these items from Fortetsa SE as obeloi.
[484] Snodgrass 1996, 590-2.
[485] Matthäus 1998, 141.
[486] Rethemiotakis and Englezou 2010.

probably represents the local elite members with similar if not identical burial customs to the Knossians. One could even argue that the use of the obeloi was more general outside Knossos and that they might also have held monetary status. However, this suggestion is hard to be accepted for this early pre-monetary period.

Fire-dogs are very closely associated with the obeloi. In fact, obeloi were often placed on two fire-dogs inside the tombs and might have also served for cooking purposes. Again, the shape of the fire-dogs from Knossos is almost identical to those discovered at Kouklia. Those from Cyprus are older and have slightly more elaborate edges. Both obeloi and fire-dogs found at Knossos were made of iron. Regarding iron technology, Dickinson[487] supports that iron technology was introduced to the Aegean from Cyprus and that around 1050 BC iron was being worked in the leading regions of the Aegean. Without a doubt, Knossos was one of those leading regions. Matthäus is not entirely negative towards this approach but also writes of the possibility that Anatolia might also have been related to this process.[488] Waldbaum's[489] argues for an independent development of iron working in the Aegean. Dickinson[490] rejects this theory based on the lack of evidence of a metallurgical background comparable to that of Cyprus and the Near East. One may also add that not only the absolute dating of the objects but also their context has shown that relations between Crete, Cyprus and Phoenicia were never severed, but were probably rather limited in periods of turbulence, such as immediately after 1200 BC.[491]

The bronze objects of this category, the four-sided stands and bronze rod tripods can be found at many places in EIA Crete and Greece and are always associated with cultic and funerary contexts.[492] Catling[493] supports that all the stands and rod-tripods found in EIA Knossos were *keimelia* (heirlooms) from the LBA and reached Crete during the SM through a process named 'The heroes return'.[494] In other words, Cretan warriors returned home after their wanderings in the East carrying prestige items and were cremated or buried with them. Matthäus[495] and Cross[496] following Gjerstad,[497] on the other hand, have argued strongly for an EIA

---

[487] Dickinson 2006, 148.
[488] Matthäus 1985, 328-329; 1998, 141.
[489] Waldbaum 1982, 336-8.
[490] Dickinson 2006, 147.
[491] Waldbaum 1982, 345-49; Sherratt 1994, 59-106.
[492] See Papasavvas 2001 for an analytical study on this subject.
[493] Catling 1984, 70-91; 1995, 123-8; 1996c, 647-9.
[494] Catling 1996c, 649.
[495] Matthäus 1988.
[496] Cross 1974.
[497] Gjerstad 1948, 403.

Cretan production of these stands. Matthäus[498] claims that most of the bronze rod tripods found in EIA contexts are Cretan productions. However, he makes a clear distinction by admitting that the earliest stands, such the four-sided stand discovered at the burial complex 200-202, is of Cypriot manufacture and might have been indeed a keimelio.[499] He also agrees with Catling maintaining that in the SM the relations between Cyprus and Crete were much stronger than the archaeological evidence reveals[500] and that it is likely that iron technology was promoted by Cypriot cultural inference. Hoffman maintains that probably all the rod-tripods and open work stands found at Crete (even the earliest from the SM) are imitations made by the locals and not imports.[501]

Matthäus' suggestion on the provenance of the bronze rod tripods has been confirmed by the study of Papasavvas.[502] The author after a meticulous examination of the material from Crete and Cyprus believes that all bronze rod tripods found in the tombs at Knossos are local imitations of at least two different workshops.[503] The four-sided stand from the 200-202 tomb is according to Papasavvas a Cypriot import of the LBA.[504] Regarding the four-sided stand from Khaniale Teke tomb, Papasavvas has demonstrated that most probably is of Cretan manufacture.[505]

A final suggestion concerning this category of objects is that, perhaps the earliest tripods and obeloi could have been imports from Cyprus (from SM to the PG) and that during the PG the Cretan bronze workshops began copying the Cypriot originals.[506] If the earlier objects are indeed imports, then one might observe that there are two different kinds of imports reaching Crete during the EIA. The first group consists of imports of Near Eastern character related to the Phoenician, North Syrian and Egyptian styles, even if these imports come from Cyprus, and the second group includes objects of Cypriot character probably associated with the LBA Aegean and its Greek-speaking inhabitants. LPG items such as the gold diadem (Tomb L, Fortetsa NE), indicate a continuity of this trait at later periods.

---

[498] Matthäus 1998, 129; 1988.
[499] Matthäus 1998, 130.
[500] Ibid., 140-141.
[501] Ibid., 117-9.
[502] Papasavvas 2001, 158-163, 195 table 5.
[503] Ibid.
[504] Ibid., 82-84, 2012, 139.
[505] Ibid., 241-242.
[506] Matthäus 1998, 141.

Karageorghis[507] also suggests two different streams of imports from the East to the Aegean, one Phoenician and one Cypriot but in later periods: the first occurred mostly in the 10th century BC, and the latter mainly from the 8th century BC and onwards. Matthäus sees the possibility of a third North Syrian stream.[508] However, the dating of early imports also suggests that the 11th century was also very important for the trading between Crete and Cyprus. While Phoenicians were famous traders during the EIA, it is probably Cypriots those who transported those SM items to Crete. As already inferred, the BoR I and II pots which also reached Knossos later than the SM could well have been carried there both by Cypriots and Phoenicians. It is hard to know whether these commercial networks acted independently especially from the PGB and onwards. Maybe this confusing situation makes perfect sense when one approaches it as a series of gift exchanges between the various elites of the Eastern Mediterranean.[509] This is an important factor, at least for the precious imports after the end of the BA and before the middle of the 9th century, when numerous imports (especially) pottery begin to arrive at Knossos. On the other hand, one may suggest that Knossians were simply far more interested in the trading of imports of the Phoenician repertoire since they were more 'exotic' or attractive to them than the imports of Aegean character, or simply different.

c. The significance of the imitations in relation to their prototypes: the pottery factor

As far as the imitations of pottery are concerned, it is of little value to seek provenance in the Near East and/or Cyprus, since it is known that they were produced locally in Crete. All of them are clay objects and therefore it has been much easier to establish a relation with the aid of chemical analysis. The total number of the clay objects which are imitations of Near Eastern shapes (almost all of them derive from original imports found in Knossos) is 160 and most of them are pots. A curious exception to the absolute predominance of pottery in this category might have been the four clay objects known as fenestrated stands. The first was discovered in Tomb 283 (KMF, catalogue no 98) and the other three were together at the Khaniale Teke Tholos Tomb (catalogue no 105, 106, 107). These objects might be distant imitations of Cypriot bronze stands.[510] However, as Boardman admits they are probably a mixture of Minoan, Cypriot and Phoenician elements[511] and are no direct imitations of bronze stands.

---

[507] Karageorghis cited in Matthäus 1998, 159.
[508] Matthäus 1998, 159.
[509] Ibid., 140,
[510] Coldstream 1996a, 368; Boardman 1967, 64.
[511] Ibid.

To obtain a better understanding of the pottery imitations in order and to establish chronological and typological relations, one must study these copies in parallel with the original imports. At this point, one could ask why pottery (both as imported prototype and imitation) must be separated from the main corpus of the evidence. The answer is, as always, 'quantity'. Pottery comprises roughly one-third of all published imports in Crete.[512] For Knossian cemeteries, the figure increases dramatically. Almost half of all the Near Eastern imports from fully published tombs consist of Near Eastern pots (45.66%). Imported pottery constitutes a very homogeneous category with Cyprus being the place from where most of the pots originate. Additionally, pottery is almost always examined as a separate category from all the other finds. Especially in the excavations at Knossos, one always finds a distinction between 'pottery' and 'small finds' in all the relevant publications. Everything else apart from pottery (and bones) is placed in the category of small finds. Finally, the reason for this distinction is perfectly understandable for a period still called 'Dark Age' by some scholars. Pottery is the material on which provenance can be safely established and in many cases, it offers a safe framework of chronology. To return to the analysis, one should make a distinction between the original pots whose copies were found at Knossos and the Near Eastern pots which were not imitated. The reason for this task is to reveal, if possible, a personal taste of the Knossians for prototype types of pottery. The different categories and distinctions can be seen in the next graph:

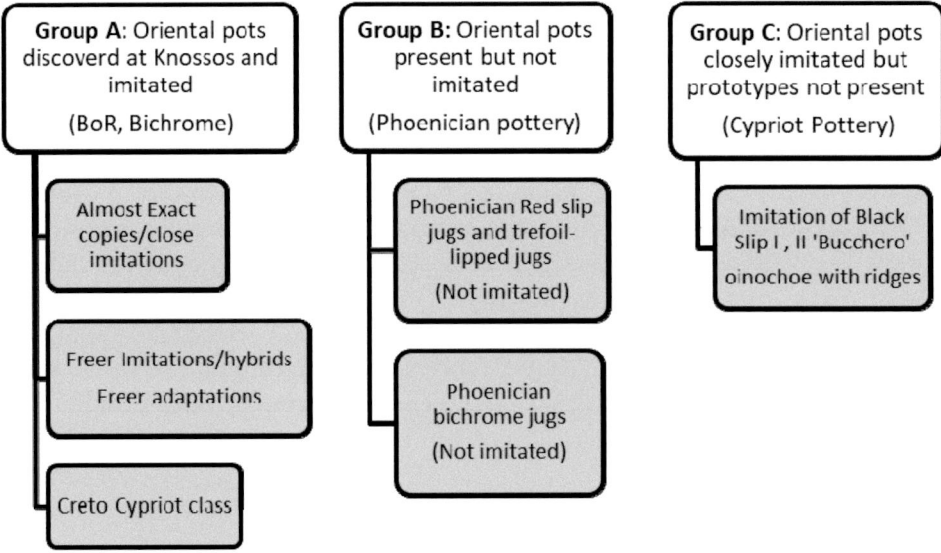

TABLE 13: CHART 1: IMPORTED AND LOCALLY MADE POTTERY.

---

[512] Hoffman 1997, 148.

As shown in the graph above, as far as the Near Eastern pots are concerned, three different groups of pottery were found at Knossos, which are not necessarily absolutely separated from each other. Group A includes pots copied or deriving mostly from BoR pottery originated in Cyprus. The vast majority of the imitations (almost 95%) belong to this group. However, there is also a minor representation of copies of bich. pots. The term 'almost exact copies' means imitations that are faithful to their prototypes apart from some minor details. Two typical examples are the BoR juglets 218.41 (Tomb 218) and 219.56 (Tomb 219) that intent to imitate even the slip of the originals. As Coldstream[513] points out the practice of polishing the surface is not typical for Cretan G pottery and for this reason these imitations are a special case. Additionally, there are other close copies with slightly different fabric and surface polishing. On the other hand, the freer adaptations of the BoR are the prototypes to what would become one of the most popular shapes: the Creto-Cypriot lekythos. This is the most numerous category of the local imitations group. They imitate the shape of the original BoR pots even though sometimes they are more biconical.

The freer imitations/hybrids such as pot 292.109 from KMF are termed like this, because no close prototypes have yet been discovered. They basically differ in the way that the original motifs are combined (more lines or circles). Coldstream[514] interprets these freer imitations as an experiment made by local potters. The other two shapes largely imitated at Knossos were the trefoil-lipped and round-mouthed jugs, and the sack-shaped trefoil-lipped juglet.

Group B of the graph includes the Phoenician pots and shapes discovered in few quantities at Knossos. There are no local imitations of these shapes. This is very important since close local imitations of Phoenician Red Slip juglets have not been discovered in Rhodes and Kos either, even though original pieces have been found there.[515]

Group C is an imitation of Cypriot shape and function unrelated to the Levantine repertoire. These are the coarse red micaceous oinochoe which imitate the shape of the Black Slip I and II vessels which derive from the Late Cypriot III ribbed jugs ware.[516] If the assumption that these pots held liquid opium is correct, then they must have been of a very important value either as narcotic for religious purposes or as painkillers for severe wounds, as it probably happened also in

---

[513] Coldstream 1984c, 132.
[514] Ibid., 134-5.
[515] Schreiber 2003, 285-306.
[516] Kotsonas 2012, 160; Schreiber 2003, 302; Stampolidis 2003, n. 57; Coldstream 2002b, 463-9; 1998, 256; 1996a, 346-7.

the Bronze Age.[517] This type of pots seems very independent from the other imitations. Perhaps the reason that no prototypes were found is that this shape was probably imitated first at Lyktos and then introduced to Knossos.[518]

There are two categories of pottery of Near Eastern character which have not been included in the catalogue. The first is a group of pots of Cypriot inspiration which probably reached Knossos either at the end of the BA or during the 10th and 9th centuries. These are the zoomorphic vessels such as the bird-askoi and a bird-kernos. They have an apparently exotic shape. However, original Cypriot pots of this type have not yet been discovered in the Knossian cemeteries and even if their shapes derive from Cyprus, their decoration has many local features. The same can also be said for a group of lentoid or pilgrim flasks which, as Coldstream[519] suspects, owe their shape to the Phoenician pilgrim flasks and not to the Cypriot vessels. However, since these flasks have bird shape neck, they cannot be included in the close imitated shapes.

As stated in the introduction and as seen in the catalogue, Near Eastern pottery is pottery coming from Phoenicia and Cyprus. The quantity of Phoenician pottery is rather limited and has been discovered only at the site of the KMF and at Fortetsa SE (5 and 2 pots respectively). This limited quantity may indicate that Knossians did not appreciate at all the Phoenician pots. On the other hand, Cypriot BoR pottery has been found at the six following sites: Fortetsa SE, Fortetsa NE, KMF, Atsalenio, Khaniale Teke and Lower Gypsades Hill. Coldstream argues that the Phoenician pots came to Knossos at an earlier period before the arrival of the Cypriot BoR.[520] The three main types of pots were the juglet or lekythos, mostly BoR and normally with one handle, the trefoil-lipped jug or oinochoe and the sack-shaped juglet (trefoil-lipped alabastron or alabastron-aryballos). Brock[521] made the first and most fundamental study of the way Near Eastern pots were imitated at Knossos. The most important part of this research on local imitations was the analysis of what he named as Creto-Cypriot lekythos and oinochoe. In addition, Coldstream made some important changes to Brocks's typology in a series of articles.[522] Moignard[523] also contributed with her study of the O period at KNC. Kotsonas[524] makes an important point as far as the distinctions of the imitations are concerned.

---

[517] Arnott 1999, 268-270.
[518] Kotsonas 2012, 164.
[519] Coldstream 1996a, 365-6; 2002, 208.
[520] Coldstream 1984c, 136.
[521] Brock 1957.
[522] Coldstream 1979, 1984c, 1996a.
[523] Moignard 1996.
[524] Kotsonas 2011b.

The following table presents the original pots alongside their imitations in an attempt to trace the evolution of the various Near Eastern types in Knossos. All the pots shown below can also be seen within their proper context in the catalogue of Chapter 3 with their references. All the examples and images used are from the KMF site and from Fortetsa SE. An additional reason for doing this presentation is to highlight the possible typological differences within these two sites and the studies of Brock and Coldstream. In the group of juglets, I have included both lekythoi and aryballoi which are the ancient Greek names of small unguent vases performing a similar if not identical function as containers of oils and perfumes. Certainly, an Attic lekythos is very different from a Corinthian aryballos but this is not the case for the Near Eastern juglets. Coldstream[525] has explained this difference in terminology on several occasions.

In this table as I did in the catalogue as well, I have used both Brock's and Coldstream's typologies: The main reason for this modification is that the pots discovered at the KMF site were much closer to the original BoR and WP juglets than those of Fortetsa SE, which were the pots in which Brock based his typology. The major difference is the orange-colour clay that the close imitations of the KMF have and which is similar but again not identical to the original BoR pots.[526] However, it must be stressed that there are few features which under a close macroscopic examination do reveal differences between BoR pots and their Cretan copies.[527] Kotsonas notes that Cretan copies, unlike their prototypes have a broader neck, they carry no slip on the surface, have similar but not identical colour and there is normally a band surrounding the base.[528] These differences can be attributed to various factors ranging from the raw material used for the pot[529] but, I also think, to a local or even Cypriot immigrant potter who wished to mark a personal attribution or differentiation from the previous tradition.

On the other hand, the typology of Brock on Creto-Cypriot lekythoi has largely remained intact. The same can be said for trefoil-lipped jugs. The close imitations were again based on Brock, while no major changes were applied to his Creto-Cypriot series. Finally, the alabastron and its typology have remained the same since Brock. Even though Type III (iv) on lekythoi departs from the originals especially in terms of decoration, it can be argued that overall most of the types remain within the BoR tradition. Apart from typology, quantity becomes again important as far as the shapes and style are concerned.

---

[525] Coldstream 1979, 1984c, 122.
[526] Kotsonas 2011a; Coldstream 1984c.
[527] Kotsonas 2012, 170.
[528] Ibid.
[529] Ibid.

108 KNOSSOS AND THE NEAR EAST

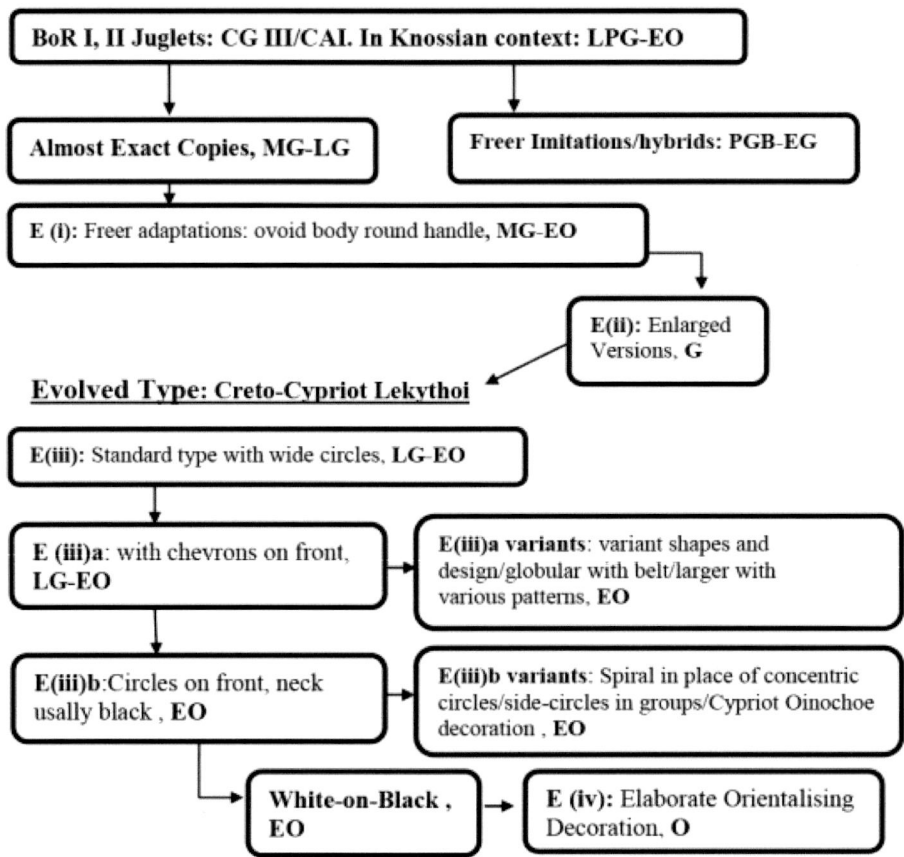

Examples from Medical Faculty (*MF*) and Fortetsa SE (*F*)
Height (H) is given in cm. All these examples with their references are also cited in the catalogue

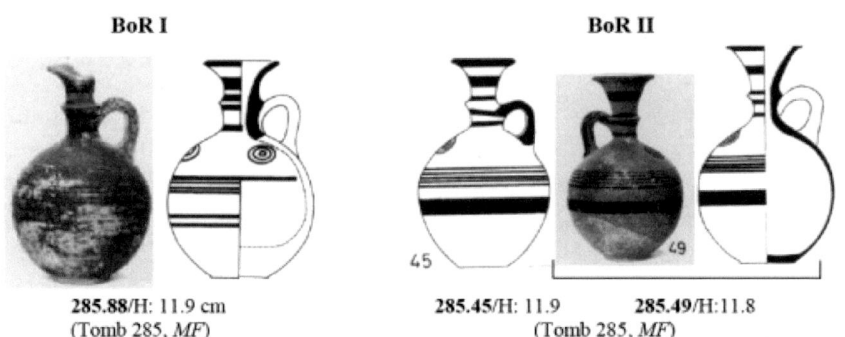

TABLE 14: CHART 2: EVOLUTION OF LOCAL SHAPES DERIVING FROM NEAR EASTERN POTS. BROCK 1957, PLATES: 34, 59, 97, 71, 68, 49, 76; COLDSTREAM AND CATLING 1996, PLATES: 115, 116, 119, 146, 148, 188, 194, 201, 206, 208, 223, 227, 239). IMAGES REPRODUCED WITH PERMISSION OF THE BRITISH SCHOOL AT ATHENS.

Chapter 4: Who gets the Imports and who the Imitations? 109

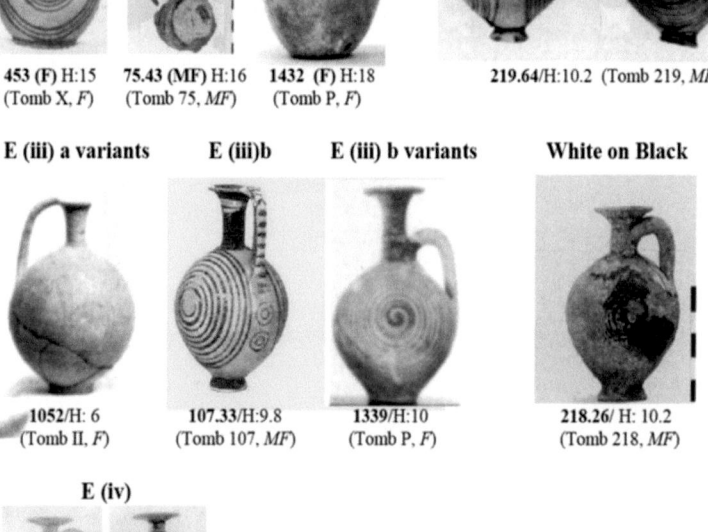

TABLE 14: CHART 2: EVOLUTION OF LOCAL SHAPES DERIVING FROM NEAR EASTERN POTS. BROCK 1957, PLATES: 34, 59, 97, 71, 68, 49, 76; COLDSTREAM AND CATLING 1996, PLATES: 115, 116, 119, 146, 148, 188, 194, 201, 206, 208, 223, 227, 239). IMAGES REPRODUCED WITH PERMISSION OF THE BRITISH SCHOOL AT ATHENS.

(2)

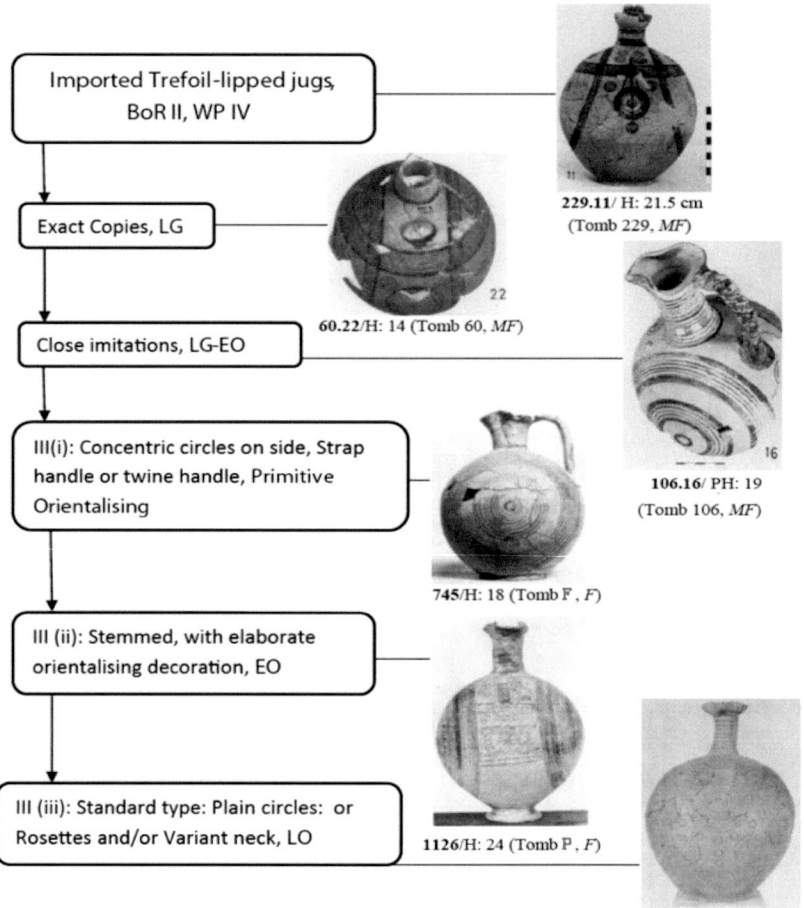

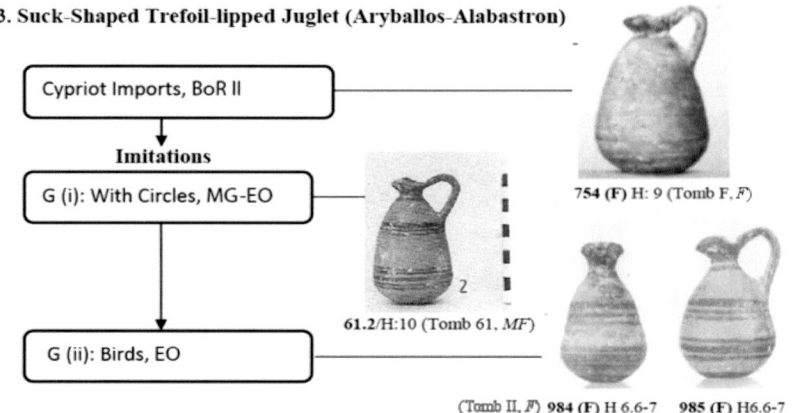

TABLE 14: CHART 2: EVOLUTION OF LOCAL SHAPES DERIVING FROM NEAR EASTERN POTS. BROCK 1957, PLATES: 34, 59, 97, 71, 68, 49, 76; COLDSTREAM AND CATLING 1996, PLATES: 115, 116, 119, 146, 148, 188, 194, 201, 206, 208, 223, 227, 239). IMAGES REPRODUCED WITH PERMISSION OF THE BRITISH SCHOOL AT ATHENS.

(3)

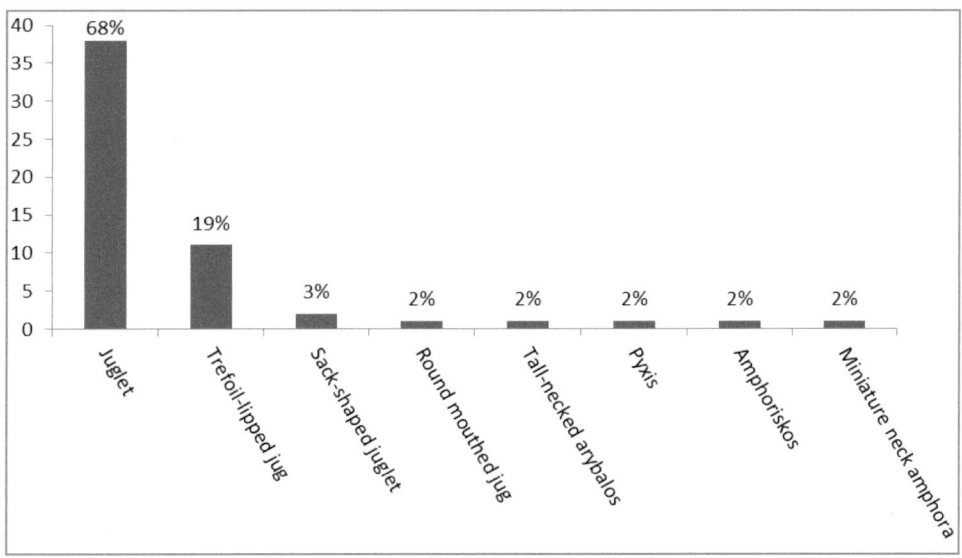

TABLE 15: GRAPH 12: SHAPES AND QUANTITIES OF NEAR EASTERN POTTERY FOUND AT KNOSSOS CEMETERIES.

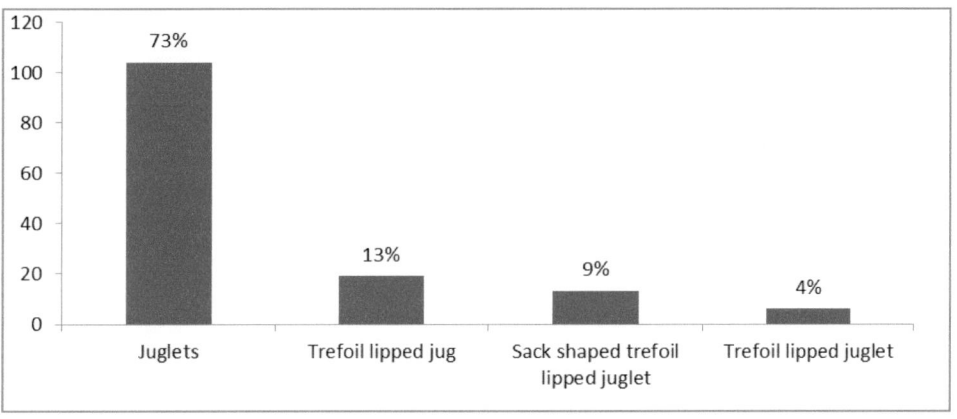

TABLE 16: GRAPH 13: SHAPES OF LOCAL IMITATIONS OF NEAR EASTERN POTTERY AND QUANTITIES FOUND AT KNOSSOS CEMETERIES.

As can be seen in Table 15, Chart 12 and Table 16, Chart 13, BoR juglets are the most numerous group. At the same BoR imitations are also the most numerous group with identical percentages.[530]

It might be coincidental but in both cases, juglets are the most numerous categories. It cannot be a coincidence that there are comparable percentages

---

[530] In the graph of the imports 6 out of 38 juglets have two handles. No imitations of double-handle juglets have been found.

between imports and imitations. The local juglets are about three times more numerous than the imports and almost the same can be said about the trefoil-lipped jugs and the sack-shaped juglets. It is not clear what this analogy suggests and one should bear in mind that the chronological span of the imitations is longer. It is tempting to think, however, that the need of the Knossians to use those shapes was similar to that of the people who created the imports back in Cyprus. Additionally, in the following graph, one can see the amount of Near Eastern pots and local imitations discovered at Knossos at any given period.

The exact copies and close imitations of the juglets cover the same time span, with most of the original Near Eastern pots from the PGB and onwards, even if they are more numerous. This fact suggests once more that the production of copies begun shortly after or even simultaneously with the arrival of the first imports. One important thing about all these juglets (both imported and local) is their deposition in cemeteries and their use burial rites. What is remarkable though is the steady increase of the imitations at the end of the LG. This is the time when the Creto-Cypriot lekythos attains a standardised form and is assimilated to the local tradition without however dismissing entirely its Cypriot characteristics.[531] With the notable exception of an unpublished Cypriot BoR II juglet discovered in the EIA settlement, these juglets have not been found outside the cemeteries.[532] Their association with funerary rituals is more than clear. Moreover, as Coldstream says[533] (referring to slow-pouring vessels, including the local and Attic types, which were not found in the cemeteries): *"even those few pots (not discovered in burial context) would also have had a*

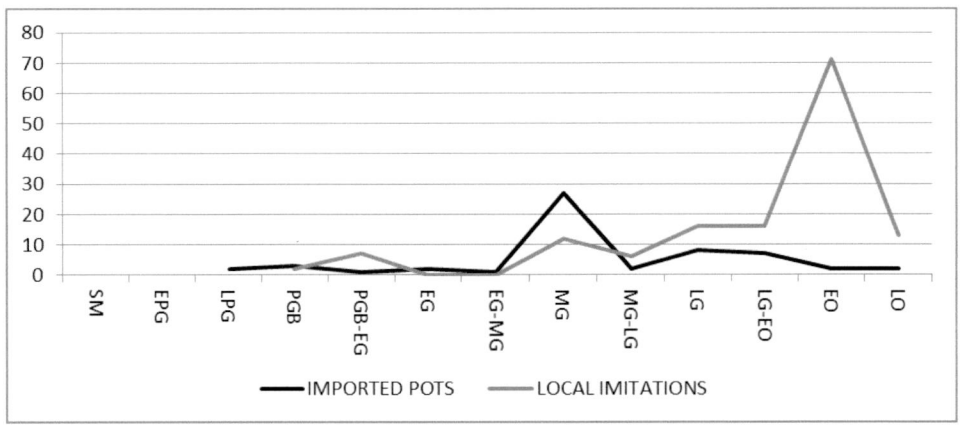

TABLE 17: GRAPH 14: CHRONOLOGICAL SEQUENCE AND QUANTITY OF IMPORTED POTS AND OF THEIR IMITATIONS.

---

[531] Coldstream 1996a, 345.
[532] Hoffman 1997, 79; Coldstream 1979, 261, no 31.
[533] Coldstream 2001, 40.

special function in anointing the dead before the burial". The exclusiveness in the use of the slow-pouring vessel in Knossos for funerary purposes is very interesting. The same also occurs at the sites of the Dodecanese (Kos and Rhodes). The situation is similar in Cyprus.[534] In the Levant, on the contrary, BoR juglets have also been found in domestic activities (ibid) and this marks a difference. The use of trefoil-lipped oinochoae of various types (BoR, Red slip, Red micaceous) is related to rituals during the burial. The aryballos-alabastron also falls into the category of closed slow-pouring vessels used in burial rituals. All the pots of this category are close imitations of BoR I and II styles also present at Knossos.

Scholars have talked about the establishment of a Phoenician or Cypriot unguent factory near Knossos, providing the local society with Levantine fragrances and oil.[535] Certainly, the vessel par excellence for transporting and using these oils was the BoR juglet. Jones,[536] Hoffman[537] and Schreiber[538] discard the possibility of a Phoenician factory. Jones sees migrating craftsmen involved in these activities.[539] Kotsonas[540] argues for the presence of at least one Cypriot potter in Knossos based on the use of different brushes for the decoration of the concentric circles on a specific oinochoe (KMF 60.22).[541] Hoffman maintains that a pot can be copied for itself and not as unguent vessel.[542] It is hard to believe however that these pots went to the richest tomb just for their nice (?) appearance.

Is it possible then that the shape of a pot, even its colour, was mostly dictated by the liquid it contained? One should mention that the Greek name for vases, such as oinochoe (for wine) and hydria (for water) etc., had a direct reference to the function of the pot. The decoration was perhaps important but it was the use of a pot that made it suitable for a task or not. I wish to explore this point further with the following ethnographic example. In 2010, I visited various pottery workshops in order to have a look at the locally produced, modern small slow-pouring vessels and understand their function. I also had the rather romantic hope to find some connections between ancient and modern pottery shapes. The workshops I visited are located on the road between Heraklion and Knossos and at the old town of Rethymnon. In general,

---

[534] Schreiber 2003, 54-5.
[535] Kotsonas 2011a; Schreiber 2003; Hoffman 1997; Jones 1993; Coldstream 1986; 1979.
[536] Jones 1993, 299-306.
[537] Hoffman 1997, 176-185.
[538] Schreiber 2003, 299-306.
[539] Jones 1993, 293.
[540] Kotsonas 2012, 170; 2011b, 142.
[541] See Catalogue.
[542] Ibid., 181.

FIGURE 12: IN THE LEFT PHOTO THERE ARE POTS FROM A MODERN KNOSSIAN WORKSHOP. IN THE RIGHT A POT FROM A RETHYMNIAN WORKSHOP (PHOTOGRAPHS BY THE AUTHOR).

the modern juglets in Crete are separated into two categories, the ones used for raki, which is the local popular spirit, and the others for pouring olive oil in small quantities in meals. Based on the vessels I saw, I noted that those used for raki have a round mouth, with a small round lip. Curiously, some share a distant resemblance to the Attic lekythoi (they had no handle either). The other category consists of trefoil-lipped juglets of the same size (about 10cm). They are used for pouring olive oil and share a similarity with the Phoenician juglets of the EIA, having only a different mouth. In the following picture, one can see those pots before the second firing, which gives them a glazed appearance.

The potters were very concerned with the final colour and glaze of the pot, besides its shape. A potter at Rethymnon told me that the red and orange colours (which are similar to the ancient frit) were very nice and attractive but, because of their chemical composition, could not hold spirits, such as raki, since their clay is very porous. As a result, few hours after the liquid is poured into the pot, a layer of moisture appears at its foot. With olive oil, however, there is no such problem, because it is thicker than raki due to its molecular composition. For this reason, they tend to use blue quartz as a glaze for raki pots, while for oil pot they prefer the red/orange glaze.

In my inquiry about the shape of the pots I was told that they do not follow any ancient tradition, but are more the results of experiments aimed at the most attractive shapes and functions. The shape is also dictated by practical reasons: for example, the oil must be poured in small quantities hence the narrow neck. The handle must also allow the hand to pour the oil with a short movement so as not to require much effort. In the photo from the Rethymnian workshop, one can see an example of a not very successful form of pot. The maker of the pot explained to me that this form demands more effort from the wrist in order to pour the oil and this was not convenient at all. For this reason, he decided not to produce this form again.

With this example, I wish to show that there is always the possibility of experimenting with pot shapes in order to get the desired results. In certain cases, the shape serves not so much an artistic need but is rather dictated by the liquid it contains. There are tourists that buy them for decorative purposes, but most of these modern pots have a domestic use, in houses or taverns in Crete. One can see that modern Cretan pottery makers are very concerned with the function of the pot and not that much with its appearance. Perhaps, ancient Cretans were also concerned with how they could carry and use oil fragrances and for this reason, they selected, experimented and eventually imitated the BoR juglets.

ii. Second-Level Analysis: Imports, Imitations and Society

In this part of the analysis, I combine the evidence from the spatial distribution of the tombs and the location of the cemeteries with the data from the distribution of the imports and their imitation discovered in these tombs. Out of the 166 tombs registered, 48 have at least one Near Eastern import in their inventory. Out of these 48 tombs, 40 are chamber tombs, and two are tholos tombs, five pit-caves and one pithos burial. The dominance of the chamber tomb structure is no surprise since it is the most widespread type of tomb in EIA Knossos. It is important, though, that other tombs and burial types are represented. No import was found in shaft graves and most of them had been emptied anyway long before their discovery.

The fact that only 48 tombs have imports indicates that not all the tombs contain Near Eastern material. Furthermore, even in cases where a few imported objects were discovered in a tomb, this does not necessarily mean that all the burials in this tomb were accompanied by Near Eastern objects. As already stated, is not always easy to associate a specific context to an import even if the tomb is undisturbed, due to the chaotic state of the tombs because of multiple burials.

In some cases, numbers can be even less encouraging: The total number of pots from published tombs is 5203 pots. Near Eastern pots represent only 1.11% of the total number and the rest of the Near Eastern objects represent only about 7% of the total number of objects in all the cemeteries of Knossos. In many cases, Near Eastern objects are restricted only to a few faience beads per tomb. This amount of evidence might seem limited to serve as an exclusive basis for an analysis of Knossian society.

However, this can become extremely valuable if one takes into consideration two very important factors: the first is the location of the discovered tombs. The second is a number of local products produced as copies of Near Eastern imports and their context.[543] The argument that the data is limited could be valid if the number of tombs was also limited. However, a total number of 48 out of 166 tombs cannot be considered as a limited amount of evidence. Furthermore, even the Attic pots, which constitute the largest amount of foreign pottery in Knossos represent no more than the 3.5% of all pots.[544] That makes Cypriot pots one of the most numerous objects coming to Knossos from overseas.

For this reason, one must seek further evidence and relations regarding the presence of imports in the tombs. This can be achieved by associating a different kind of data. One could start from the fact that there are tombs that do not contain imports at all and others that do. Thus, one can attempt an initial comparison between the tombs with and without imports. In the case of the Knossian tombs, the presence and the quality of imports has been hitherto linked to the richest and most powerful members of the society or even in some rare cases to rich foreigners.[545]

For this comparison, I will use the three categories of objects as analysed in the previous chapter and three different quantified groups of objects: group A, with tombs with less than ten pots and other objects irrespective of their kind. Group B, which includes the tombs where the total number of pots and objects is less than 50; and group C, which contains the richest and best furnished tombs, with a total number of pots and objects ranging from 50 to 524. The latter figure represents the tomb with the largest number of finds, which is Tomb P at Fortetsa SE.

The first category includes the tombs with Near Eastern imports which belong to each group (A, B or C). In the same way, the second one includes the tombs with imports or imitations of tombs. Finally, in the third category I have placed tombs containing imitations.

The majority of the tombs belong to Group A, while the minority to Group C. The 41 tombs of Group C are the richest in general but also are most of the tombs containing Near Eastern imports, imports or imitations and imitations also belong to Group C. This indicates that most of the evidence in this study is confined to the richest tombs and that those Near Eastern imports and their imitations were a privilege of the richest or more prominent members of the elite.

---

[543] As explained in the previous section.
[544] Coldstream 1996a; 2002.
[545] Boardman 1967.

Objects per Tomb	Total number of Tombs per group	Tombs with Near Eastern Imports per group	Tombs with Imports or Imitations per group	Tombs with Imitations per group
(Group A) 0-9	66	1 out 66 (1.51%)	0 out 66 (0%)	4 out 66 (6.06%)
(Group B) 10-49	59	15 out 59 (25.42%)	4 out 59 (6.77%)	7 out 59 (11.86%)
(Group C) 50-524	41	29 out 41 (70.73%)	12 out 41 (29.26%)	26 out 41 (63.41%)

TABLE 18: CLASSIFICATION OF TOMBS ACCORDING TO IMPORTS.

In a further analysis of the evidence one may see that as far as the Near Eastern imports are concerned, 29 tombs of the group C are tombs containing the largest amount of Near Eastern pots and objects in comparison to the other two groups. This distribution though is by no means even. Some tombs contain much more imports than others even within group C. The distribution of the finds of uncertain provenance (category two in the catalogue and fourth column on the Table 18) is much more limited.

The objects falling in this category (bronze rod tripods, obeloi and fire-dogs) are found only in sixteen tombs. Even though this is the most limited of the three catalogue categories, again 75% of the tombs containing these objects falls also into group C. Nothing associated with this category was found in group A.

What initially seems to be a surprise is that almost the 65% of the tombs containing imitations are also found in group C. This is rather unexpected because in archaeology it is commonly thought[546] that an imitation is produced in order to satisfy the need of people (normally poorer) who cannot acquire the original object that other people (normally richer) can. However, this analysis has shown that imitations, which are pots in their vast majority, are found in the richer Knossian tombs.

---

[546] The most celebrated example is Vickers and the theory on Black and Red figure Attic pottery (Vickers and Gill 1994).

Concerning the Near Eastern imports, Tombs P from Fortetsa SE, Tomb II from Khaniale Teke and Tombs 292, 285, 219 from the KMF, apart from being five of the tombs with the largest amount of pots and objects (together they contain 22.5% of all finds), are also those with the highest number of Near Eastern imports. These five tombs contain almost 49% of the imports in all the cemeteries. The same tombs contain about 63% of the objects of uncertain provenance but only about 30% of the imitations. The amount of imported material and locally produced material makes these five tombs exceptionally rich.

These five tombs were used, not always uninterruptedly, during most of the EIA: from the LPG to the LO for Tombs P, 285 and 219, from the PGB to the EO for Tomb II[547] at Khaniale Teke and from the PGB/EG to the LO for Tomb 292. Especially, the use of Tombs 285 (KMF) and Tomb P (Fortetsa SE) was uninterrupted. At the same time, though, there are burials of a totally different type which also contain quite a few imports as well. For example, an isolated pithos burial (Tomb 78, KMF) is the next richer in imports following the five ones mentioned above and contains faience amulets, such scarabs and faience figurines of Egyptian deities.

The main difference of this tomb though is its late date (LG/EO) and probably its function. According to Webb[548] this tomb must have belonged to a child of foreign (perhaps Near Eastern?) origin. In any case, this is not a typical dead. In the KMF site, in general, no infants and very young children have been found.[549] On the other hand, inferences for Near Eastern people, most probably Phoenicians, buried at Knossos have been found from partly published tombs: at Atsalenio area a reused Phoenician cippus was found inside a chamber tomb.[550] Another anthropomorphic cippus discovered at KNC.[551] Finally, the bowl with the Phoenician inscription (Tomb J, Teke) could also indicate another foreigner.

To return to the subject of the richness of the tombs, it is also true that all the chamber tombs at Knossos are associated with the elite, as shown in Chapter 2, even if this elite is hierarchical in a pyramid shape.[552] In the following chart, one can see the ten richest/best furnished tombs across all Knossian cemeteries in relation to the Near Eastern and non-Near Eastern objects and pots they contain.

---

[547] I am only referring to the reuse of the tomb after the initial LBA use.
[548] Webb 1996, 606.
[549] Musgrave 1969, 680.
[550] Kourou and Karetsou 1998, 243-251.
[551] Kourou and Grammatikaki 1998.
[552] Snodgrass 1996, 596.

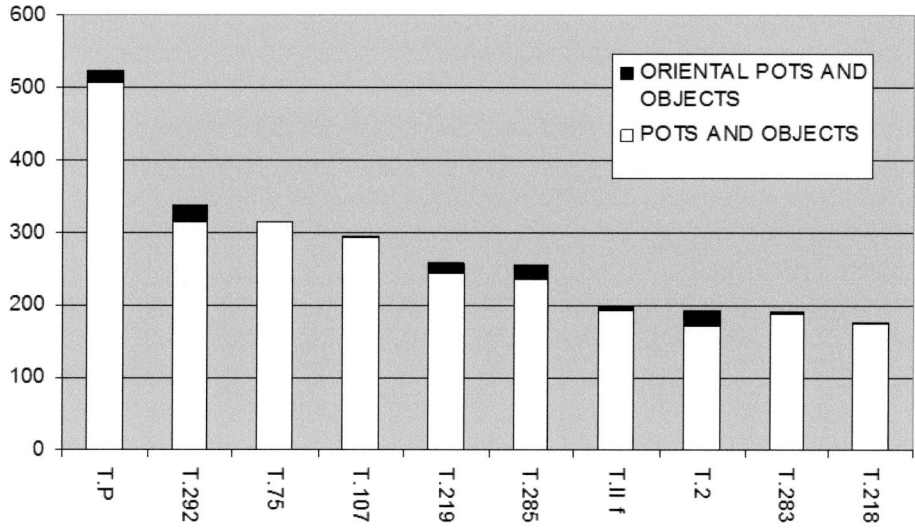

TABLE 19: GRAPH 15: THE TEN RICHEST TOMBS ACROSS ALL CEMETERIES.

The five tombs which contain 49% of all the Near Eastern imports are naturally present on this graph. Tombs P and 292 are the richest while the remaining are in positions 5(Tomb 219), 6 (Tomb 285) and 8 (Khaniale Tholos tomb). The rest of the rich tombs also contain some imported material but in considerable smaller quantities. Based on this chart one can assume that the increased presence of Near Eastern imports is a sign of wealth, but on the other hand, the limited presence or even the absence of Near Eastern imports does not necessarily mean the opposite. This means that not all the elite members of Knossos shared the same taste for imported material. For example, the undisturbed tomb 75 at KMF site, one of the wealthiest of all tombs, despite its 226 pots and 89 objects, it has only one glass bead (75.109), probably originated from Near East.

In this case and in order to approach the issue of the presence of imports in more depth, one should examine the distribution of the tombs individually within each cemetery, since most of them are organised in smaller groups (clusters). The formation of tombs in clusters apparently indicates a kind of connection between tombs belonging to the same group. The site that deserves more discussion regarding tomb clusters is the KMF where most of them are located. On this site which is one of the oldest burial grounds of the EIA, at least seven clusters have been identified.[553] At the same time, it is the most intensively used not only by Iron Age tombs but also by Hellenistic and early Christian graves.

---

[553] At least seven clusters were noted by Cavanagh (1996, 657). He also includes in these clusters one from the Teke Cemetery. In the present study, however, this cluster is treated separately.

It is the site where Knossians probably had their main cemetery until the Arab conquest and the final decline of the city.

If Catling and Coldstream are right and this site was established (or better saying re-established) as a cemetery after the end of the LM, then the first clusters created there are beyond doubt the group of tombs around the complex of SM pit-caves 200-202 and pit-cave 186. The complex of 200-202 forms one burial structure which must have been of great importance for SM Knossians:[554] *"Tomb 200 contained the remains of a single individual (probably a woman). Tomb 201 had the remains of two adults (perhaps man and woman) and, less certainly, a child. Tomb 202 was empty except for tiny scraps of bone"*.[555] Tomb 186 had only one chamber and the cremated remains of a not very old person, probably a man were found there.[556] The grave offerings were weapons, such as an iron knife, a dirk and whetstones.

The bronze stand from Cyprus found in this tomb (201.1) is also an ancient import, even probably by SM standards. Catling calls it an heirloom and dates it to the 12th century BC.[557] Even if this stand is not an heirloom the fragmentary boar's tusk helmet (201.14) found in the same grave definitely is. This is a clear example of how the LBA 'warlike' past was appreciated. Despite the fact that imports do appear in this cluster in such an early period, most of the SM tombs do not contain imports. In fact, they are the poorest tombs in terms of Near Eastern material. Moreover, all the imports in the burial complex 200-202 are associated with Cyprus and not with the Phoenician coast. It must be pointed out that this tomb does not really belong to any cluster.[558] Rather, the clusters of the chamber tombs were probably formed having this tomb as a point of reference[559] at the same time or slightly later (since they are also dated to the SM times). South of this burial complex, there are only a few scattered tombs with no obvious association with each other.

On the contrary, the development of the later cemetery was towards the north. In other words, from a geographical and spatial point of view, the burial monument 200-202 and Tomb 186 are the starting point from which all the clusters of the chamber tombs began the site of KMF. In the following map, one can see the distribution of the imports according to the distribution of

---

[554] Coldstream and Catling 1996, 715.
[555] Coldstream and Catling 1996, 192.
[556] Ibid., 191.
[557] Coldstream and Catling 1996, 193.
[558] Clusters I and II in the following map.
[559] A similar phenomenon of satellite burials has been observed at Lefkandi. However, the monumental Euboean burial structure is an isolated phenomenon.

the tombs and clusters. Clusters I, II, III, IV and VIII are grouped around the same area while clusters V and VI much further north. Most of the tombs have only one import (blue colour).[560] The rest with more than one import are highlighted in red. In the exceptional case where a tomb has more than ten imports, is highlighted with green colour. The reason I have chosen the amount of ten imports per tomb as an indication is that not many tombs with such high number of imports can be found at Knossos.

Clusters I (Tombs 16, 40, 106, 112) and II (24, 25, 30, 45, 56), which were constructed next to 200-202, contain almost no other Near Eastern imports except few faience beads and one Phoenician juglet (56.10). Overall, most of the tombs of cluster VIII[561] are much later than the tombs of Clusters I and II, which are dated to the SM. This cluster is different than I and II, only because Tomb 219 is part of it. As already mentioned this is one of the five tombs with the largest number of Near Eastern imports and one of the richest in general. It must be said though that Tomb 219 differs in many aspects from the other tombs of this cluster. It is bigger and has a slightly different orientation. It is also positioned at the north edge of the cluster. It is of a much earlier date in comparison to the rest of the tombs.

This tomb was also found next to a fence of an early Christian church and perhaps was associated with other (destroyed) tombs. I believe that Tomb 219 must be seen individually and not in association with cluster VIII. This tomb contains ivory handles, which might also be another direct reference to the highest level of the Knossian society. Tomb 218 (another extremely rich tomb) is also an isolated phenomenon due to the partially excavated area north of 219. Clusters III and IV contain a few imported pots and beads.

However, the cluster with the largest amount of imports in the KMF site is cluster VI which is located on the other extreme of the site (about 200m away from cluster I). Cluster VI has the largest amount of imported material because Tombs 285 and 292 are part of it. In the same cluster, there are other tombs, such as 283, which also contains one import. At the same time, Tombs 283 and 285 contain almost all the obeloi and fire-dogs found in the Knossian cemeteries. Tomb 219 has the second higher quantity of obeloi.

Cluster VI is probably one of the latest clusters in date (at the end of LPG). In fact, most of the tombs were probably constructed in the PGB. The fact that

---

[560] Cavanagh and Mee (2009, 185) used colours for highlighting tombs with different architectural features, in the map of Perati cemetery (Iakovides 1970, 12). In the present thesis different colours are marking the quantity of the imports in each tomb.
[561] I use VIII instead of VII because Cavanagh used number VII for the cluster at Teke tombs.

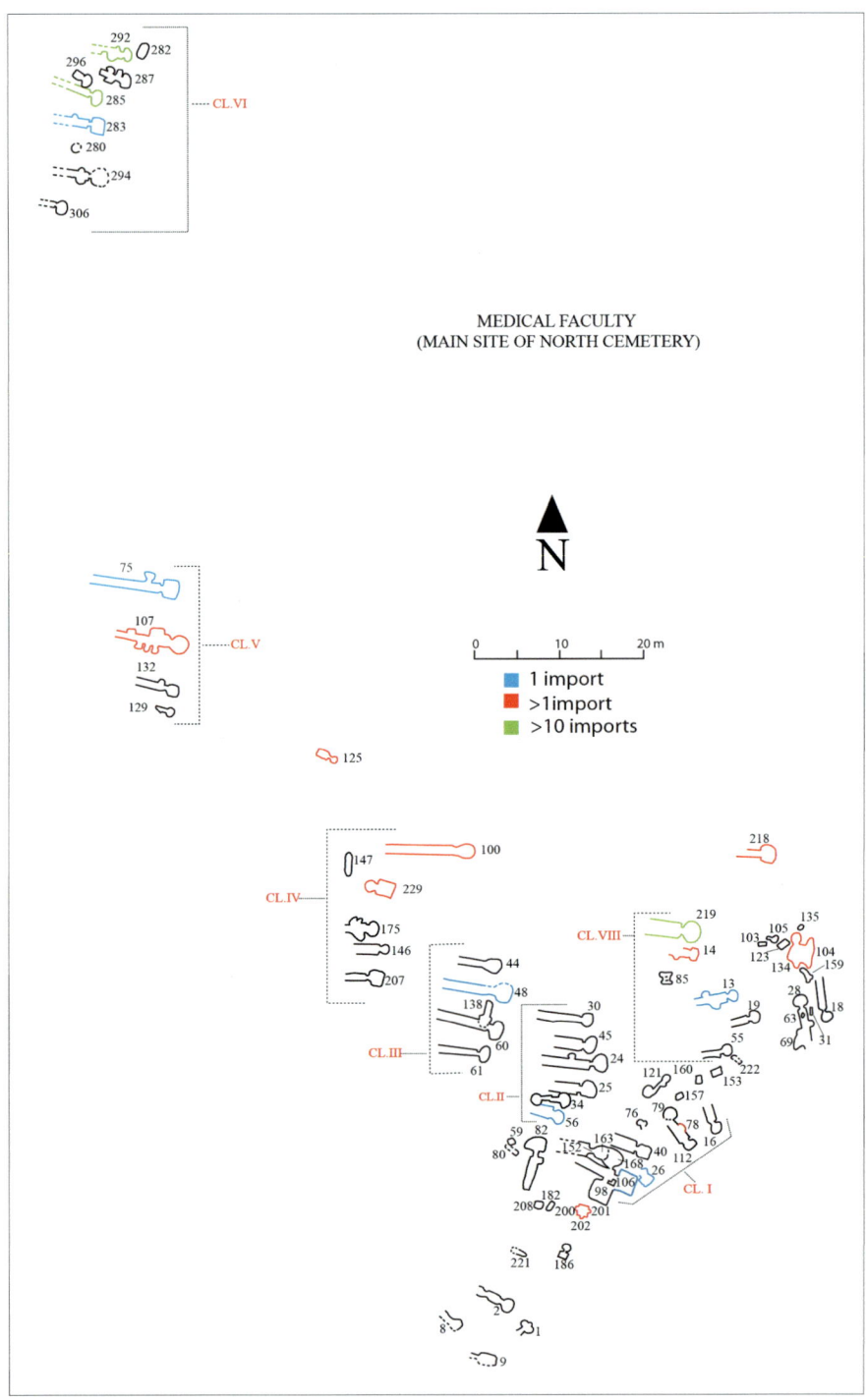

FIGURE 13: DISTRIBUTION OF IMPORTS AT KMF (AFTER COLDSTREAM AND CATLIN 1996, FIGURE 1). REPRODUCED WITH PERMISSION OF THE BRITISH SCHOOL AT ATHENS.

this group is at such a significant distance from the SM centre of the cemetery might signify the existence of a different class of people or families. It may also imply the existence of another elite group which emerged as a competitive class after the establishment of the initial elite of the cemetery whose members were lying around the core (200-202) of the old cemetery.

Clusters I and II continue to receive burials until the end of the EIA. This probably means that within the same cemetery different elites (probably associated with family ties as well) manifested their competition through lavish funerals. Clusters I and II, being so near to the most aristocratic tombs, reveal that the people who constructed them were much more interested in maintaining close bonds to tombs 200-202 and 186. The need for a part of the Knossian population to be buried near the area of the first SM tombs can be seen in the plan of tomb 106[562] which depicts only a small part of Cluster I which is the most crowded of the whole cemetery.

On the other hand, cluster VI is at the northernmost limit of the KMF burial site and for this reason, the people who constructed these tombs might have wanted to manifest their own status as a social class or elite. From this short survey, it becomes evident that tombs containing more than ten Near Eastern imports (except for tomb 219 at the margin of cluster III) are found only in a specific part of the site. Furthermore, the amount of the imports that this cluster contains represents 39% of all the Near Eastern imports of the cemetery. I believe that the distance between Clusters I and VI reveals a political diversity in the highest rank of the Knossian society at the LPG and at the beginning of the PGB. Furthermore, the fact that cluster V which is nearer to the core of the cemetery than cluster VI, begun its function in PGB after the inauguration of cluster VI is very important. It reveals that for choosing a location for constructing a tomb there must have been reasons unrelated to the suitability of the terrain. Apart of the imports, one should have a look at the categories import or imitation and local imitation. As far as the category of imports or imitations is concerned, Tomb 285 has at least 25 items, while regarding imitations, Tomb 292 contains ten pots.

However, despite the fact Cluster VI and Tomb 219, made by people displaying luxurious items during funeral rituals and expensive oils and fragrances (i.e. BoR juglets), those tombs were still part of the North Cemetery. Therefore, this emerging elite, despite the possible political and/or aesthetic differences with clusters I, II and III, still maintained a position (though remote) in the central

---

[562] Coldstrean and Catling 1996, figures 33-34.

cemetery. One should bear in mind that despite their differences, the people buried in all these tombs and clusters came from the same settlement.

As far as the dating of the clusters is concerned all clusters except cluster VI have tombs dated back to SM. Two of them (and probably the most celebrated) are the burial structure 200-202 and Tomb 186 which are probably the earliest. In these two tombs after the initial burials entered the tomb, no other activity occurred. In most of the other cases, all tombs were reopened and used for more than one generation. This practice does not differentiate the tombs with imports from the ones without imports because the vast majority of the tombs do contain multiple burials for more than one generation. It seems also that in the KMF one can also observe a clash between different traditions, where each group could choose a heritage. However, before making any conclusion, it is worth having a look at the rest of sites and cemeteries.

Heading to the Teke burial site, most of the tombs were not found very disturbed but contained rather few imports. In this site, six out of the thirteen tombs contained at least one import. Most of the tombs in this cluster were in use during the same period (PGB). The dating of the finds though can be quite different. An example already mentioned before is the bronze bowl with the Phoenician inscription with a date ranging from 1100 to 900 BC. This bowl together with the other two bronze bowls (a mesomplalos phiale and a lotus handle jug) found in tomb G can be interpreted either as luxury gifts or as personal belongings of the diceased, or both. The two Near Eastern pots (a Bich. III and BoR I juglets from tombs A and H), on the other hand, fit better to the general dating of the tombs in which they were discovered. No local imitations of Near Eastern pottery were found. In the following map, one can see the spatial distribution of the Teke Tombs.

As far as the grouping of the tombs is concerned, one can notice that the few Near Eastern imports are located only in the first cluster This group of tombs is at a considerable distance from the KMF and one can again observe a degree of independence from the main funeral site. Imports are not too many but the quality and significance of the bronze bowls might reveal a special relationship of gift exchanges with foreign people or trade.

A site which was found in a very poor state of preservation is the Fortetsa NE, which constitutes another part of the North Cemetery. I have attempted a reconstruction of the different tomb groups that apparently belong to the same burial site in Figure 15.

The location of the most important tombs at this site was lost after their excavation before World War II (TFT, L and Π). However, the gold diadem from

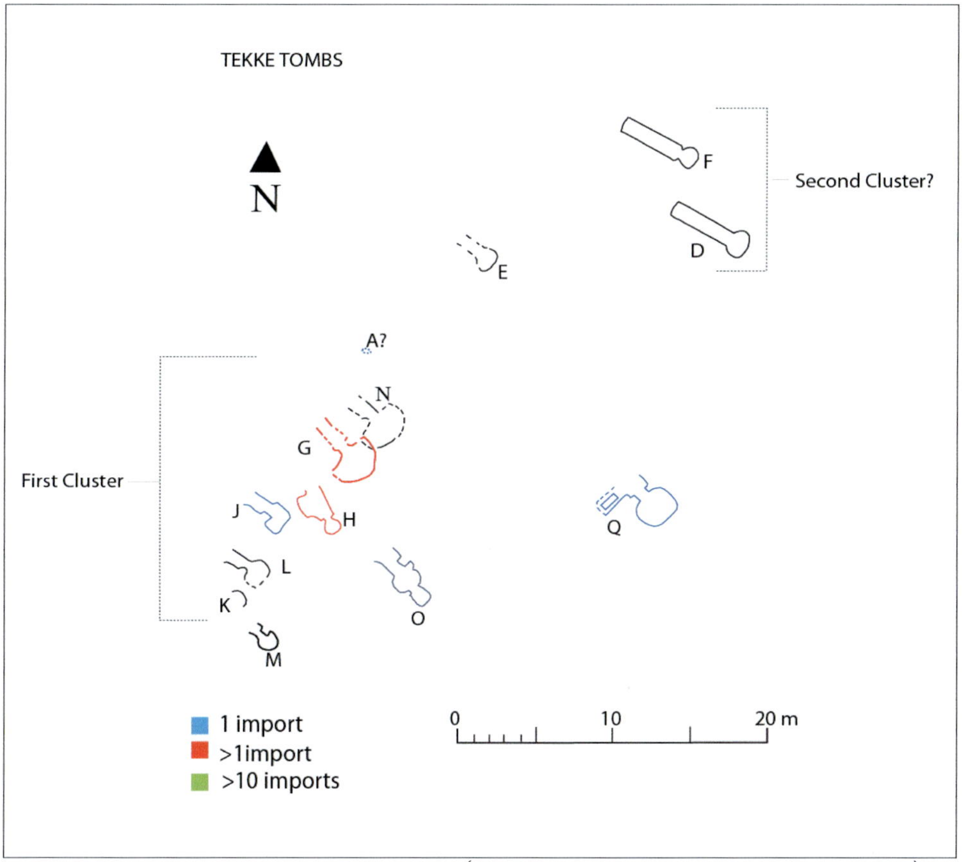

CHAPTER 4: WHO GETS THE IMPORTS AND WHO THE IMITATIONS?   125

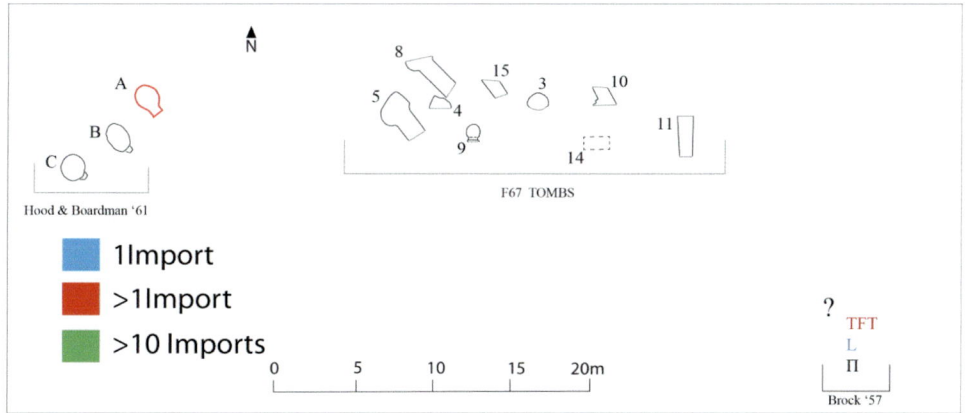

FIGURE 14: DISTRIBUTION OF IMPORTS AT TEKE (AFTER COLDSTREAM AND CATLING 1996, FIGURE 2). REPRODUCED WITH PERMISSION OF THE BRITISH SCHOOL AT ATHENS.

FIGURE 15: DISTRIBUTION OF IMPORTS AT FORTETSA NE (AFTER COLDSTREAM AND CATLING 1996, FIGURES 1-6; HOOD AND BOARDMAN 1961, 68). THE PRESENT AUTHOR MADE THE SYNTHESIS OF MAPS OF DIFFERENT EXCAVATIONS. REPRODUCED WITH PERMISSION OF THE BRITISH SCHOOL AT ATHENS.

Cyprus (tomb L) and finds from TFT tomb suggest that this lost cluster must have been the most important at this site. The distance from the main core of the cemetery is again considerable.

A great need for Near Eastern objects can also be seen in the Khaniale Teke tombs, even if two of these tombs were found almost destroyed. Boardman[563] suggested that the gold jewellery from the tholos tomb could have belonged to a Near Eastern craftsman and his family. This hypothesis has been criticised by Hoffman[564] and Kotsonas[565] on the grounds of the social hierarchy. Both have stressed the link between the circulation of metals and their control by the elite of the region. Living aside this debate, a large amount of imported material has been discovered in this tomb. Apart from two pots from Cyprus, all the other imported finds are related to ornaments and metalwork. This fact reveals how misleading the partial study of pottery alone can be.

Most of the products originated from the Levantine coast and were probably Phoenician imitations of Egyptian products. This means that the people buried in the tomb had an obvious taste for all these Near Eastern products. It appears however that the Knossians who used this tomb did not share the same taste for Near Eastern pottery, as they did for metal objects. The vast majority of

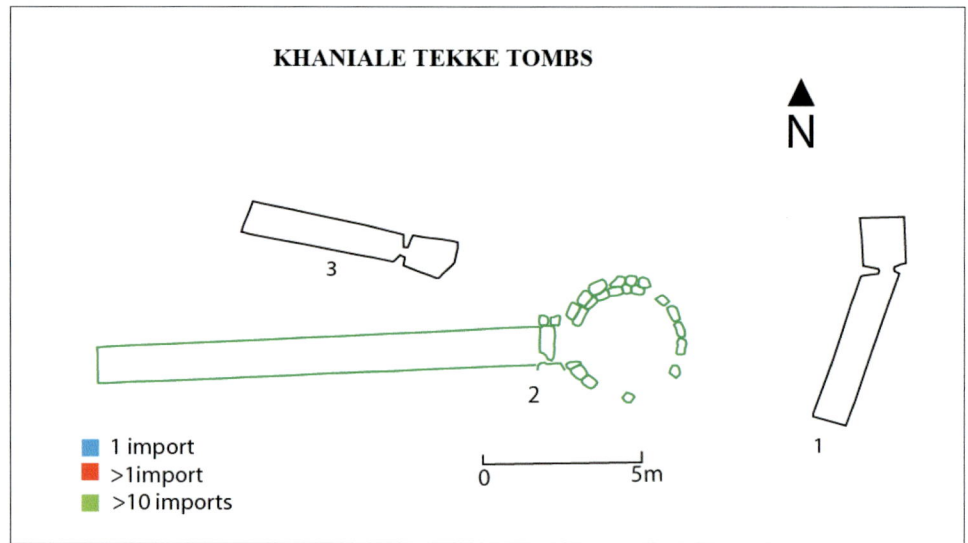

FIGURE 16: DISTRIBUTION OF IMPORTS AT KHANIALE TEKE (AFTER HUTCHINSON AND BOARDMAN 1954, 215). REPRODUCED WITH PERMISSION OF THE BRITISH SCHOOL AT ATHENS.

---

[563] Boardman 1967, 57-67.
[564] Hoffman 1997, 191-234.
[565] Kotsonas 2006, 149-172.

pots are either local or come from Athens and the Aegean. This impression, however, changes slightly if one takes into consideration six Creto-Cypriot lekythoi found in the tombs. The fact that a LM tomb is reused reveals a clear connection with the Minoan past. A broken symbol of 'horns of consecration' was discovered in the tomb. Despite the fact the Teke Tholos Tomb has been found in a looted state, it reveals that those who used this tomb in the PGB were very fond not only of the Minoan past but also of imports coming from the East. This feature suggests once more that these tombs must have belonged to a PGB elite, which was either inventing a connection with a LM tomb and its past or that the people buried there did not want to associate themselves to those buried at the KMF site.

The next site is Fortetsa SE, which all the archaeologists who have written about EIA Knossos agree is a separated site from KMF. Evidence from the surveys, suggests that there were not EIA tombs between the site of Fortetsa SE and the North Cemetery. This site is smaller than the KMF and much more restricted in comparison to the extended North Cemetery (including all its sub-groups), it also had a different character. The following map illustrates the distribution of the imports.

The fact that ten tombs were found almost intact is of great importance. From the point of view of the Near Eastern imports, the significance of this cemetery is probably of equal importance to that of the KMF. At Fortetsa SE more than half of the tombs have at least one Near Eastern import. Tomb P, which contains more pots and objects than any other tomb across all the cemeteries, is apparently positioned between two different groups of tombs (first and second group). In his study of the iron objects from the North Cemetery, Snodgrass[566] makes a comparison between the two cemeteries (KNC and Fortetsa SE). He separates the tombs in groups according to the kind of iron objects they contained (arms, tools etc.) and states that both groups that used the cemeteries had similar customs and *"an individual in one group, of whatever status, would have his close counterpart in the neighbouring group"*.[567] In terms of the iron objects, Snodgrass must be right, but this might not be the case for Near Eastern imports. First, the Fortetsa SE cemetery inaugurated its function in the end, or after the end of the SM. The distribution of the tombs in a linear arrangement is much clearer than in the KMF cemetery, where there is a persistence of burying the dead near the 200-202 complex. At Fortetsa SE, people did not construct new tombs after MG but continued to use the same ones instead of constructing pit-tombs or other tomb types,

---

[566] Snodgrass 1996, 596.
[567] Ibid.

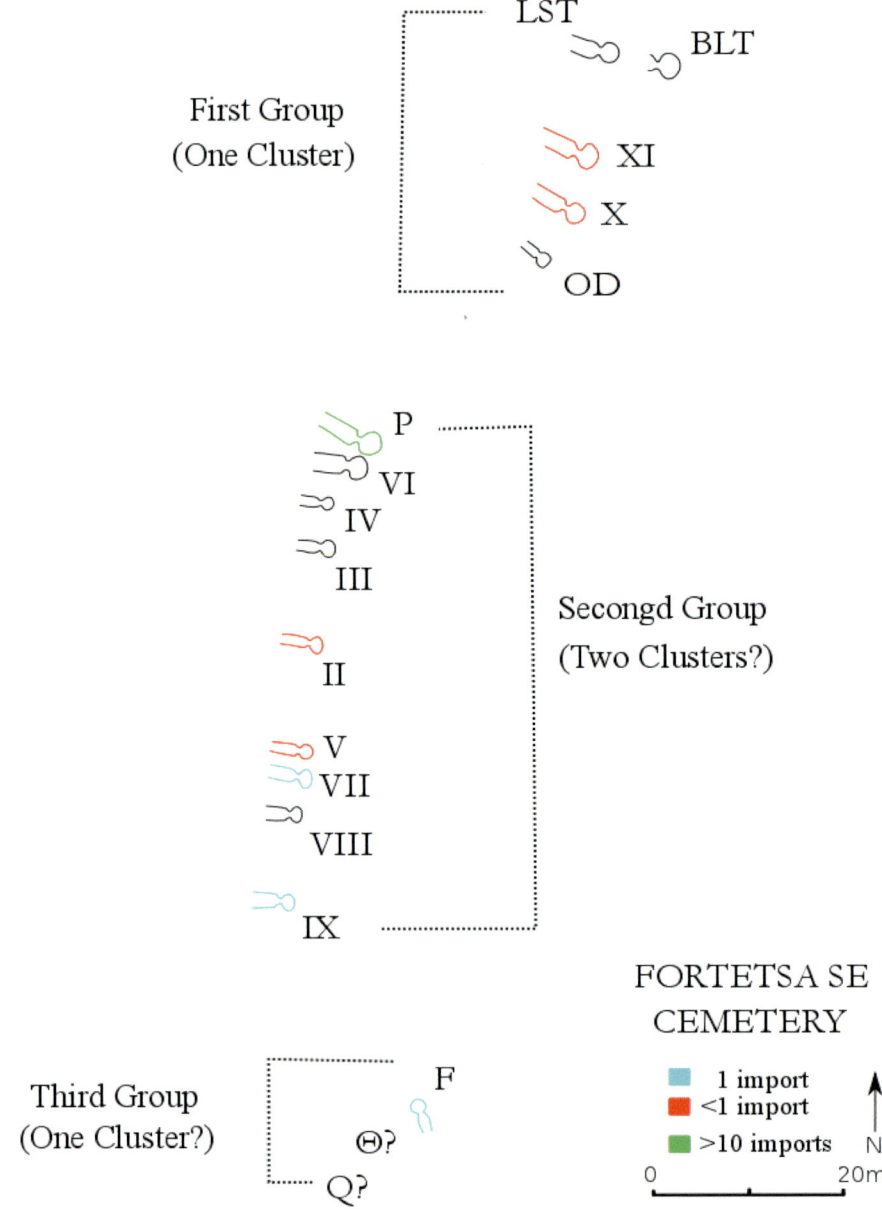

Figure 17 Distribution of imports at Fortetsa NE (after Brock 1957, figure 2). Reproduced with permission of the British School at Athens.

which are easier to construct than a chamber tomb. Overall, there seems to be a strict hierarchic order at the Fortetsa SE that is not found in the chaotic KNC. The fact that tomb P, the richest tomb (at least of offerings) and the with the most burials of all Knossian tombs is located at the Fortetsa SE cemetery reveals that the surrounding tombs were not meant to compete this tomb. Tomb P dominates the cemetery.

At the Kephala Ridge cemetery, the amount of evidence is very limited. Not many things can be said about the location of the tombs, except that all of them seem to have been constructed before the EIA and, thus, the cluster of these tombs is more associated with those of the SM cemeteries. However, it is interesting to highlight that in the SM a part of the Knossian society did not choose to bury its people at the North Cemetery. Importantly, three out of seven tombs contain at least one import. No imported pottery or imitations were found. The bronze tripod found there is considered either as an import or as a faithful imitation.

At Ayios Ioannis, even though at least two tombs were discovered with rich content in terms of furniture, (Tomb I and Tomb VIII), the only Near Eastern imports found there were a few fragments of faience beads. It must be pointed out that tomb I contained 59 pots and four objects respectively, while Tomb VIII contained 15 pots and five small finds, but none of them was Near Eastern.

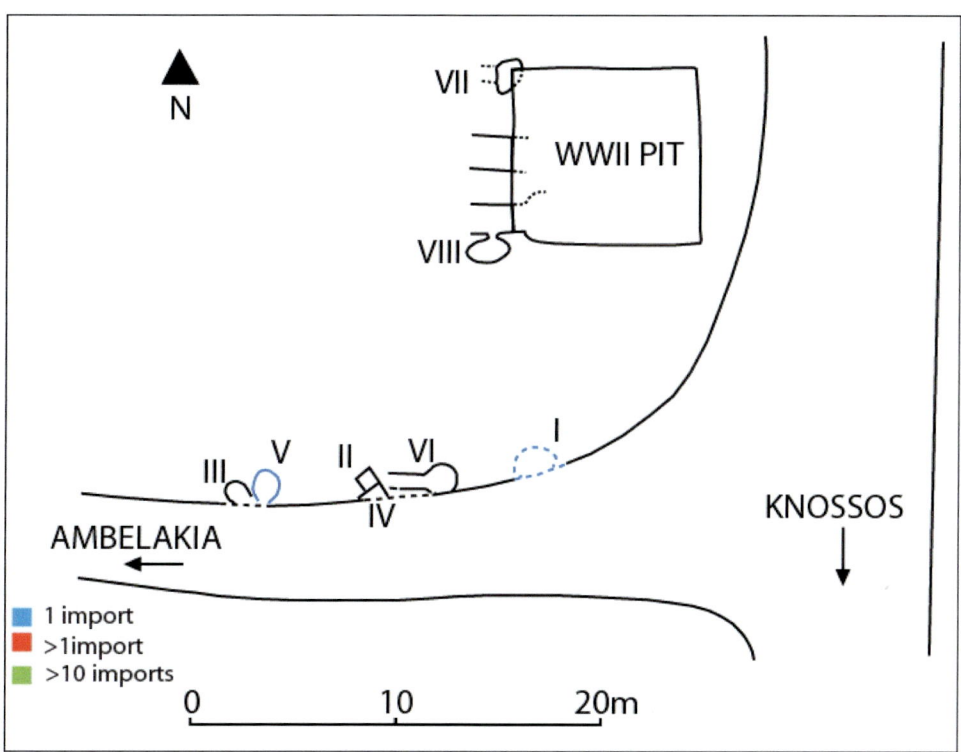

FIGURE 18: DISTRIBUTION OF IMPORTS AT AYIOS IOANNIS (AFTER BOARDMAN 1960, 128). REPRODUCED WITH PERMISSION OF THE BRITISH SCHOOL AT ATHENS.

The absence of Near Eastern finds and close imitations of Near Eastern products is either due to the destruction and looting of the tombs or because the people buried there did not have a taste for such goods. Tomb I, for example, even though it contained at least 59 pots and was in use during the same period as tomb V, has no imports in its context.

In Atsalenio, there are G tombs which have not been fully published. It is more than clear that this burial site is distinct from the North Cemetery. It is also clear that the use of Near Eastern pottery must have been important to the people buried there and therefore exact copies and freer imitations were also used in this cemetery, for example in Tomb A. The date of Tomb A and its context though is more similar to the Fortetsa SE than to the North Cemetery. Perhaps the smaller satellite cemeteries had more in common with each other than with the central one. Tombs A and B at Atsalenio, which are of identical construction and date, contain a small but interesting portion of Near Eastern pottery and local imitations. Tomb A has one Cypriot oinochoe and one local imitation and maybe this reveals the need to copy something that at that time was not abundant.

The isolated tomb at the Lower Gypsades Hill contains only a few imports but its importance lies more in its isolation and in the fact that a considerable number of pots (at least ten) are adaptations of BoR juglets. Finally, in the reused Minoan cemeteries of Upper Gypsades and Mavro Spilio no imports were found apart from an iron knife in tomb VII at Upper Gypsades. The main difference between the two cemeteries is that Upper Gypsades was reused only at the end of the BA, while Mavro Spilio almost at the end of the EIA. It is a surprise, though, that in the reused tombs at Mavro Spilio not even one Creto-Cypriot lekythos was found in a period that this pot was very popular among the Knossian society (LG-LO).

Returning to the imports, so far it has been suggested that the tombs which contained imports belonged to the highest rank of the Knossian elite. The use of imports is probably related to the manifestation of the status a dead person and a lavish ritual during the funeral. It also related to a part of the Knossian society whose eclecticism served as means of differentiating itself from the rather more conservative people buried at the old centre of the KMF Cemetery. Regarding imitations and spatial distribution, it must be noted that from the 160 pots which are either imitations of Near Eastern imports, 20 are juglets deriving from prototypes not found in Knossos (Red micaceous clay oinochoe, imitation of Cypriot Black slip I-II). From the remaining 140 pots, about 40 are close copies of BoR I or II. The majority of these juglets are in Tombs 283, 219, 293 (KMF) and P (Fortetsa SE). All these tombs represent an elite which fully emerged in the 9th century. The fact however that certain tombs were used for first time in the end of SM/EPG (tomb XI at Fortetsa SE) perhaps reveals some earlier attempts of these elite groups.

Inside these tombs Near Eastern pots and their contemporary imitations were found in close association, probably accompanying the same burial. Knossians needed to use the unguents coming from the East inside in BoR juglets and initially, this need was covered by creating close imitations of Near Eastern imports that presumably carried the same content. However, a few years later, several free imitations and adaptations stepped in to satisfy the demand. The Creto-Cypriot lekythos is the most famous example. Although it partly departed from the original pot, it still maintained the basic Near Eastern features of the prototype, without any influence from local or Attic traditions. Only in LO the Creto-Cypriot lekythoi acquire some local decoration of local pedigree.[568]

What is striking, though, is that Tombs P and 219 are again the ones containing the highest number of Creto-Cypriot lekythoi, even though these pots are more evenly distributed than other shapes. It also seems that the earliest Creto-Cypriot lekythoi were used first in the MG in Tomb 292 together with Bich. III juglets. If one also considers that in each tomb no more than three (maximum seven) burials were deposited per generation, then there is again the possibility that both original pots and imitations were used in the same burial. BoR juglets and their imitations were most probably considered of equal importance. Wealthy Knossians probably did not even distinguish between imports and faithful local imitations. However, the opposite view can also be that there were the rich Knossians who created a demand for Knossian imitations, because of a probable shortage in the importation of the originals or because they wanted to control the production of this product. For the Knossians, the shape and decoration of the jug must have been the trademark indicating the oils and scents that those jugs were carrying.

iii. Cluster Analysis

Another way to approach this large amount of evidence is the combination of a series of variables using average linkage, in order to get a deeper understanding of the mortuary and social aspects of the Knossians. This will be a combination not only of the distribution of the imports, but also the size of each tomb and the number of burials found in each one of them. As shown above, there is a series of tombs such as Tomb P at Fortetsa SE, Tombs 292, 285, 219 at the KMF

---

[568] Coldstream 2002b, 42.

and Tomb II at Khaniale Teke), which have been associated with all the possible different categories related of Near Eastern pots and their imitations.

The dating of these tombs in relation to their location has also revealed that they belonged to a part of the elite which did not wish any longer to be a part (after LPG) of the elite which was buried around Tombs 200-202 and 186 Tombs at the KMF site. The use of Near Eastern imports was an instrument of differentiation. In order to test this hypothesis, one should run a cluster analysis with a wide use of variables. In this way, data are interpreted from a totally different point of view. The variables to be used will be related not only to Near Eastern objects but also to how rich or not a tomb can be and certainly how many burials it might contain. Namely, the variables are:

1. number of pots per tomb
2. number of Near Eastern pots per tomb
3. number of finds per tomb
4. number of Near Eastern finds per tomb
5. number of imports or imitations per tomb
6. number of imitations per tomb
7. number of burials per tomb
8. chamber's surface area

The combination of eight variables seems to be a safe tool to analyse all the different kinds of evidence from the study of the catalogues of the cemeteries. Cremation burials were calculated by counting cremation urns even if they were empty, as explained in Chapter 2. All the data can be seen in Appendices I and II at the end of the book. With inhumations, it was relatively easier. The biggest difficulty was calculating the chambers' surface because this is not provided in the various catalogues. In order to find out the surface, I had to redraw the plans of the chambers using the AutoCAD program in a specific scale. The results of the cluster analysis are shown on Table 20, Graph 16's dendrogram.

Four groups were indicated as representing a breakdown of the data, the rest of the tombs were finally dismissed by the cluster analysis program as insignificant for these variables.

The groups are:

A: 1 tomb (P Fortetsa SE)
B: 5 tombs (219, 285, 218, 283 KMF and II Khaniale Teke)
C: 3 tombs (292, 107, 75 KMF)
D: 7 tombs (100 KMF, XI, VI Fortetsa SE, 3 Kephala Ridge, 201, 45, 24 KMF)

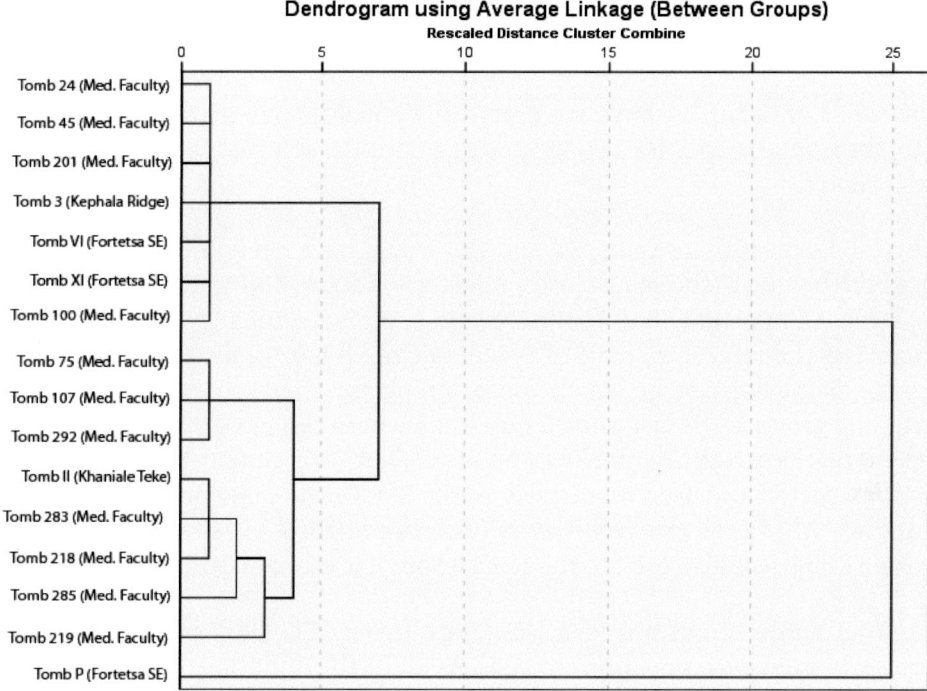

TABLE 20: GRAPH 16: DENDROGRAM OF TOMB CLUSTERS.

An initial surprise could be that Tomb P does not belong to any group but, on the contrary, forms a group on its own. This, however, could have been expected, since this tomb has an outstanding presence of all the categories but one (number of imports or imitations: bronze tripods were not found and the recovered oboloi were relatively few). In the variables 3, 5 and 1, P is also the tomb with the highest numbers, while as far as Near Eastern finds and pots are concerned it is also among the first. Unfortunately, it is one of the few tombs with unknown dimensions, but it is known that it was not a tholos tomb and that it was probably constructed in LPG. Therefore, its dimensions must have been at least more than 4m² for the chamber.[569] For this dendrogram, Tomb P is the outlier.

The next group includes all the tombs which in the second level analysis were considered as exceptionally rich and part of the new elite which made extensive use of Near Eastern objects. The date of construction for most of them is LPG. Only 283 and Tomb II at Knhaniale Teke have a slightly later date (PGB). The only

---

[569] For Brock a chamber with 4m² surface is considered a big chamber. The average size of a chamber at Fortetsa SE was probably 3 m² (Brock 1957, 41).

tomb of cluster VI of KMF which does not belong to this group is the tomb 292 since it belongs to the next one (Group 3). This group is as rich as the previous ones and even richer. The variable which might make the difference is that the dimensions of Group 3 tombs are practically equal (about 3.5m²).[570] Moreover, all tombs from Group 3 are also located at a considerable distance from the old burial centre.

One would expect that tombs 292 and 285 would have been in the same group since both belong to the same cluster (cluster VI) at the KMF site. Perhaps Tomb 285 is more important than tomb 292 and the reason might well be that the former has the largest amount of obeloi out of all the tombs and cemeteries. The use of obeloi can be much more important than expected. The most intriguing group is the last one (Group four) where the most important tombs of the old aristocratic 'regime' can be seen. First, it is the pit-cave 201 which was constructed and used exclusively in the SM. Of the same period are tombs 24 and 45, which are at a few meters' distance at the KMF site. Tomb 3 from Kephala Ridge was also used in the SM, although it was constructed earlier.

The other three tombs are of a later date (from EPG-LPG) and contain few imports, but not even one imported pot. As far as the imitations are concerned, only an oinochoe, imitation of Cypriot Black slip I-II (Tomb VI)[571]$2$1 was discovered, which represents another function unrelated to the vast majority of the Near Eastern juglets. I would risk saying that this group is one of the most revealing because it shows that Near Eastern pottery and its imitations were finally an important way for manifesting the difference between the elites. Once again what becomes obvious is a separation between the different groups of tombs at Knossos. This separation probably reveals a division among the Knossians, since it marks the different ideological means they used to acclaim a social position.

IV. Conclusion

Concluding Chapter 4 and the second part of this book I would like to highlight an important aspect of this research. So far, I have attempted to demonstrate that from about the end of the SM and onwards people used the new clusters of KMF, at Teke, at Fortetsa NE, at Fortetsa SE and later at Khaniale Teke and Mavro Spilio. Those Knossians decided to be buried at a considerable distance from the 200-202 burial complex and its satellite clusters. The reason for choosing the specific sites though needs some further explanation. I think this reason

---

[570] It seems that the size of the tomb must have been an important factor. Cavanagh and Mee (2009, 187) in their study on Perati cemetery argue that there is a tendency for richer tombs to be larger.
[571] Brock 1957, 14, catalogue no 92.

is related to the fact that all these sites have demonstrated evidence for BA funerary activities: Tomb 294 at cluster VI, Tomb 75 at cluster V, tomb 219 at cluster VIII at KMF, Tomb Q at Teke, probably Tomb TFT at Fortetsa NE, the larnax associated with Tomb P at Fortetsa SE, the LM tholos tomb at Khaniale Teke and the LM cemetery at Mavro Spilio. Certainly, the suitability of terrain (i.e. the presence of Kouskouras) and the slopes of the low hills must have played their role in the construction of the chamber tombs. The existence, however, of older tombs in each site was the best possible indication of such suitability. The Knossians who wanted to dissociate themselves with those buried in tombs 200-202 and 186, they found other burial monuments around Knossos that could connect them to a different or alternative Minoan/BA (?) past and thus to enhance their social identity in a different way.

Finally, from the entire synthesis of this chapter one could deduct some conclusions concerning the use of imports and imitations in the EIA tombs and at the same time to respond to the questions mention in the introduction of this book: Judging from the context of both imported and imitated pots, but also from the bronzes (rod-tripods, for sided stands) and the iron objects (obeloi), one can claim that Knossians treated both imports and imitations as items of the same symbolic and apparently economic value. One cannot tell with absolute certainty if Knossians could discriminate between an import and a close imitation, but I would think that they could not. It has very been hard even for scholars to make such distinctions: As Kotsonas[572] points out there were BoR copies so faithful to the prototype that Humfry Payne was uncertain if they were indeed imports from Cyprus.[573] The same stands from the bronze rod tripods since it took more than fifty years for scholars to decide whether a tripod was of Cypriot or Cretan manufacture. Finally, judging from the wealth and size of the tombs that held the imports and their imitations, I believe that the use of those items was under the control of certain elite members. Those Knossians wished to manifest their social status by the conspicuous consumption of those imports and of their imitations.

---

[572] Kotsonas 2012, 159.
[573] Ibid; Payne 1927 – 28, 256, nos 119 – 22.

Conclusion: An Overview of the Knossian Early Iron Age Society

As explained in Chapter 1, the method employed in this book does not strictly follow a single theoretical approach. On the contrary, it combines the different methods of processual, post-processual and interpretive approaches, in order to interpret certain aspects of the EIA society. The present book was not written as a new historic explanation to the relations of the Knossians with the Near East neither it was planned as a synthesis of the whole island of Crete. Knossos is a particular case and perhaps not the most representative for Crete of the LBA and EIA. There are other sites such as Karphi and Kavousi that reflect the end of the BA in a different way. The diversity of the island has been noted by all the specialists of this period. In conclusion however, I consider appropriate to include an overview of the Knossian society from the beginning of the EIA to the LO, based on the mortuary evidence in relation to the use of the Near Eastern imports as presented and analysed in this book.

The SM covers the 11th century and is represented by 36 tombs. At least six of them were constructed in the BA and the rest of them were probably constructed in the SM. From those 36 tombs, 12 of them were exclusively used in the SM, while the rest were also used in later periods without necessarily continuous use. In the beginning of the SM, immediately after the LM IIIC, some people still used Minoan burial sites (Kephala Ridge, Ayios Ioannis), while others began c.1050 BC to bury their dead in pit-caves at KMF, where no Minoan tombs were found in its core. In this site, one can see 'warrior' burials of traditional Homeric fashion. Around this core, the first clusters of SM chamber tombs were formed.

The differentiation in the use of old and new tombs can be explained only up to a certain point. The fact that not everyone was able to reuse older tombs suggests that the appropriation of the visible past was an elite activity.[574] This exclusiveness occurs not only in the SM but also in later periods. From an archaeological point of view, there is only one major difference in the rites between the burials using BA tombs and the burials placed in newly constructed tombs. The SM intrusive burials at Kephala Ridge, Ayios Ioannis and Upper Gypsades are inhumations and thus follow the pre-existing rite of the Minoan tomb; on the contrary, the burials in the new tombs at KMF, in their vast majority,[575] are cremations. Coldstream and Catling[576] link this difference to

---
[574] Wallace 2003, 270 n. 79.
[575] Fourteen inhumations and 352 cremations for the KMF Cemetery.
[576] Coldstream and Catling 1996, 715.

the funeral rites with political disputes between those who are buried during the SM in the KMF site and those buried elsewhere. Perhaps the different rite is more evident and important for the archaeological record than for those Knossians.

This is also the period that imports from the Near East begin to reach Crete if there never was a real interruption between those two regions. The fact, however, that these imports are often dated to the LM does not help explaining whether the imports reached Crete earlier and were used in SM as heirlooms, or they were valuable gifts that reached Crete as part of the gift-exchange process or trading between the elites of Crete and the Near East. There is also a third case mentioned by Catling.[577] He thinks that those items were the personal property of heroes who returned to Crete after their wanderings in the East.[578] This explanation should still fit in the gift-exchange process. It must be said that there is only a limited amount of such imports. Few of them can be seen in Tombs 200-202 which have been characterised as warrior graves or at least as graves that echo a strong symbolism of arms and warrior activity. In a period of limited trade where only the most prominent members of the society seem to receive a proper and elaborate burial, is probably where the gift exchanges of the Homeric society feet best. Cyprus appears to have a leading role both in the trade, but probably in the gift exchanges as well.

The 10th century is mostly represented by the end of the SM, the entire EPG (970-920) and the beginning of the MPG (920-870). There is a considerable increase in the construction of the tombs. At least 60 tombs were constructed in the 10th century after the end of the SM. In the end of the first quarter of the century, a very important incident occurs. It is the inauguration of the Fortetsa SE cemetery. This is also the period that Cluster VI at the KMF site is created. Imports continue to arrive from Near East but not in high numbers.

My interpretation is that in this period some of the Knossians did not want to be associated further with the SM past and its successors, which was represented by the people buried around Tomb 200-202. For this reason, they decided to create new burial groups inside the site of the KMF, and as well as a new cemetery at Fortetsa SE. According to the evidence provided by the settlement and the cult activity, those Knossians buried at Fortetsa SE were residents of the central settlement. This cemetery is located near the Acropolis of Knossos and in the west limits of the settlement. All these new burial sites were associated with BA tombs. This demonstrates a need for a symbolic attachment to a remote past.

---

[577] Catling 1996c, 649.
[578] Ibid.

The 9th century follows the traits established in the end of the 10th century BC. First, numbers of Near Eastern imports that reach Knossos and end up in tombs are much higher than before. The Phoenicians are now actively involved in the trading of these items. The second is the even more intense interest of certain Knossians for their remote Minoan (and not Sub-Minoan) past. For this reason, they reused, in PGB, the tholos tomb at Teke and possibly some Minoan chamber tombs at KMF site. Similarly, the same apparently group also used LM IIIA and LM IIIB larnakes as coffins for their children. At the same time, in certain tombs with a broad use of Minoan symbols, there was also an abundance of Near Eastern imports and local imitations. Such tombs are the Khaniale Teke, the cluster VI at KMF and Tomb P in Fortetsa SE and the tombs that surround it accept a significant amount of Near Eastern imports unparalleled to any other burial sites or clusters All of them are located at a considerable distance from tomb 200-202 and the old SM centre of the KMF.

Coldstream[579] describes this as the nostalgia of some Knossians for a "*Heroic*"[580] past, probably in a Homeric sense. I think, however, that Minoans had nothing to do with the heroic Homeric past. This heroic past must belong to the SM with the cremated 'warriors', and their prestige grave goods buried together with women, as represented in Tomb 200-202, or in Tomb 40 at Kourion, Kaloriziki, or slightly later in the Toumba at Lefkandi in Euboea.[581]

During the 8th century, it is even easier to see an association between the exotic material from the East and the scenes of the Minoan past that made these Knossians differentiate themselves as an elite alternative to the old one. Other traits of Near Eastern art can also be found in pottery art and metalwork, which means that people were particularly attracted to this iconography. However, the acquisition of original imports and close imitations must have belonged only to a specific part of the society. These are the people buried in the richest tombs and they could afford this high-cost deliberate destruction of wealth during a burial. These tombs continue to receive large quantities of imports until the middle of the 8th century (MG), especially BoR II juglets. Near Eastern imports begin to have a wider distribution but still not very wide. Not all the newly established tombs contain Near Eastern imports.

The appreciation of imports led to the production of almost identical copies as well as other kinds of adaptations. These different adaptations might be related to perfume production, which was used for the preparation of the dead. After LG, imported juglets almost cease to appear, but local imitations continue to be

---

[579] Coldstream 1998, 60; Coldstream and Catling 1996, 715.
[580] Coldstream 1998, 59.
[581] Matthäus 1998, 140.

produced until the LO. Since most of the imports and the imitations are confined in the tombs and in the same cluster of tombs, one can at least talk for a kind of personal taste by a specific group of Knossians who had the economic status of acquiring them. It is not known whether the occupants of these wealthy tombs were the most aristocratic, but they were probably the wealthiest. In the 7th century there was a vast production of Creto-Cypriot lekythoi during the EO. Most of the imports, however, were now limited to faience amulets and beads, which could have been produced everywhere, even on the Aegean islands. On the other hand, this seems to indicate what happened at the end of the LO at Knossos in 630 BC, when the use of the cemeteries was probably halted.

The evidence for the settlement of Knossos and for cult activity is also very specific. One must accept that the development of the city of Knossos had nothing in common to those of the Greek mainland and the Aristotelian model of synoecism. In Knossos, there was a central extended settlement, and most probably all people buried in the surrounding cemeteries had lived in it. Thus, the various social mechanisms regarding competition and status were developed inside the same settlement and manifested during the burials of its prominent members. All Classical sanctuaries discovered in the settlement of Knossos (Demeter's temple included) had probably a prior open-air cult established in the same sites. During the entire EIA, a strong presence of nature goddesses is detected in all these activities. These goddesses have a special connection with the burial activities of the Knossians.

As far as Near Eastern imports are concerned, I believe that this book has made clear that a contextual study of the imports in close comparison with their imitations can change the way one understands and evaluates an ancient society. The importance of such a study is not related to whether there was a production of BoR juglets by foreigners or by Cretans at Knossos. It is extremely important that there was a need for Near Eastern imports, such as pots by the Knossian elite, which considered them suitable to accompany to the tombs the most prominent persons of the region. This elite was so satisfied with these pots that it also used (and perhaps ordered) local imitations thereof. There are also few imports of which the context indicates some religious affinities with the Phoenicians.

Another question that could arise is whether all these prestige items made of precious metals were exotic for the Knossians. I believe that the answer is no. Except for the pendant from Luristan at Tomb P (Fortetsa SE), Near Eastern imports did not come to Knossos from very distant places but just from its eastern 'neighbourhood', since the LM, the Knossians were very familiar with the Phoenicians, Cypriots and North Syrians who crafted those prestige items.

Maybe this long-established commercial relation could explain the appreciation of imports by the Knossians. Snodgrass[582] argues that that Knossian society was conservative. This seems to be true, but perhaps it reflects only a part of the Knossian elite, which competed with other elite groups by different means. While, this part used the glorious SM heroic past (clusters around 200-202 and 186 tombs), another part of the society was attracted by the Near Eastern imports and a third one, which was not so spatially distinguishable from the second, turned to the Minoan era.

Moreover, Whitley[583] has made clear how different the EIA Athens and Knossos were. The scholar has interpreted the 9th-century Athenian aristocracy as a class *"that went to great lengths to preserve other groups from usurping its symbolic privileges"*.[584] It seems that the class which ruled Knossos, from the SM to at least the beginning of the LPG, was not able to exercise the same control. On the contrary, from the end of the 10th century onwards, it is difficult to find more than a couple of Near Eastern imports in the traditional burial ground at the centre of the KMF site. The irony is that after the end of the BA, the first dead who made use of the connection with Cyprus, was the one buried in tomb 201 with his bronze four-sided stand. However, few decades after his funeral, the emerging elite groups which buried its members mainly at cluster VI of the KMF and at Fortetsa SE took control of this connection.

The study of EIA Knossos has become very important in the last thirty years and acquired, even more, importance after the excavation of KNC. Around the archaeological area of the BA Palace, there is still farmland which remains unexcavated. Hopefully, more evidence for the settlement and the structure of this period's society will come from systematic future investigations, like the KULP project. Rescue excavations are very important, but they only occur during the construction of new buildings. New constructions normally signify the destruction of the archaeological remains. Before new and costly systematic excavations begin in the distant future, one really hopes for the full publication of all those tombs at the north of Knossos near and inside Heraklion. These publications will help us understand the distribution of the cemeteries located at a considerable distance from the EIA settlement but apparently are still associated with it.

---

[582] Snodgrass 1996, 596.
[583] Whitley 1994, 60.
[584] Ibid.

Appendix I: The Tombs and the Burials

Tomb	Type	Location	Dating	Disturbed	Inhum.	Crem.	Chamber	Publication
I	ch. tomb	Khaniale Teke	O?	YES			2.06m²	Hutchinson and Boardman 1954
II	tholos tomb	Khaniale Teke	PGB-EO	YES		21		Hutchinson and Boardman 1954
III	ch. tomb	Khaniale Teke	PGB-EO	YES		17	1.54m²	Boardman 1967
A	ch. Tomb	Teke	PGB-LG	YES		3		Coldstream and Catling 1996
B	Niche?	Teke	?	YES		1		Coldstream and Catling 1996
D	ch. tomb	Teke	LPG-PGB	YES		1	1.88m²	Coldstream and Catling 1996
E	ch. tomb	Teke	LPG	YES	2		1.50m²	Sacket 1976
F	ch. tomb	Teke	LPG-EO	YES		6	1.66m²	Coldstream and Catling 1996
G	ch. tomb	Teke	MPG-EG	YES		11	5.63m²	Coldstream and Catling 1996
H	ch. tomb	Teke	MG-EO	YES		7	0.71m²	Coldstream and Catling 1996
J	ch. tomb	Teke	EPG-PGB	NO		2	2.13m²	Coldstream and Catling 1996
K	ch. tomb	Teke	EPG-LPG	YES				Coldstream and Catling 1996
L	ch. tomb	Teke	MPG-PGB	YES		3	2.25m²	Coldstream and Catling 1996
M	ch. tomb	Teke	EG-LG	YES		5	1.00m²	Coldstream and Catling 1996
N	ch. tomb	Teke	LPG-EG	YES		5	5.26m²	Coldstream and Catling 1996
O	ch. tomb	Teke	PG-LG	YES?		18	1.34m²	Coldstream and Catling 1996
Q	ch. tomb	Teke	MPG-O	YES		19	4.67m²	Coldstream and Catling 1996
-	ch. tomb	Teke	EPG	YES	2			Coldstream 1963
1	ch. tomb	KMF	MG-EO?	YES		7	1.57m²	Coldstream and Catling 1996
2	pit-cave	KMF	SM	YES	1	1	1.64m²	Coldstream and Catling 1996
8	ch. tomb	KMF	LG	YES		2	1.70m²	Coldstream and Catling 1996
9	pit?	KMF	?	YES				Coldstream and Catling 1996
13	ch. tomb	KMF	PGB-EG	YES		10	1.09m²	Coldstream and Catling 1996
14	ch. tomb	KMF	G-LO	YES		7	1.25m²	Coldstream and Catling 1996
16	ch. tomb	KMF	SM-MG?	NO	1		1.37m²	Coldstream and Catling 1996
18	ch. tomb	KMF	SM-MG*	NO		2	1.88m²	Coldstream and Catling 1996

19	ch. tomb	KMF	LG-EO	NO		4	1.83m²	Coldstream and Catling 1996
24	ch. tomb	KMF	SM-EPG	YES		3	2.80m²	Coldstream and Catling 1996
25	ch. tomb	KMF	SM-EO	YES		1	2.59m²	Coldstream and Catling 1996
26	ch. tomb?	KMF	SM-LO*	YES		4	2.62m²	Coldstream and Catling 1996
28	ch. tomb	KMF	LPG-EO	NO		2	2.27m²	Coldstream and Catling 1996
30	ch. tomb	KMF	EPG-O	YES			1.91m²	Coldstream and Catling 1996
31	larnax burial?	KMF	MG-LG	YES				Coldstream and Catling 1996
34	ch. tomb	KMF	LO	YES		4	2.20m²	Coldstream and Catling 1996
40	ch. tomb	KMF	SM-LO*	YES		8	2.75m²	Coldstream and Catling 1996
44	ch. tomb	KMF	?	YES			2.90m²	Coldstream and Catling 1996
45	ch. tomb	KMF	SM-LO	YES	1	1	2.07m²	Coldstream and Catling 1996
48	ch. tomb	KMF	SM-LO*	YES		4	4.28m²	Coldstream and Catling 1996
55	ch. tomb	KMF	EPG	YES			1.45m²	Coldstream and Catling 1996
56	ch. tomb	KMF	SM-LO*	YES		3	1.78m²	Coldstream and Catling 1996
57	ch. tomb	KMF	LO	YES		2	1.53m²	Coldstream and Catling 1996
59	pit	KMF	O	YES		2		Coldstream and Catling 1996
60	ch. tomb	KMF	?	YES?		7	2.4m²	Coldstream and Catling 1996
61	ch. tomb	KMF	SM-LO*	YES			1.86m²	Coldstream and Catling 1996
63	cremation pit?	KMF	PGB-MG	YES?		1		Coldstream and Catling 1996
69	pithos burial?	KMF	EO-LO	YES		1		Coldstream and Catling 1996
75	ch. Tomb	KMF	EG-LO	NO		44	3.49m²	Coldstream and Catling 1996
76	ch. tomb?	KMF	LG-EO	YES		2		Coldstream and Catling 1996
78	pithos burial	KMF	LG-EO	NO?				Coldstream and Catling 1996
79	pit	KMF	LG-EO	YES		2		Coldstream and Catling 1996
80	undifined	KMF	EPG	YES				Coldstream and Catling 1996

APPENDIX I: THE TOMBS AND THE BURIALS 143

82	ch. tomb	KMF	LO	YES		3	3.91m²	Coldstream and Catling 1996
85	pit-tomb?	KMF	LG ?	YES		1		Coldstream and Catling 1996
86	pit-tomb?	KMF	?	YES				Coldstream and Catling 1996
98	pit-cave?	KMF	SM-EO*	YES?	1	3		Coldstream and Catling 1996
100	ch. tomb	KMF	EPG-EG	YES		4	3.18m²	Coldstream and Catling 1996
103	larnax grave?	KMF	M-LG	YES				Coldstream and Catling 1996
104	side chamber	KMF	PGB-LG	YES		6		Coldstream and Catling 1996
105	ch. Tomb	KMF	G	YES				Coldstream and Catling 1996
106	ch. tomb	KMF	EG-LO	YES		4	5.84m²	Coldstream and Catling 1996
107	ch. tomb	KMF	PGB-LO	YES		31	3.32m²	Coldstream and Catling 1996
111	pithos burial	KMF	EO	NO?	1			Coldstream and Catling 1996
112	ch. tomb	KMF	SM	YES	1	1	1.53m²	Coldstream and Catling 1996
113	larnax grave?	KMF	LG	YES				Coldstream and Catling 1996
121	pit-cave	KMF	SM	NO?	3		1.44m²	Coldstream and Catling 1996
123	ch. tomb?	KMF	G-LO	YES		1		Coldstream and Catling 1996
125	ch. tomb	KMF	MG	YES		3	0.48m²	Coldstream and Catling 1996
126	undefined	KMF	O	YES				Coldstream and Catling 1996
129	ch. tomb	KMF	EG-LO	YES		2	0.70m²	Coldstream and Catling 1996
132	ch. tomb	KMF	MG-LO	YES		14	1.74m²	Coldstream and Catling 1996
134	pit-tomb?	KMF	LPG-EO	YES?		1		Coldstream and Catling 1996
135	pit?	KMF	MG	YES				Coldstream and Catling 1996
138	ch. tomb	KMF	LG-O	YES		1	2.14m²	Coldstream and Catling 1996
146	ch. tomb	KMF	LO	YES			0.77m²	Coldstream and Catling 1996
147	ch. tomb?	KMF	PGB-O?	YES		4		Coldstream and Catling 1996
149	Shaft grave	KMF	SM?	YES	1			Coldstream and Catling 1996

144 KNOSSOS AND THE NEAR EAST

152	ch. tomb	KMF	G	YES			2.64m²	Coldstream and Catling 1996
153	Shaft grave	KMF	SM	NO				Coldstream and Catling 1996
159	undefined	KMF	EO	YES	1	2		Coldstream and Catling 1996
160	Shaft grave	KMF	SM	YES	1			Coldstream and Catling 1996
163	pit	KMF	LG	YES?		2		Coldstream and Catling 1996
168	ch. tomb	KMF	LG-EO	YES			3.51m²	Coldstream and Catling 1996
175	ch. tomb	KMF	EPG-O	YES		11	1.96m²	Coldstream and Catling 1996
176	cremation pit?	KMF	?	YES?				Coldstream and Catling 1996
182	pit	KMF	LPG-PGB	YES?				Coldstream and Catling 1996
186	pit-cave	KMF	SM	NO		1		Coldstream and Catling 1996
200	pit-cave	KMF	SM	NO?		1		Coldstream and Catling 1996
201	pit-cave	KMF	SM	NO?		1		Coldstream and Catling 1996
202	pit-cave	KMF	SM	NO?				Coldstream and Catling 1996
207	ch. tomb	KMF	SM-LPG	YES	2		3.57m²	Coldstream and Catling 1996
208	pit-cave	KMF	SM	YES				Coldstream and Catling 1996
218	ch. tomb	KMF	LPG-O	NO?		18	4.31m²	Coldstream and Catling 1996
219	ch. tomb	KMF	LPG-LO	YES		3	4.57m²	Coldstream and Catling 1996
221	ch. Tomb	KMF	O?	YES				Coldstream and Catling 1996
222	ch. tomb?	KMF	?	YES			1.52m²	Coldstream and Catling 1996
229	ch. tomb	KMF	MG-EO	NO?		8	1.50m²	Coldstream and Catling 1996
242	ch. tomb?	KMF	MPG-PGB	YES				Coldstream and Catling 1996
247	ch. tomb?	KMF	?	YES				Coldstream and Catling 1996
280	pithos burial	KMF	EG	NO?		1		Coldstream and Catling 1996
282	shaft grave	KMF	SM	YES				Coldstream and Catling 1996
283	ch. tomb	KMF	PGB-LO	YES		17	2.93m²	Coldstream and Catling 1996
285	ch. tomb	KMF	LPG-LO	NO		20	2.50m²	Coldstream and Catling 1996
286	ch. tomb	KMF	EG	YES		3	0.96m²	Coldstream and Catling 1996

Appendix I: The Tombs and the Burials

287	ch. tomb	KMF	LPG-LO	YES		5	1.75m²	Coldstream and Catling 1996
292	ch. tomb	KMF	PGB-LO	YES		32	3.48m²	Coldstream and Catling 1996
294	ch. tomb	KMF	MG-LO	YES		14	2.84m²	Coldstream and Catling 1996
306	ch. tomb	KMF	LG-EO	YES		10	2.48m²	Coldstream and Catling 1996
ʹ	ch. tomb	Low. Gypsades	PGB-LO	No?		35		Coldstream et al 1981
III	ch. tomb	Kephala Ridge	MPG	YES	1			Coldstream 1963
V	ch. tomb	Kephala Ridge	PG-O	YES		1		Coldstream 1963
1	ch. tomb	Kephala Ridge	SM-PG	YES				Coldstream 2002
2	ch. tomb	Kephala Ridge	?	YES				Coldstream 2002
3	ch. tomb	Kephala Ridge	PGB-EO	YES		1		Coldstream 2002
4	ch. tomb	Kephala Ridge	SM-PG?	YES				Coldstream 2002
5	ch. Tomb	Kephala Ridge	SM	NO	2			Coldstream 2002
6	tholos tomb	Kephala Ridge	PG	YES				Coldstream 2002
II	ch. tomb	Fortetsa SE	LPG-LO	NO		28	2.58m²	Brock 1957
III	ch. tomb	Fortetsa SE	PG	NO		3	1.30m²	Brock 1957
IV	ch. tomb	Fortetsa SE	PG	NO		2	1.89m²	Brock 1957
V	ch. tomb	Fortetsa SE	PG	YES?		1	1.05m²	Brock 1957
VI	ch. tomb	Fortetsa SE	SM/EPG	NO?		4	3.48m²	Brock 1957
VII	ch. tomb	Fortetsa SE	MPG-O	NO		14	1.16m²	Brock 1957
VIII	ch. tomb	Fortetsa SE	EPG-G*	YES		6	2.08m²	Brock 1957
IX	ch. tomb	Fortetsa SE	PG	YES			1.96m²	Brock 1957
X	ch. tomb	Fortetsa SE	PGB-LG	NO		21	2.92m²	Brock 1957
XI	ch. tomb	Fortetsa SE	EPG?	NO		4	4.06m²	Brock 1957
BLT	ch. tomb	Fortetsa SE	PG?	YES			1.69m²	Brock 1957
F	ch. tomb	Fortetsa SE	PGB-EO	YES		14	0.57m²	Brock 1957
LST	ch. tomb	Fortetsa SE	PG-LG	YES				Brock 1957
OD	ch. tomb	Fortetsa SE	PGB	NO		4		Brock 1957
P	ch. tomb	Fortetsa SE	LPG-LO	YES		80		Brock 1957

P2	ch. tomb	Fortetsa SE	LG-EO	NO		18		Brock 1957
Θ	ch. tomb	Fortetsa SE	EPG	YES		2	2.36m²	Brock 1957
Q	ch. tomb	Fortetsa SE	PG-G	YES				Brock 1957
Lf	ch. tomb	Fortetsa NE	PG-PGB	NO?	1	2		Brock 1957
TFT	ch. tomb	Fortetsa NE	PGB-EO	NO?		15	1.16m²	Brock 1957
Π	ch. tomb	Fortetsa NE	SM-O*	YES			4.79m²	Brock 1957
F/67:1	ch. tomb	Fortetsa NE	PG-O	YES		2		Coldstream and Catling 1996
F/67:3	ch. tomb	Fortetsa NE	PG-LG	YES			1.25m²	Coldstream and Catling 1996
F/67:4	ch. tomb	Fortetsa NE	MG-EO	YES		6		Coldstream and Catling 1996
F/67:5	ch. tomb	Fortetsa NE	SM-EO*	YES	1	4	2.91m²	Coldstream and Catling 1996
F/67:8	ch. tomb	Fortetsa NE	PG-G	YES			2.04m²	Coldstream and Catling 1996
F/67:9	ch. tomb	Fortetsa NE	LG-EO	YES		1	0.66m²	Coldstream and Catling 1996
F/67:10	ch. tomb	Fortetsa NE	PG-G	YES				Coldstream and Catling 1996
F/67:11	ch. tomb	Fortetsa NE	PG-LG	YES				Coldstream and Catling 1996
F/67:14	ch. tomb	Fortetsa NE	SM-G*	YES				Coldstream and Catling 1996
F/67:15	ch. tomb	Fortetsa NE	?	YES				Coldstream and Catling 1996
A	ch. tomb	Fortetsa NE	LPG-EO	YES	1	7		Hood & Boardman 1961
B	ch. tomb	Fortetsa NE	PG?	YES	2			Hood & Boardman 1961
C	ch. tomb	Fortetsa NE	PG?	YES	1			Hood & Boardman 1961
—	ch. tomb	Ayios Ioannis	SM	YES	2			Hood & Coldstream 1968
I	ch. tomb	Ayios Ioannis	SM-LPG	NO	1	8		Boardman 1960
II	pit-tomb?	Ayios Ioannis	EPG?	NO?	1			Boardman 1960
III	pit-tomb?	Ayios Ioannis	SM-EPG?	NO		1		Boardman 1960
IV	pit-tomb?	Ayios Ioannis	SM-EPG?	YES	1	1		Boardman 1960
V	ch. tomb	Ayios Ioannis	EPG-MPG	YES?		2		Boardman 1960
VI	ch. tomb	Ayios Ioannis	SM-EPG	NO	4			Boardman 1960
VII	ch. tomb	Ayios Ioannis	SM-EPG	YES?	1			Boardman 1960
VIII	side ch.	Ayios Ioannis	EPG-MPG	NO	1	3		Boardman 1960

APPENDIX I: THE TOMBS AND THE BURIALS   147

A	ch. tomb	Atsalenio	LPG-LO	YES		17	Davaras 1968
B	ch. tomb	Atsalenio	LPG-LO	YES		7	Davaras 1968
VIa	ch. tomb	Up. Gypsades	SM	YES?	?		Hood et al 1958-1959
VII	ch. tomb	Up. Gypsades	SM	YES?	3?		Hood et al 1959-1959
4	ch. Tomb	Mavro Spilio	LG-LO	YES		3	Coldstream 2000
7	ch. tomb	Mavro Spilio	LG-LO	YES		1	Coldstream 2000
17	ch. tomb	Mavro Spilio	LG-LO	YES			Coldstream 2000

Note: I have left blank the cells which show no information instead of simply potting '0', because this is a calculation based on indirect evidence such as the number of pithos urns for cremations or that an empty shaft grave once probably held an inhumation. I have also only calculated the surface of the chamber tombs of which their plan is published and do not constitute part of Minoan. In the re-used LM tombs and larnx graves I have noted only the EIA use.

*An interruption in the use of the tomb

**Tomb P at Fortetsa SE includes the finds of tomb I.

***Inhum.: Inhumation, Crem.: Cremation, Chamber: Chambers' surface.

Appendix II: Imports and Imitations

Tomb	Location	Pots	Finds	NE[1] Pots	NE Finds	Import or imitation	Imitations
I	Teke Khaniale	8	4				
II	Teke Khaniale	112	80	2	14	1	9
III	Teke Khaniale	61	13				
A	Teke	7	0	1			
B	Teke	3	0				
D	Teke	43	10				
E	Teke	10	1				
F	Teke	14	0				
G	Teke	141	13		2		5
H	Teke	39	6	1	1		
J	Teke	65	14		1		
K	Teke	5	0				
L	Teke	18	3				
M	Teke	22	2				
N	Teke	41	24				
O	Teke	48	5		1		
Q	Teke	116	26		1		1
-	Teke	18	2				
1	KMF	18	3				1
2	KMF	3	14				
8	KMF	2	0				
9	KMF	1	2				
13	KMF	51	4		1		1
14	KMF	52	11		2	0	2
16	KMF	3	2			0	
18	KMF	16	9			0	
19	KMF	29	5			0	2
24	KMF	10	9			1	
25	KMF	6	13				
26	KMF	20	13		1		
28	KMF	20	10				
30	KMF	9	10				

31	KMF	19	1				
34	KMF	40	40				
40	KMF	46	18				
44	KMF	0	0				
45	KMF	8	10			1	
48	KMF	16	22		1		
55	KMF	4	2				
56	KMF	40	74	1			
57	KMF	11	9				
59	KMF	6	6				
60	KMF	35	12				1
61	KMF	3	0				1
63	KMF	9	0				
69	KMF	3	0				
75	KMF	226	89		1	5	1
76	KMF	5	0				
78	KMF	12	30		8		
79	KMF	9	0				
80	KMF	2	0				
82	KMF	15	11				
85	KMF	2	0				
86	KMF	5	0				
98	KMF	21	9				
100	KMF	79	42		5	3	
103	KMF	2	0				
104	KMF	129	14	2			1
105	KMF	0	0				
106	KMF	42	5	1			3
107	KMF	218	78	3	2	1	9
111	KMF	2	0				
112	KMF	3	0				
113	KMF	2	0				
121	KMF	7	3				
123	KMF	9	14				
125	KMF	16	2	1	1		
126	KMF	13	9				
129	KMF	7	3				
132	KMF	42	5				

134	KMF	77	10	1			2
135	KMF	1	2				
138	KMF	3	3				
146	KMF	2	3				
147	KMF	6	0				
149	KMF	0	1				
152	KMF	1	3				
153	KMF	0	0				
159	KMF	4	3				
160	KMF	1					
163	KMF	9	1				
168	KMF	1	1				
175	KMF	75	34	1			2
176	KMF	0	0				
182	KMF	2	2				
186	KMF	6	0				
200	KMF	4	13		2		
201	KMF	0	19		7	1	
202	KMF	0	0				1
207	KMF	77	6				
208	KMF	1	9				
218	KMF	140	37		2	1	12
219	KMF	100	166	5	14	18	2
221	KMF	1	2				
222	KMF	1	0				
229	KMF	35	8	1	3		3
242	KMF	2	1				
247	KMF	0	1				
280	KMF	10	1				
282	KMF	0	0				
283	KMF	108	91	1		13	7
285	KMF	163	109	7	7	27	2
286	KMF	8	0				
287	KMF	43	6				
292	KMF	246	91	11	13	2	10
294	KMF	64	19				2
306	KMF	39	22				2
-	Lower Gypsades	117	15	2	1		10

Appendix II: Imports and Imitations

III	Kephala Ridge	2	2				
V	Kephala Ridge	10	4		1		
1	Kephala Ridge	3					
2	Kephala Ridge						
3	Kephala Ridge	24	1			1	
4	Kephala Ridge	6					
5	Kephala Ridge	2					
6	Kephala Ridge	19	1		2		1
II	Fortetsa SE	140	53		6		10
III	Fortetsa SE	8	3				
IV	Fortetsa SE	13	0				
V	Fortetsa SE	22	0				
VI	Fortetsa SE	66	15		4	2	1
VII	Fortetsa SE	47	7	1			4
VIII	Fortetsa SE	50	11				
IX	Fortetsa SE	17	0		1		
X	Fortetsa SE	149	24	2			6
XI	Fortetsa SE	51	14		6	2	
BLT	Fortetsa SE	1	0				
F	Fortetsa SE	58	12	1			2
LST	Fortetsa SE	25	4				
OD	Fortetsa SE	38	2				
P**	Fortetsa SE	408	116	7	11	4	27

P2	Fortetsa SE	67	3	1	2		9
Θ	Fortetsa SE	19	4				
Ϙ	Fortetsa SE	1	1				
Lf	Fortetsa NE	65	5		1		
TFT	Fortetsa NE	82	8	2	1		6
Π	Fortetsa NE	33	2				
F/67 1	Fortetsa NE	12	2				
F/67 3	Fortetsa NE	0	0				
F/67 4	Fortetsa NE	14	4				2
F/67 5	Fortetsa NE	9	0				
F/67 8	Fortetsa NE	0	0				
F/67 9	Fortetsa NE	5	1				
F/67 10	Fortetsa NE						
F/67 11	Fortetsa NE						
F/67 14	Fortetsa NE						
F/67 15	Fortetsa NE						
A	Fortetsa NE	30	9	1			
B	Fortetsa NE		4				
C	Fortetsa NE		1				
-	Ayios Ioannis	3	3		1		
I	Ayios Ioannis	59	4				
II	Ayios Ioannis	3	3				
III	Ayios Ioannis	5	1				

IV	Ayios Ioannis	6	4				
V	Ayios Ioannis	26	11		1		
VI	Ayios Ioannis	4	1				
VII	Ayios Ioannis	1					
VIII	Ayios Ioannis	15	5				
A	Atsalenio	74	4	2			1
B	Atsalenio	24					2
4	Mavro Spilio	17					
7	Mavro Spilio	2					1
17	Mavro Spilio	2					
VIa	Upper Gypsades	4?					
VII	Upper Gypsades	6?	1		1		

**Tomb P at Fortetsa SE includes the finds of tomb I, since the latter is part of tomb P.

Bibliography

Alexiou, M. (1974) *The Ritual Lament in Greek Tradition*, Cambridge.

Alexiou, S. (1958) Η Μινωϊκή θεά μεθ' υψωμένων χειρών, PhD Thesis.

Alexiou, S. (1950) 'Παραστάσεις πολύποδος επί πρωτοελληνικών αγγείων εκ Κρήτης', *Kretika Chronica* 4, 294-318.

Andreadaki-Vlasaki, M. (1990) 'Παρατηρήσεις στην Πρωτογεωμετρική Κεραμεική της Κρήτης,' in V. Niniou-Kindeli (ed.) Πεπραγμένα του ΣΤ' Διεθνούς Κρητολογικού Συνεδρίου, Χανιά, 24-30Αυγούστου 1986, Vol. Α1, Chania, 93-104.

Antonaccio, C.M. (2006) *Religion, Basileis and Heroes* in Deger-Jalkotzy S. and Lemos I.S. (eds.) *Ancient Greece: From the Mycenaean Palaces to the Age of Homer*, Edinburgh Leventis Studies 3, Edinburgh, 381-398.

Antonaccio, C.M. (1995) *An Archaeology of Ancestors: Tomb cult and hero cult in early Greece*, Lanham.

Antoniadis, V. (2012) *Early Iron Age Cemeteries at Knossos: The Appreciation of Oriental Imports and their Imitations by Knossian Society*, PhD Thesis.

Appadurai, A. (ed.) *The social life of things: Commodities in cultural perspective*, Cambridge.

Arnott, R. (1999) 'Opium', in Y. Tzedakis, (ed.) (2002) *Minoans and Mycenaeans: flavors of their time: NationalArchaeological Museum, 12 July-27 November 1999*, Athens.

Aubet, M.E. (2004) 'The Iron Age Cemetery' in M. E. Aubet, (ed.) *The Phoenician cemetery of Tyre-Al Bas: Excavations 1997-1999*, Baal Hors: Serie 1, Beirut.

Aubet, M.E. (2001) *The Phoenicians and the West: Politics, Colonies and Trade*, (Translated by Mary Turton) Cambridge.

Balensi, J. (1980) *Les fouilles de R. W. Hamilton ů Tell Abu Hawam effectuies en 1932-1933 pour la compte du Dιpartementdes Antiquitιs de la Palestine sous mandat Brittanique. Niveaux IV et V. Dossier sur l'histoire d'un port Mιditerranιen durant les ages du Bronze et de Fer*, PhD Thesis.

Barnett, R.D. (1935) 'The Nimrud Ivories and the Art of the Phoenicians', *IRAQ* 2, 180-210.

Bennet, J., Whitelaw, T., Grammatikaki, E. and Vasilakis, A. (2006) 'The Knossos Urban Landscape Project,' *Pasiphae* I, 103-109.

Bernal, M. (1987) *Black Athena: Afroasiatic Roots of Classical Civilization*, London.

Bernal, M. (1991) *Black Athena: Afroasiatic Roots of Classical Civilization:The Archaeological and Documentary Evidence*, Vol. II, London.

Bernal, M. (2001) *Black Athena writes back: Martin Bernal responds to his critics*, London.

Betancourt, P.P. (2008) 'Minoan Trade' in C.W Shelmedrine (ed.) *The Cambridge Companion to the Aegean BA*, New York, 209-229.

Biehl, P. F. and Rassamakin Y.Ya (2008) 'Import and Imitation in Archaeology: An Introduction' in P. F. Biehl and Y.Ya. Rassamakin (eds.) *Import and imitation in archaeology*, Langenweissbach.

Bikai, P.M. (1987) *The Phoenician pottery of Cyprus.* Nicosia.
Binford, L.R. (1982) 'Meaning, inference, and the material record' in A.C. Renfrew and S. Shennan (eds.) *Ranking resource and exchange*, Cambridge, 160-163.
Binford, L.R. (1972) 'Mortuary practices: Their study and their potential.' in L.R. Binford (ed.) *An Archaeological Perspective*, New York, 208-53.
Binford, L.R. (1962) 'Archaeology as Anthropology', *AmerAnt* 28, 217-225.
Boardman, J. (1990) 'The lyre player group of seals, An encore', *AA*, 1-17.
Boardman, J. (1980) *The Greeks Overseas: Their early colonies and trade*, London.
Boardman, J. (1967) 'The Khaniale Tekke Tombs II', *BSA* 62, 57–75.
Boardman, J. (1961) *The Cretan Collection in Oxford: The Dictaean Cave and Iron Age Crete*, Oxford.
Boardman, J. (1960) 'Protogeometric graves at Agios Ioannis near Knossos', *BSA* 55, 128–148.
Bourogiannis, G. (2012) 'Pondering the Cypro-Phoenician conundrum. The Aegean view of a bewildering term', in M. Iacovou (ed.) *Cyprus and the Aegean in the early Iron Age: The legacy of Nicolas Coldstream*, Nicosia, 183-206.
Bourogiannis, G. (2008) Κυπριακή και φοινικική κεραμική στο Αιγαίο κατά τους Πρώιμους Ιστορικούς χρόνους: Εμπορικά δίκτυα και το πρόβλημα του ρυθμού *Black-on-Red*, PhD Thesis.
Bradley R. (1981) 'Various styles of Urn: Cemeteries and settlement in Southern England c.1400-1000 BC' in R. Chapman, I. Kinnes, and K. Randsborg (eds.) *The archaeology of death*, Cambridge, 93-104.
Braun, D. (1981) 'A critique of some recent North American studies', *American Studies Antiquity* 46, 398-416.
Brock, J.K. (1957) *Fortetsa: Early Greek Tombs near Knossos*, Cambridge.
Brown, J.A. (1981) 'The search for rank' in R. Chapman, I. Kinnes and K. Randsborg (eds.) *The archaeology of death*, New York, 25-37.
Brown, A. (1993) Before Knossos: Arthur Evans's Travels in the Balkans and Crete, Oxford.
Cadogan, G. (1976) *Palaces of Minoan Crete*, London.
Cadogan, G. (1967) 'Late Minoan IIIC Pottery from the Kephala Tholos Tomb near Knossos', *BSA* 62, 257-266.
Castleden, R. (1990) *The Knossos labyrinth: A new view of the 'Palace of Minos' at Knossos*, London.
Catling, H.W. (1996a) 'Bronze', in J.N. Coldstream and H.W. Catling, (eds.) *Knossos North Cemetery. Early Greek Tombs,* BSA Suppl. 28. Vol. II, London, 542–574.
Catling, H.W. (1996b) 'The objects other than pottery in Sub-Minoan tombs', in J.N. Coldstream, and H.W. Catling, (eds.) *Knossos North Cemetery: Early Greek Tombs*, Vol. II, BSA Suppl. Vol. 28, 517–537.
Catling, H.W. (1996c) 'The Sub-Minoan phase in the North Cemetery at Knossos', in J.N. Coldstream, and H.W. Catling, (eds.) *Knossos North Cemetery: Early Greek Tombs*, Vol. II, BSA Suppl. Vol. 28, 639–649.
Catling, H.W. (1996d) 'The Sub-Minoan Pottery', in J.N. Coldstream, and H.W. Catling, (eds.) *Knossos North Cemetery: Early Greek* Tombs, Vol. II, BSA Suppl. Vol. 28, 295-310.

Catling, H.W. (1995) 'Heroes Returned? Subminoan burials from Crete' in J.B. Carter and S.P. Morris (eds.) *The Ages of Homer: A Tribute to Emily Townsend Vermeule*, Austin, 123–36.

Catling, H.W. (1984–5) 'Archaeology in Greece 1984–5', *AR*, 3–69.

Catling, H.W. (1984) 'Workshop and heirloom: Prehistoric Bronze Stands in the East Mediterranean', *RDAC*, 69-91.

Catling, H.W. (1982-3) 'Archaeology in Greece 1982–3', *AR*, 3–62.

Catling, H.W. (1979-80) 'Knossos 1978', *AR*, 43-58.

Catling, H. W., Smyth, D., Musgrave, J. H., and Jones, G. (1976) 'An Early Christian Osteotheke at Knossos', BSA 71, 25-47.

Cavanagh, W.G. (1996) 'The burial customs' in J.N. Coldstream and H.W. Catling, (eds.) *Knossos North Cemetery. Early Greek Tombs,* BSA Suppl. 28. Vol. II, London, 651–75.

Cavanagh, W.G. (1977) *Attic burial customs ca. 2000-700 B.C*, PhD Thesis.

Cavanagh W. and Mee, C. (2009) 'Perati kai Para Pera' in D. Daniilidou (ed.) Δώρον: τιμητικός τόμος για τον καθηγητή Σπύρο Ιακωβίδη, Athens, 169-189.

Cavanagh W. and Mee, C. (1998) A Private Place: Death in Prehistoric Greece. *Studies in Mediterranean Archaeology*, Vol. 125, Jonsered.

Chaniotis, A. (2011) 'Cultural Identity, Ethnicity, and Cultural Transformation in Crete from the Dark Ages to the Archaic Period', in G. Rizza (ed.) *Identità culturale, etnicità, processi di trasformazione a Creta fra Dark Age e Arcaismo. Convegno di Studi per i cento anni dello scavo di Priniàs, 1906-2006 (Atene 9-12 novembre 2006)*, Catania, 421-432.

Chapman, S.V. (1972) 'A catalogue of Iron Age Pottery from the cemeteries of Khirbet, Silm, Joya, Qrayé and Qasmieh of South Lebanon', *Berytus* 21, 55-194.

Childe, V.G. (1929) *The most ancient East: The oriental prelude to European prehistory*, New York.

Christenson, A.L. (1989) *Tracing Archaeology's Past: The Historiography of Archaeology*, Carbondale.

Clarke, D. (1973) 'Archaeology: the loss of innocence', *Antiquity* 47, 6-18.

Coldstream, J.N. (2016) 'Geometric and Archaic Crete. A hunt for the elusive polis', in W.-D. Niemeier, O. Pilz, I. Kaiser (eds.) *Kreta in der geometrischen und archaischen Zeit: Akten des Internationalen Kolloquiums am Deutschen Archäologischen Institut, Abteilung Athen, 27.-29. Januar 2006.* Athenaia, Vol. 2. München.

Coldstream, J.N. (2006) 'Knossos in Early Greek Times' in Deger-Jalkotzy, S. and Lemos I.S. (eds.) *Ancient Greece: From the Mycenaean Palaces to the Age of Home*, Edinburgh Leventis Studies 3, Edinburgh, 581-596.

Coldstream, J.N. (2002) 'Knossos: 'Geometric tombs' excavated by D.G. Hogarth, 1900', *BSA* 97, 201–216.

Coldstream, J.N. (2001) 'The Early Greek period' in J.N. Coldstream and L.J. Eiring, (eds.) *Knossos Pottery Handbook. Greek and Roman.* BSA Studies 7, London, 23–76.

Coldstream, J.N. (2000a) 'Evans Greek Finds: The Early Greek Town of Knossos, and its Encroachment on the Boarders of the Minoan Palace, *BSA* 95, 260–299.

Coldstream, J.N. (2000b) 'A Strange Prelude to the Cypriot Unguent Trade in Crete', in G.K. Ioannides and S.A. Chadistyllis (eds.) Πρακτικά του Γ´ Διεθνούς

Κυπρολογικού Συνεδρίου, Λευκωσία, 16-20 Απριλίου 1996, Vol. Ά , Nicosia, 463-469.

Coldstream, J.N. (1998) 'Minos Redivivus: some nostalgic Knossians of the ninth century BC (a summary),' in W. G. Cavanagh, and M. Curtis (eds.) *Post-Minoan Crete. Proceedings of the First Colloquium on Post-Minoan Crete held by the British School at Athens and the Institute of Archaeology, University College London, 10-11 November 1995*, London, 58-61.

Coldstream, J.N. (1996a) 'The Protogeometric and Geometric pottery' in J.N. Coldstream and H.W. Catling, (eds.) *Knossos North Cemetery. Early Greek Tombs* BSA Suppl. 28, Vol. II, London, 311-420.

Coldstream, J.N (1996b) 'Minos Redivivus: Some nostalgic Knossians of the ninth century B.C.,' *PraktAkAth* 71:2, 236-262.

Coldstream, J.N. (1988) 'Early Greek visitors to Cyprus and the eastern Mediterranean', in V. Tatton-Brown (ed.) Cyprus and the East Mediterranean in the Iron Age: Proceedings of the 12th *British Museum Classical Colloquium*, London, 90–97.

Coldstream, J.N. (1986) 'Kition and Amathus: some reflections on their westward links', in V. Karageorghis, (ed.) Acts of the International Archaeological Symposium 'Cyprus between the Orient and the Occident', Nicosia, 8–14 September 1985, Nicosia: Department of Antiquities, 321–329.

Coldstream, J.N. (1984a) 'Dorian Knossos and Aristotle's Villages' in N. Claude (ed.) *Aux Origines del'Hellénisme. La Crète et la Grèce. Hommage à Henri Van Effenterre,* Paris, 311–232.

Coldstream, J.N. (1984b) 'A Protogeometric nature goddess from Knossos', *BICS* 31, 93–104.

Coldstream, J.N. (1984c) 'Cypriaca and Cretocypriaka from the North Cemetery of Knossos', *RDAC* 1984, 122–137.

Coldstream, J.N. (1983) 'Gift exchange in the eighth century BC', in R. Hägg (ed.) *The Greek renaissance of the eighth century B.C.: Tradition and innovation: Proceedings of the second International Symposium at the Swedish Institute in Athens, 1-5 June, 1981,* Stockholm, 201-206.

Coldstream, J.N. (1982) 'Greeks and Phoenicians in the Aegean', in H. G. Niemeyer, (ed.) *Phönizier im Westen, Die Beiträge des Internationalen Symposiums über die phönizische Expansion im westlichen Mittelmeerraum, in Köln vom 24 bis 27 April 1979,* Mainz, 261–275.

Coldstream, J.N. (1979) 'Some Cypriot traits in Cretan pottery c. 950-750 BC in V. Karageorghis (ed.) *Acts of the International Archaeological Symposium Cyprus and Crete, c.2000-500 BC, Nicosia, 16-22 April 1978,* Nicosia: Department of Antiquities, Nicosia, 258-263.

Coldstream, J.N. (1977) *Geometric Greece: 900-700 BC*, London.

Coldstream, J.N. (1972) 'Knossos: 1951-61: Protogeometric and Geometric Pottery from the Town', *BSA* 67, 63-98.

Coldstream, J.N. (1968) *Greek Geometric Pottery: a Survey of Ten Local Styles and their Chronology*, London.

Coldstream, J.N. (1963) 'Five tombs at Knossos', *BSA* 58, 30–43.

Coldstream, J.N. and Catling, H.W. (1996) (eds.) *Knossos North Cemetery: Early Greek Tombs*, Vols. I-IV, BSA Suppl. Vol. 28, London.

Coldstream, J. N. and Hatzaki, E. (2003) 'Knossos: Early Greek Occupation Under the Roman Villa Dionysos', *BSA* 98, 280-306.

Coldstream J. N., Eiring, L. J., Forster G. (2001) *Knossos Pottery Handbook: Greek and Roman*. BSA Studies Vol. 7, London.

Coldstream, J.N. and Huxley, G. L. (1999) 'Knossos: the Archaic gap', *BSA* 94, 289–307.

Coldstream, J. N. and MacDonald, C. (1997) 'Knossos: Area of South-West Houses, Early Hellenic Occupation', *BSA* 92, 191-245.

Coldstream, J.N., Callaghan, P. and Musgrave, J.H. (1981) 'Knossos: An early Greek Tomb on Lower Gypsadhes Hill', *BSA* 76, 141–166.

Coldstream, J.N. (ed.) (1973) Knossos: *The Sanctuary of Demeter*, BSA Suppl. Vol. 8, Oxford.

Cross, T.M (1974) *Bronze Tripods and Related Stands in the Eastern Mediterranean from the Twelve-Seventh Centuries BC*, PhD Thesis.

D'Agata, A. L. (2006) 'Cult activity on Crete in the Early Dark Age: Changes, continuities and the development of a 'Greek' cult system' in Deger-Jalkotzy S. and Lemos I.S. (eds.) *Ancient Greece: From the Mycenaean Palaces to the Age of Homer*. Edinburgh Leventis Studies 3, Edinburgh, 397-416.

D'Agata, A. L.(2001) 'Religion, society and ethnicity in Crete at the end of the Late BA: A contextual framework for LM IIIC cult activities', in R. Laffineur and R. Hägg (eds.) *Potnia: Deities and Religion in the Aegean Bronze Age. Proceedings of the 8, 11 International Aegean Conference, Göteborg, Göteborg University, 12-15 April 2000*, Liège, 345-354.

D'Agata, A. L.(1997) 'Shrines on the Piazzale dei Sacelli at Ayia Triadha: the LM IIIC and SM material: a summary', in J. Driessen and A. Farnoux (eds.) *La Crète Mycénienne: actes de la Table Ronde Internationale organisée par l'Ecole française d'Athènes, 26-28 Mars 1991*, Athens, 85–100.

Danford, L. M. (1982) *The death rituals of Rural Greece*, Princeton.

Davaras, C. (1968) 'Two Geometric Tombs at Atsalenio near Knossos', *BSA* 63, 133-146.

Davies, J. L and Bennet, J. (1999) 'Making Mycenaeans: Warfare, territorial expansion and representation of the other in the Pylian kingdom' in R. Laffineur (ed.) *Polemos: Le contexte guerrier en Egée à l'âge du Bronze: Actes de la 7e Rencontre égéenne internationale, Université de Liège, 14-17 avril 1998*, Liège, 107-120.

Deger-Jalkotzy S. and Lemos I.S. (eds.) *Ancient Greece: From the Mycenaean Palaces to the Age of Homer*. Edinburgh Leventis Studies 3, Edinburgh.

Demitriou, A. (1978) 'Die Datierung der Periode Cypro-Archaic I nach Fundzusammenhangen mit griechischer Keramik', *AA* 1978, 12-25.

Desborough V.R.d'A (1972) *The Greek Dark Ages*, London.

Desborough V.R.d'A (1964) *The Last Mycenaeans and their successors; an archaeological survey, c. 1200-c. 1000 B.C.*, Oxford.

Desborough V.R.d'A (1952) *Protogeometric Pottery*, Oxford.

Dickinson, O.T.P.K. (2006) *The Aegean from Bronze Age to Iron Age: continuity and change between the twelfth and eighth centuries B.C.*, London.
Dickinson, O.T.P.K. (1994) *The Aegean Bronze Age*, Cambridge.
Dickinson, O.T.P.K. (1983) 'Cist Graves and Chamber Tombs', *BSA* 78, 55-67.
Dörpfeld, W. and Goessler, P., (eds.) (1927) *Alt-Ithaka: Eein Beitrag zur Homer-Frage, Studien und Ausgrabungen aus der Insel Leukas-Ithaka,* Vol. I, München.
Evans, A.J. (1931) *The earlier religion of Greece in the light of Cretan discoveries*, London.
Evans, A.J. (1928) *The Palace of Minos*, vol. 2, London.
Evans, A.J. (1921) *The Palace of Minos*, vol.1. London.
Evans, A.J. (1901) 'Mycenaean tree- and pillar-cult and its Mediterranean relations', *JHS* 31, 135-38.
Evans, A.J. (1906) *The Prehistoric Tombs of Knossos*, London.
Evans, A.J. (1899-1900) 'The Palace', *BSA* 6, 3-69.
Fermor, P.L. (2003) 'J. Pendlebury and the Battle of Crete' in A. Cooper (ed.) *Words of Mercury*, London.
Foley, A. (1988) *The Argolid 800-600 B.C.: An archaeological survey: Together with an index of sites from the Neolithic to the Roman period*, Gtsteborg.
Forsdyke, J. (1956) *Greece before Homer: Ancient Chronology and Mythology*, London.
Forsdyke, J. (*1926-7*) 'The Mavro Spelio cemetery at Knossos', *BSA* 28, 243-298.
Gallis, K. (1982) Καύσεις νεκρών στη Θεσσαλία, Athens.
Gamer-Wallert, I. (2004) 'The Scarabs' in M.E. Aubet (ed.) *The Phoenician cemetery of Tyre-Al Bas: Excavations 1997-1999.* Beirut, 397-413.
Geertz, C. (1973) *The Interpretation of Cultures*, New York.
Gere, C. (2009) *Knossos and the Prophets of Modernism,* Ghicago.
Gjerstad, E. (1948) *The Swedish Cyprus Expedition, vol. IV, part 2: The Cypro-Geometric, Cypro-Archaic and Cypro-Classical Periods*, Stockholm.
Goody J. (1962) *Death, Property and the Ancestors: A Study of the Mortuary Customs of the Lodagaa of West Africa*, London.
Grammatikaki, E. (1993) 'Αμπελόκηποι' *ArchDelt* 48, B' 2, 448-450.
Haggis, D.C. (2001) 'A Dark Age settlement system in East Crete, and a reassessment of the definition of refuge settlements', in V. Karageorghis and C.E. Morris (eds.) *Defensive settlements of the Aegean and the eastern Mediterranean after c. 1200 B.C.: proceedings of an international workshop held at Trinity College Dublin, 7th-9th May, 1999*, Nicosia, 41–59.
Hales, S and T. Hodos (eds.) (2008) *Material culture and social identities in the ancient world*, Cambridge.
Hallager, E. (1977) *The Mycenaean Palace at Knossos: Evidence for Final Destruction in the III B Period*, Stockholm.
Hansen, S. (2008) 'Preface' in P. F. Biehl and Y. YA. Rassamakin (eds.) *Import and imitation in archaeology*, Langenweissbach.
Helbig, W. (1900) 'Zu den homerischen bestattungsbräuchen'. *AbhMünch* 1900, 199-279.
Hertz, R. (1960) *Death and the Right Hand*, (transl. R. Needham and C. Needham) New York.
Higgins, R.A. (1996) 'Jewellery' in Coldstream, J.N. and Catling, H.W. (eds.) *Knossos North Cemetery. Early Greek Tombs*, London, BSA Suppl. Vol. 28 II, 539-542.

Hodder, I. (1991) 'Interpretative archaeology and its role', *AmerAnt* 56, 7-18.
Hodder, I. (1986) *Reading the Past*, Cambridge.
Hodder, I. (1982) (ed.) *Symbolic and Structural Archaeology*, Cambridge.
Hodder, I. (1982b) *The present past: An introduction to anthropology for archaeologists*, London.
Hodder, I. (1982c) 'Theoritical Archaeology: a reactionary review', in I. Hodder (ed.) *Symbolic and Structural Archaeology*, Cambridge, 1-16.
Hodos, T. (2006) *Local responses to colonization in the Iron-Age Mediterranean*, London.
Hoffman, G.L. (1997) *Imports and immigrants: Near Eastern contacts with Iron Age Crete*, Ann Arbor.
Hogarth, D.G. (1899–1900) 'Knossos: Early Town and Cemeteries', *BSA* 6, 70–85.
Hood, M.S.F. (1960) 'Late Minoan tombs south of the Palace', *ArchDelt* 16, 266.
Hood, M.S.F. and Smyth, D. (1981) *Archaeological survey of the Knossos area*, BSA Suppl. Vol. 14. Oxford.
Hood, M. S. F. and Boardman, J. (1961) 'Early Iron Age tombs at Knossos', *BSA* 56, 68–81.
Hood, M. S. F. and Coldstream, N. (1968) 'A Late Minoan tomb at Ayios Ioannis near Knossos', *BSA* 63, 205–2.
Hood, M. S. F. and de Jong, P. (1952) 'Late Minoan Warrior-Graves from Ayios Ioannis and the New Hospital Site at Knossos', *BSA* 47, 243–277.
Hood, M. S. F., Huxley, G. L. and Sandars, N. (1958-1959) 'A Minoan cemetery on Upper Gypsades', *BSA* 53–4, 194–262.
Hood, M. S. F., Warren, P. and Cadogan, G. (1964) 'Travels in Crete, 1962', *BSA* 59, 50-100.
Hutchinson, R.W. and Boardman, J. (1954) 'The Khaniale Tekke Tombs', *BSA* 49, 215–230.
Iacovou, M. (2004) 'Review: Phoenicia and Cyprus in the first millennium B.C.: Two distinct cultures in search of their distinct archaeologies: The Cypro-Phoenician Pottery of the Iron Age by Nicola Schreiber', *BASOR* 336, 61-66.
Iacovou, M. (2002) 'Amathous: an EIA Polity in Cyprus. The Chronology of its Foundation', *RDAC*, 101-126.
Iacovou, M. (1999) 'The Greek Exodus to Cyprus: The Antiquity of Hellenism', *Mediterranean Historical Review*, 14:2, 1-28.
Iakovidis, S. E. (1970) Περατή: Το νεκροταφείο. Athens.
Jacopi, G. (1938) *Clara Rhodos: Studi e materiali pubblicati a cura dell'Istituto storico-archeologico di Rodi*, Vol. 19, Rhodes.
Jones, D. W. (2000) *External relations of Earle Iron Age Crete, 1100-600 B.C*, Boston.
Jones, D. W. (1993) 'Phoenician Unguent Factories in Dark Age Greece. Social Approaches to Evaluating the Archaeological Evidence', *OJA* 12, 293-303.
Jones, S. (1997) *The archaeology of Ethnicity: Constructing Identities in the Past and Present*, London.
Karageorghis, V. (2006) 'Cypriote' styles beyond Cyprus from the Late Bronze Age to the end of the Archaic period', in E. Herring, I. Lemos, F. Lo Schiavo, L. Vagnetti, R. Whitehouse and J. Wilkins(eds.) *Across Frontiers. Etruscans, Greeks, Phoenicians and Cypriots. Studies in honour of David Ridgway and FrancescaRomana Serra Ridgway*. Accordia Specialist Studies on the Mediterranean 6, London, 77-87.

Karageorghis, V. (1983) *Palaepaphos-Skales. An Iron Age Cemetery in Cyprus*, Konstanz.
Karageorghis, V. (1979) 'Some reflections on the relations between Cyprus and Crete during the Late Minoan IIIB period', in V. Karageorghis (ed.) *Acts of the International Archaeological Symposium 'Cyprus and Crete, c.2000-500 BC, Nicosia, 16-22 April 1978, Nicosia: Department of Antiquities*, Nicosia,199–204.
Karageorghis, V. (1976) *View from the Bronze Age: Mycenaean and Phoenician discoveries at Kition*, Dutton.
Karageorghis, V. (1974) 'Pikes and Obeloi from Cyprus and Crete' in *Antichità Cretesi Studi in Onore di Doro Levi*, Vol. 2, Catania, 168-172.
Kearsley, R. A. (1999) 'Greeks Overseas in the 8th Century B.C.: Euboeans, Al Mina and Assyrian Imperialism', in G. R. Tsetskhladze (ed.) *Ancient Greeks, West and East*, Leiden.
Kern, H (2000) *Through the Labyrinth: Designs and Meanings over 5,000 Years*, New York.
Keswani, P. (2004) *Mortuary ritual and society in Bronze Age Cyprus*, Sheffield.
Keswani, P. (1993) 'Models of local exchange in Late Bronze Age Cyprus', *BASOR* 292, 73–83.
Keswani, P. (1989) 'Dimensions of social hierarchy in Late Bronze Age Cyprus: an analysis of the mortuary data from Enkomi', *JMA*, 49–86.
Khalifeh, I.A. (1988) *Sarepta II: The Late Bronze and Iron Age Periods of Area II, X*, Beirut.
Killebrew, A.E. (1998) 'Aegean and Aegean-style material culture in Canaan during the 14th-12th centuries BC' in E. Cline and D. Harris-Cline (eds.) *Trade colonization, diffusion or migration? The Aegean and the orient in the second millennium*, Aegeum Vol. 18, 149–170.
Klein, N. L. (1997) 'Excavation of the Greek Temples at Mycenae by the British School at Athens', *BSA* 92, 247-322.
Knapp, A. B. (2008) *Prehistoric and Protohistoric Cyprus: Identity, Insularity, and Connectivity*, New York.
Kontrarou-Rassia, N. (2010) '3.000 στρέμματα στην Κνωσσό ελεύθερα για χτίσιμο', *Eleutherotypia*: http://www.enet.gr/?i=news.el.article&id=196829, (date accessed: 15/3/2011).
Kopaka, K. (1995) 'Ο Μίνως Καλοκαιρινός και οι πρώτες ανασκαφές στην Κνωσσό' Πεπραγμένα Ζ' Διεθνούς. Κρητολογικού Συνεδρίου, Α1, *Ρέθυμνο 1991*, Rethymno, 501-511.
Kopytof, L. (1986) 'The cultural biography of things: commoditization as process' in A. Appadurai (ed.) *The social life of things: commodities in Cultural Perspective*, Cambridge, 64–91.
Kossinna, G. (1911) *Die Herkunft der Germanen. Zur Methode der Siedlungsarchäologie. Kabitzsch*, Würzburg.
Kotsonas, A. (2016a) 'Politics of Periodization and the Archaeology of Early Greece', *AJA* 120, 239-270.
Kotsonas, A. (2016b) 'Greek and Roman Knossos: The pioneering investigations of Minos Kalokairinos', *BSA* 111, 299-324.

Kotsonas, A. (2012) "Creto-Cypriot' and 'Cypro-Phoenician' complexities in the archaeology of interaction between Crete and Cyprus', in M. Iacovou (ed.) *Cyprus and the Aegean in the Early Iron Age: The legacy of Nicolas Coldstream*, Nicosia, 155-182.

Kotsonas, A. (2011a) 'Quantification of Ceraminc from Early Iron Age Tombs', in S. Verdan, T. Theurillat and A. Kenzelmann-Pfyffer (eds.) Early Iron Age Pottery: A Quantitative Approach Proceedings of the International Round Table organized by the Swiss School of Archaeology in Greece, Oxford, 129-138.

Kotsonas, A. (2011b) 'Foreign Identity and Ceramic Production in Early Iron Age Crete' in G. Rizza (ed.) *Identità Culturale, Etnicità, Processi di trasformazione a Creta fra Dark Age e Arcaismo*. Per i cento anni dello scavo di Priniàs 1906-2006 Convegno di Studi (Atene 9-12 novembre 2006), Catania, 133-155.

Kotsonas, A. (2011c) 'Review of S.A. Wallace, (2010) *Ancient Crete: From Successful Collapse to Democracy's Alternatives, Twelfth to Fifth Centuries BC'*, BMCR 2011.04.52.

Kotsonas, A. (2006) *The Archaeology of Tomb A1K1 of Orthi Petra in Eleutherna: The Early Iron Age Pottery*, Athens.

Kotsonas, A. (2006) 'Wealth and Status in Iron Age Knossos', OJA 25, 149-172.

Kotsonas, A., Vasilakis A. and Whitelaw, T. (2012) 'Η Κνωσός της Πρώιμης Εποχής του Σιδήρου: Τα νέα δεδομένα από το πρόγραμμα επιφανειακής έρευνας (KULP) in M. Adrianakis, P. Varthalitou, I. Tzachili (eds.) *Αρχαιολογικό έργο Κρήτης 2: Πρακτικά της 2ης Συνάντησης: Ρέθυμνο, 26-28 Νοεμβρίου 2010*, Rethymnon, 219-229.

Kourou, N. (2000) 'Phoenician presence in EIA Crete reconsidered', in Aubet, M.E. and Barthélemy, M. (eds.) *Actas del IV Congreso Internacional de Estudios Fenicios y Púnicos, Cádiz, de 2 al 6 de Octubre de 1995*, Cádiz, 1067–1081.

Kourou, N. (1997) 'Αιγαίο και Κύπρος κατά την Πρώϊμη Εποχή του Σιδήρου: Νεώτερες εξελίξεις' in Πρακτικά του Διεθνούς Αρχαιολογικού Συνεδρίου ‹Η Κύπρος και το Αιγαίο στην αρχαιότητα›: *από την προϊστορική περίοδο ως τον 7ο αιώνα μ.Χ.: Λευκωσία, 8-10 Δεκεμβρίου 1995*, Nikocia, 217-230.

Kourou, N. and Karetsou, A. (1998) 'An Enigmatic Stone from Knossos. A Reused Cippus?', in in V. Karageorghis and N.C. Stampolidis (eds.) *Eastern Mediterranean. Cyprus–Dodecanese–Crete 16th–6th cent. B.C. Proceedings of the International Symposium held at Rethymnon-Crete in May* 1997, Athens, 243- 255.

Kourou, N. and Grammatikaki, E. (1998) 'An Anthropomorphic Cippus from Knossos, Crete', in R. Rolle and K.Schmidt (eds.) Archäologische Studien in Kontaktzonen der antiken Welt, Hamburg, 237- 251.

Kroll, J.H. (2003) Weights, Bullion Currency, Coinage. In N.C. Stampolidis, and V. Karageorghis, (eds.) *Sea Routes: From Sidon to Huelva. Interconnections in the Mediterranean, 16th–6th c. BC. Proceedings of the International Symposium held at Rethymnon, Crete, September 29th–October 2nd 2002*, Athens, 41–79.

Lebessi, A. (1970) 'Ανασκαφικαί έρευναι εις Ανατολικήν Κρήτην', *Prakt*, 256-297.

Lehmann, G. (2005) Al Mina and the East: A report on research in progress' in A. Villing (ed.) *The Greeks in the East*, London, 61-92.

Lemos, I. (2002) *The Protogeometric Aegean. The archaeology of the late 11th and 10th centuries BC*, Oxford.
Leonard, Jr. A., Hughes, M., Middleton, A. and Schofield, L. (1993) 'The making of Aegean stirrup jars. Technique, tradition and trade', *BSA* 88, 105–123.
Lewartowski, K., (2000) *Late Helladic simple graves: a study of Mycenaean burial customs*, Oxford.
Liddy, D. J. (1996) 'Pottery analysis by Atomic Absorption', in J.N. Coldstream, and H.W. Catling, (eds.) *Knossos North Cemetery: Early Greek Tombs*, Vol. II, BSA Suppl. Vol. 28, 465-516.
Lipínski, E. (1983) 'Notes d'épigraphie phénicienne et punique', *Orientalia Lovaniensia Periodica* 14, 129-165.
Lorimer, H.L. (1950) *Homer and the Monument*, London.
Luke, J. (2003) *Ports of Trade: Al Mina and Geometric Greek Pottery in the Levant*, Oxford.
Luntley, M. (1984) 'The Sense of A Name', *The Philosophical Quarterly* 34, 265-282.
Macdonald, C. (1986) 'Problems of the 12th century in the Dodecanese', *BSA* 81, 125–151.
Malinowski, B. (1948) 'Magic, science and religion' in B. Malinowski (ed.) *Magic, Science and Religion and other essays*, New York, 10-87.
Marchand, S. L., (1996) *Down from Olympus: archaeology and philhellenism in Germany, 1750 - 1970*, Princeton.
Marinatos, S. (1933) 'Funde und Forschungen auf Kreta', *AA* 48, 303-307.
Markoe, G. (1998) 'The Phoenicians on Crete: transit trade and the search for ores', in V. Karageorghis and N.C. Stampolidis (eds.) *Eastern Mediterranean. Cyprus-Dodecanese-Crete 16th-6th cent. B.C. Proceedings of the International Symposium held at Rethymnon-Crete in May 1997*, Athens, 233–240.
Masson, E. and Masson, O. (1983) 'Les objets inscrits de Palaepaphos-Skales', in Karageorghis, V. (ed.) *Palaepaphos-Skales: An Iron Age Cemetery in Cyprus*, Konstanz, 411–415.
Matthäus, H. (1998) 'Cyprus and Crete in the Early First Millennium B.C', in V. Karageorghis and N.C. Stampolidis (eds.) *Eastern Mediterranean. Cyprus-Dodecanese-Crete 16th-6th cent. B.C. Proceedings of the International Symposium held at Rethymnon-Crete in May 1997*, Athens, 127–158.
Matthäus, H. (1988) 'Heirloom or Traditon? Bronze Stands of the Second Millenium and Early First Millennium BC in Cyprus, Greece, Italy', in French and Wardle (eds.) *Problems in Greek Prehistory. Papers Presented at the Centenary Conference of the British Scholl of Archaeology at Athens, Manchester, April 1986*, Bristol, 285-300.
Matthäus, H. (1985) *Metallgefässe und Gefässuntersätze der Bronzezeit der geometrischen und archaischen Periode auf Cypern: Mit einem Anhang der bronzezeitlichen Schwertfunde auf Cypern*, München.
McFadden, G.H. (1954) 'A Late Cypriot III Tomb from Kourion', *AJA* 58, 131-42.
McGillivray, J.A. (2000) *Minotaur: Sir Arthur Evans and the Archaeology of the Minoan Myth*, New York.
Mee, C.B. and Cavanagh W. G. (1984) 'Mycenaean Tombs as Evidence for Social and Political Organisation', *OJA* 3, 45-64.

Melas, M. (2001) 'Καύσεις νεκρών: Προς μία αρχαιολογία του φόβου' in N. Stampolidis (ed.) Καύσεις στην εποχή του χαλκού και την πρώιμη εποχή του σιδήρου: πρακτικά του συμποσίου, Ρόδος, 29 Απριλίου-2 Μαΐου 1999, Rhodes, 15-29.

Melas, M. (1984) 'The origins of Aegean cremations', Ανθρωπολογικά 5, 21-34.

Miller, M. (2011) *The funerary landscape at Knossos: A diachronic study of Minoan burial customs with special reference to the warrior graves*, Oxford.

Miller, N. (1927) 'Some Aspects of the Name in Culture-History', *American Journal of Sociology* 32:4, 585-600.

Moignard, E. (1996) 'The Orientalising Pottery', in J.N. Coldstream, and H.W. Catling, (eds.) *Knossos North Cemetery: Early Greek Tombs*, Vol. II, BSA Suppl. Vol. 28, 421-462.

Morgan, C. (2009) 'The Early Iron Age' in K.A. Raaflaub and H. van Wees (eds.) *A companion to Archaic Greece*, Chichester.

Morgan, C. (1999) 'Some thoughts on the production and consumption of EIA pottery in the Aegean', in J.P. Crielaard, V. Stissi and G.J. Van Wijngaarden (eds.) *The complex past of pottery: Production, circulation and consumption of Mycenaean and Greek pottery (sixteenth to early fifth centuries BC), Proceedings of the ARCHON international conference, held in Amsterdam, 8-9 November 1996*, Amsterdam, 213-259.

Morris, I. (1998) 'An archaeology of equalities?', in D. L. Nichols, and T. H. Charlton, (eds.) *The Archaeology of City-States: Cross-Cultural Approaches*, Washington, 91–107.

Morris, I. (1997) 'Periodization and the Heroes: Inventing a Dark Age', in M. Golden and P. Toohey, (eds.) *Inventing Ancient Culture? Historicism, Periodization, and the 'New Classics'*, London, 96-131.

Morris, I. (1993) 'Response to Papadopoulos (I). The Kerameikos Stratigraphy and the Character of the Greek Dark Age', *JMA* 6:2, 207-221.

Morris, I. (1992) *Death-Ritual and Social Structure in Classical Antiquity*, Cambridge.

Morris, I. (1989) 'Circulation, deposition and the formation of the Greek Iron Age', *Man* 24:3, 502–519.

Morris, I. (1988) 'Tomb cult and the Greek renaissance: the past in the present in the eighth century BC', *Antiquity* 62, 750–761.

Morris, I. (1987) *Burial and Ancient Society: The Rise of the City-State*, Cambridge.

Morris, I. (1986) 'Gift and commodity in Archaic Greece', *Man* 21:1, 1–17.

Morris, S. (1997) 'Greeks and Near Eastern Art in the Age of Homer,' in S. Langdon (ed.) *New light on a Dark Age: Exploring the culture of Geometric Greece*, London, 57-71.

Musgrave, J.H. (1996) 'The human bones', in J.N. Coldstream, and H.W. Catling, (eds.) *Knossos North Cemetery: Early Greek Tombs*, Vol. II, BSA Suppl. Vol. 28, 677–693.

Myers, W.J., Myers and E.E. Cadogan, G. (1992) *The Aerial Atlas of Ancient Crete*, Berkeley.

Mylonas, G.E. (1948) 'Homeric and Mycenaean burial customs', *AJA* 52, 56-81.

Negbi, O. (1992) 'Early Phoenician presence in the Mediterranean Islands: A reappraisal', *AJA* 96:4, 599-615.

Nowicki, K. (2001) 'Sea-raiders and refugees: problems of defensible sites in Crete c. 1200B.C.', in V. Karageorghis and C.E. Morris (eds.) *Defensive settlements of the Aegean and the eastern Mediterranean after c. 1200 B.C.: proceedings of an international workshop held at Trinity College Dublin, 7th-9th May, 1999*, Nicosia, 23–40.

Nowicki, K. (2000) *Defensible sites in Crete, c. 1200-800 B.C. (LM IIIB/IIIC through Early Geometric)*, Liège.

O' Shea, J. M. (1984) *Mortuary variability: An archaeological Investigation*, New York.

Orton, C. (1993) 'How many pots make five? An Historical overview of pottery quantification', *Archaeometry* 35, 169-184.

Orton C., Tyers P, and Vince A. (1993) *Pottery in archaeology*, Cambridge.

Orton C., Tyers P. (1990) 'Statistical analysis of ceramic assemblages' *Archaeologia e Calcolatori* 1, 81-110.

Paidoussis, M. and Sbarounis, C. (1975) 'A study of the cremated bones from the cemetery of Perati,' *OpAth* 11, 129–160.

Panagiotaki, M. (2004) 'Knossos and Evans: buying Kephala' in Cadogan, G., Hatzaki (eds.) *Knossos: Palace, City, State*, BSA Studies 12, 513-530.

Papadopoulos J. K. (2005) 'Inventing the Minoans: Archaeology, Modernity and the Quest for European Identity,' *JMA* 18, 87-149.

Papadopoulos J. K. (1996) 'Dark Age Greece,' in B.M. Fagan, (ed.) The Oxford Companion to Archaeology, Oxford, 253-255.

Papadopoulos J. K. (1994) 'Early Iron Age potters' marks in the Aegean', *Hesperia* 63:4, 437-507.

Papadopoulos J. K. (1993) 'To Kill a Cemetery: The Athenian Kerameikos and the EIA in the Aegean,' *JMA* 6:2, 175-206.

Papasavvas, G. (2012) 'Cretan bronze stands of Cypriot types from sanctuaries and cemeteries: Cretan society in the Early Iron Age', in M. Iacovou (ed.) *Cyprus and the Aegean in the Early Iron Age: The legacy of Nicolas Coldstream*, Nicosia, 129-154.

Papasavvas, G. (2001) Χάλκινοι Υποστάτες απο την Κύπρο και την Κρήτη: Τριποδικοί και Τετράπλευροι Υποστάτες απο την Ύστερη Εποχή του Χαλκού έως την Πρώιμη Εποχή του Σιδήρου, Nicosia.

Parker Pearson, M. (1999) *The Archaeology of Death and Burial*. Sutton.

Parker Pearson, M. (1993) 'The powerful dead: Relationships between the living and the dead. *CAJ* 3, 203-229.

Parker Pearson, M. (1984) 'Economic and Ideological change: cyclical growth in the pre-statesocieties of Jutland' in D. Miller and C. Tilley (eds.) *Ideology power and prehistory*, Cambridge, 69-92.

Parker Pearson, M. (1982) 'Mourtuary practices, society and ideology: an ethnoarchaeological study' in I. Hodder (ed.) *Symbolic and Structural Archaeology*, Cambridge, 92-113.

Payne, H.G.G. (1927-1928) 'Early Greek Vases from Knossos', *BSA* 29, 224-298.

Pendlebury (1963) *The Archaeology of Crete: An introduction*, New York.

Popham, M. R. (1994) 'Precolonisation: Early Greek contact with the East', in Tsetskhladze, G.R. and De Angelis, F. (eds.) *The archaeology of Greek Colonisation: essays dedicated to Sir John Boardman*, Oxford, 11-34.

Popham, M. R. (1992) 'Section 2. The Sun-Minoan Pottery' in L.H. Sackett (ed.) *Knossos from Greek city to Roman colony: Excavations at the Unexplored Mansion II*, BSA Suppl. Vol. 21, Oxford, 59-66.

Popham, M. R. (1979) 'Connections between Crete and Cyprus between 1300–1100 BC', in V. Karageorghis (ed.) *Acts of the International Archaeological Symposium Cyprus and Crete, c.2000-500 BC, Nicosia, 16-22 April 1978, Nicosia: Department of Antiquities*, Nicosia, 258-263

Popham, M. R. (1978) 'Notes from Knossos, Part II.', *BSA* 73, 179–87.

Popham, M. R. (1970) *The Destruction of the Palace at Knossos: Pottery of the Late Minoan IIIA Period*, Göteborg.

Poulsen, F. (1905) *Die Dipylongräber und die Dipylonvasen*, Leipzig.

Prent, M. (2009) 'The goddesses with upraised arms', in *Archaeologies of cult: Essays on ritual and cult in Crete in honor of Geraldine C. Gesell*, Hesperia Suppl. 42, 231-238.

Preston, L. (2008) 'Late Minoan II to IIIB Crete' C.W. Shelmedrine (ed.) *The Cambridge Companion to the Aegean BA*, New York, 310-326.

Preston, L. (2005) *Cretan sanctuaries and cults: continuity and change from Late Minoan IIIC to the Archaic period*, Leiden.

Renfrew, C. (1986) 'Varna and the emergence of wealth in prehistoric Europe', in A. Appadurai (ed.) *The Social Life of Things: Commodities in Cultural Perspective*, Cambridge, 141-168.

Renfrew, C. (1985) *The archaeology of cult: The sanctuary at Phylakopi*, BSA Suppl. Vol. 18, London.

Renfrew, C. (1972) *The Emergence of Civilisation: The Cyclades and the Aegean in The Third Millennium BC*, London.

Rethemiotakis, G., Englezou, M. (2010) Το Γεωμετρικό νεκροταφείο της ‹Ελτυνας, Heraklion.

Ridgeway, W. (1901) *The early age of Greece*, Vol. 1, Cambridge.

Riis, P.J. (1939) 'Rod Tripods', *ActaArch* 10, 1-30.

Rousaki, M. and Anagnostaki, G. (2012) 'Νέο τμήμα του ονομαζόμενου Βόρειου Νεκροταφείου Κνωσσού στον Άγιο Ιωάννη (Αμπελόκηποι-Τεκές): Μια πρώτη προσέγγιση', in M. Adrianakis, P. Varthalitou, I. Tzachili (eds.) Αρχαιολογικό έργο Κρήτης 2: Πρακτικά της 2ης Συνάντησης: Ρέθυμνο, 26-28 Νοεμβρίου 2010, Rethymnon, 230-238.

Ruppenstein, R. (2013) 'Cremation Burials in Greece from the Late Bronze Age to the Early Iron Age. Continuity or Change?,' in M. Lochner and F. Ruppenstein (eds.) *Cremation burials in the region between the Middle Danube and the Aegean, 1300-750 BC: Proceedings of the international symposium held at the Austrian Academy of Sciences at Vienna, February 11th-12th, 2010*, 181-196.

Sackett, H. and Musgrave, J.H. (1976) 'A new figured crater from Knossos', BSA 71, 117-125.

Sallares, R. (1991) *The ecology of the ancient world*, London.

Saxe, A. A. (1971) Social Dimensions of Mortuary Practices in a Mesolithic Population from Wadi Halfa, Sudan', in J.A. Brown (ed.) *Approaches to the social dimensions of mortuary practices*, Memoirs of the Society for American Archaeology 25, 39-57.

Saxe, A. A. (1970) *Social dimensions of mortuary practices*, PhD Thesis.
Schreiber N. (2003) *The Cypro-Phoenician pottery of the Iron Age*, Leiden.
Shanks, N. and Tilley, C. (1987) *Social Theory and Archaeology*, Cambridge.
Shanks, N. and Tilley, C. (1982) 'Ideology, symbolic power and ritual communication: a reinterpretation of Neolithic mortuary practices', in I. Hodder (ed.) *Symbolic and Structural Archaeology*, Cambridge, 129-154.
Shaw, J.W. (1989) 'Phoenicians in southern Crete', *AJM* 93, 165–184.
Sherratt, S. (1994) 'Commerce Iron and Ideology: Metallurgical Innovation in Twelfth-Eleventh Century Cyprus', in V. Karageorghis (ed.) *Cyprus in the eleventh century BC: Proceedings of the International Symposium: Nicosia, 30-31 October 1993*, Nicosia, 59-106.
Sherratt S. and A. Sherratt (1993) 'The Growth of the Mediterranean Economy in the Early First Millennium B.C.', *WorldArch* 24, 361-378.
Sjögren, L. (2003) *Cretan locations: discerning site variations in Iron Age and Archaic Crete (800-500 B.C.)*, Oxford.
Skon-Jedele, N. J (1994) *'Aigyptiaka': A catalogue of Egyptian and Egyptianizing objects excavated from Greek archaeological sites, ca. 1100-525 BC, with Historical commentary*, PhD Thesis.
Skon-Jedele, N. J. and Dabney, M. K. (2000) 'Scarabs', in J.W. Shaw and M.C. Shaw (eds.) *Kommos IV, The Greek Sanctuary*, Princeton, 351.
Snodgrass, A. M. (2002) 'A paradigm shift for classical arcaheology?', *CAJ* 12:2, 180-93.
Snodgrass, A. M. (2000) *The Dark Age of Greece: An Archaeological Survey of the Eleventh to the Eighth centuries BC* (2nd ed.), London.
Snodgrass, A. M. (1996) 'Iron', in J.N. Coldstream, and H.W. Catling, (eds.) *Knossos North Cemetery: Early Greek* Tombs, Vol. II, BSA Suppl. Vol. 28, 575-598.
Snodgrass, A. M. (1987) *An archaeology of Greece: The present state and future scope of a discipline*, London.
Snodgrass, A. M. (1980) *Archaic Greece: The Age of Experiment*, London.
Snodgrass, A. M. (1964) *Early Greek armour and weapons from the end of the Bronze Age to 600 B.C.*, Edinburgh.
Snycer, M. (1979) 'L' inscription phénicienne de Tekke, pres de Cnossos', *Kadmos* 18, 89-93.
Stampolidis, N. C. (ed.) (2004) *Eleutherna: Polis – Acropolis – Necropolis*, Athens.
Stampolidis, N. C. (1990) 'A funerary cippus at Eleutherna-Evidence of Phoenician Presence?' *BICS* 37, 99-106.
Stampolidis and Kotsonas (2006) 'Phoenicians in Crete' in Deger-Jalkotzy S. and Lemos I.S. (eds.) *Ancient Greece: From the Mycenaean Palaces to the Age of Homer. Edinburgh Leventis Studies 3*, Edinburgh, 337-360.
Tarlas, S. (1994) *Social change organization and cremation in prehistoric Greece*, PhD Thesis.
Van Gennef, A. (1960) *The rites of passage*, (1st publication in French 1909), London.
Vavritsas, A. (1968) 'Λαύριον: Δοκιμαστική έρευνα εις την 'Σπηλιά του Κίτσου'', *AAA* 1, 234-236.
Vickers M. and Gill, D. (1994) *Artful Crafts: Ancient Greek Silverware and Pottery*, Oxford.

Waldbaum, J. C. (1997) 'Greeks in the East or Greeks and the East?: Problems in the Definition and Recognition of Presence', BASOR 305, 1–17.

Waldbaum, J. C. (1982) 'Bimetallic Objects from the Eastern Mediterranean and the Question of the Dissemination of Iron' in J.D. Muhly, R. Maddin and V. Karageorghis, (eds.) *Early metallurgy in Cyprus, 4000-500 B.C.: Acta of the International Archaeological* Symposium, Early Metallurgy in Cyprus, 4000-500BC, Larnaca, Cyprus 1-6 June 1981, Nicosia, 325-349.

Waldbaum, J. C. (1978) *From Bronze to Iron: The Transition from the Bronze Age to the Iron Age in the Easter Mediterranean*, Göteborg.

Wallace, S.A. (2010) *Ancient Crete: From Successful Collapse to Democracy's Alternatives, Twelfth to Fifth Centuries BC*, Cambridge.

Wallace, S.A. (2003) 'The perpetuated past: Re-use or continuity in material culture and the structuring of identity in EIA Crete, 12th to 7th centuries BC', *BSA* 97, 251–277.

Warren, P. M. (1983) 'Knossos: Stratigraphical Museum Excavations, 1978-82, Part II' *AR* 29, 63-87.

Webb, V. (1996) 'Faience and Glass', in J.N. Coldstream, and H.W. Catling, (eds.) *Knossos North Cemetery: Early Greek* Tombs, Vol. II, BSA Suppl. Vol. 28, 599-610.

Webb, V. (1978) *Archaic Greek Faience: Miniature Scent Bottles and Related Objects from East Greece 650-500*, Warminster.

Welch, F.B. (1899-1900) 'Knossos: Notes on the Pottery', *BSA* 6, 85-92.

Whitelaw, T., Bredaki, M. and Vasilakis, A. (2008) 'The Knossos Urban Landscape Project', *AR* 54,100-102.

Whitley, J. (2013) 'Homer's Entangled Objects: Narrative, Agency and Personhood in and out of Iron Age Texts', *CAJ* 23, 395-416.

Whitley, J. (2004) 'Style Wars: towards an explanation of Cretan exceptionalism', in Cadogan, G., Hatzaki (eds.) *Knossos: Palace, City, State*, BSA Studies 12, 433-442.

Whitley, J. (2002) 'Objects with attitude: Biographical facts and fallacies of Late Bronze Age and Early Iron Age warrior graves', *CAJ*, 12, 217–232.

Whitley, J. (2001) *The Archaeology of Ancient Greece*, Cambridge.

Whitley, J. (1998) 'Knossos without Minos', *AMJ* 102, 611–613.

Whitley, J. (1994) 'Protoattic Pottery: A contextual Approach', in I. Morris (ed.) *Classical Greece: ancient histories and modern archaeologies*, Cambridge, 51-71.

Whitley, J. (1991) *Style and Society in Dark Age Greece: The changing face of a pre-literate society 1100-700 BC*, Cambridge.

Whitley, J. (1986) *Style, Burial and Society in Dark Age Greece*, PhD thesis.

Wijngaarden, G.J. van (2008) 'The Relevance of Authenticity. Mycenaean-Type Pottery in the Mediterranean', in P.F. Biehl and Y.YA. Rassamakin (eds.) *Import and imitation in archaeology*, Langenweissbach.

Wijngaarden, G.J. van (2002) *Use and appreciation of Mycenaean pottery in the Levant, Cyprus and Italy (ca. 1600-1200 BC)*, Amsterdam.

Woolley, L.C. (1953) *A Forgotten Kingdom: Being a record of the results obtained from the excavation of two mounds*, Baltimore.

Woolley, L.C. (1948) 'The Date of Al Mina', *JHS* 68, 148.